FRONT LINES

This selection first published in 2022 by Cipher Press

105 lnk Court
419 Wick Lane
London, E3 2PX

Paperback ISBN: 978-1-8383900-8-2
eBook ISBN: 978-1-8383900-9-9

Printed and bound in the UK by TJ Books

Distributed by Turnaround Publisher Services

Cover Design by Wolf Murphy-Merrydew

Typeset by Laura Jones

www.cipherpress.co.uk

FRONT LINES

TRANS JOURNALISM
2007-2021

JULIET JACQUES

Cipher
press

ARTS

INTRODUCTION

I never believed any journalism was objective, nor that there was any point in even trying to be. I didn't simply conceive of journalism as a way to advance a political position: I always thought one should be flexible on this, being prepared to shift if the facts necessitate it, although the rampant inequality and injustice of 21st century Britain means I've barely moved since I was a teenager, scrawling hammers and sickles across my notebooks, partly because it seemed to annoy everyone I wanted to annoy. But I did think journalism could be a good forum to propagandise for the things I cared about: my tastes in literature, film, music and art, often quite obscure; and for the rights and representation of trans people, who I rarely saw speaking in their own voices or on their own terms.

I wrote extensively about my experiences of seeing trans and non-binary people in print and broadcast media during my youth, and how I became part of a generation of writers who were determined to change that media, in *Trans: A Memoir*, published by Verso in September 2015. That book also discusses my decision to document my transition in my *Transgender Journey* series which ran in the *Guardian* from June 2010 to November 2012 as part of an attempt to challenge that newspaper's historically poor trans coverage, the alienation I then felt from the journalistic circles it drew me towards, and the psychological implications of being so public about one's private life. So I won't do that again here – journalism is repetitive enough already, demanding one to keep saying whatever the discourse requires of you at any given point. But I do want to talk about my time as 'The Transgender Journalist', as I was half-jokingly called on a panel about trans people and the media with Roz Kaveney and CN Lester in 2011, and the tension between wanting to focus on art and culture and needing to counter the dishonest, damaging things being published about us in virtually every national newspaper, discussed that year by Trans Media Watch at the Leveson Inquiry.

I fell into that role, then, because I kept using the platform I'd found in mainstream media to advocate a particular cause. While I've divided them into sections here, this made my writing about politics and culture hard to separate, not least because plenty of it was about the media itself – a place where politics and culture most obviously meet. The question about objectivity or opinionising applies differently to different types of journalist: reporters are supposed to be objective; columnists are expected to give opinions; and critics are meant to approach things objectively and then give opinions. When I first thought about going into journalism, as an undergraduate back in 2002, I wanted to be a critic, hoping to make a living from my interest in the arts. Historically, this was never easy, but still looked plausible then (just). I ended up becoming a reporter, columnist and critic simultaneously, largely because the internet broke the industry's financial model, which meant aspiring writers had to become far more versatile, and the borders between these categories collapsed. But even if I had wanted to be a journalist mainly to fund my more creative writing, I always took it seriously, unlike some of the generation above mine, who just seemed to revel in the generous salaries for their columns, or some of my contemporaries, who saw easy money in being mouthpieces for conservative or corporate interests (a gig that was especially lucrative if they claimed to be anti-establishment). Whatever journalism I wrote, I thought the point was not just to chronicle our times, but to try to change them.

All this meant I constantly had to weigh up the need for money, and career advancement – as I was hoping journalism might be a way out of the mundane office jobs I'd been doing for years – against the ethics of writing for each outlet who approached me. This varied according to whether my relationship with a publication would be one-off, temporary or permanent, and whether it was adversarial, writing against previous transphobic content, or collegiate. Before I finished my *Guardian* series, I took up a blog spot with the *New Statesman*, who allowed me to write on art, literature, film, music, wider political history and theory, with the space allowing me to make an intervention on trans issues whenever I felt it necessary. I liked this enough to decline a slot on the *Guardian*'s opinion section in 2013, as they wanted me to focus almost exclusively on trans issues. (I didn't ask if this would have paid enough to quit the day job, and I never found out.) At the time, I felt the project of improving our representation had progressed to the point where we could cover other subjects – and that it would be useful for us to do so, presenting ourselves as rounded individuals rather than the crude stereotypes that our opponents, who'd primarily encountered us through our typecast media personas, portrayed us as.

However, a backlash was brewing, with anti-trans feminist and conservative columnists finding common cause in opposition to trans rights. Their arguments and methods are outlined in an article included here, 'Compromise is Neither Desirable Nor Possible', written in response to the death of trans teacher Lucy Meadows in 2013 after a press campaign against her, and published by the *New Statesman*. This British reaction became even more intense after *Time* ran their famous 'Transgender Tipping Point' article in May 2014, arguing that trans rights and visibility campaigns had now reached a level where they couldn't be stopped, with *Orange is the New Black* star Laverne Cox on the cover: our opponents took this as a direct challenge, stepping up their attacks on us. Once a year, I would report for the *Statesman* on the relationship between trans people and the British media. These grew longer and angrier each time, as they published more 'gender critical' op-eds, making me feel that I couldn't justify my position there unless I devoted it solely to refuting them. Rather than yield to that demand, I wrote an 8,500-word essay 'On the 'Dispute' Between Trans People and Radical Feminism' in August 2014 and then stood down. I haven't included it here because its arguments became the basis for *Trans: A Memoir,* which I was then redrafting – that essay going viral, even trending on Twitter, gave me the confidence to make that book far more of a critique of the media than I'd previously imagined.

That piece also offered a depressing insight into the funding disparities between liberal and conservative media. Its popularity led an editor at the *Telegraph* to ask me to write about boxing promoter Kellie Maloney, who had recently come out as transsexual, and her history of making homophobic comments. I decided to do it, hoping to reach readers with attitudes like my (recently deceased and sadly missed) *Telegraph*-reading grandmother, who might be persuaded by a simple, emotive argument for tolerance. This took a morning to write whereas the *Statesman* essay had taken a week, yet the latter could only pay me £30 more.

By now, I had worked out that journalism wasn't going to be any more remunerative than the experimental short fiction I'd wanted to write as a student, and, having just been made redundant from my NHS admin job, sought an alternative way of living. I cut my overheads by moving into a cheap shared house in east London, signed on, finished the memoir and applied for funding for a Creative and Critical Writing PhD at the University of Sussex. Before I knew the outcome, I turned down an offer to become BuzzFeed UK's LGBT editor, knowing I wouldn't fit into their "optimistic and upbeat" new media culture, and doubtless wouldn't have lasted. I was ecstatic when I got the funding, most likely thanks to my prior journalism. For three years, I could focus on what would become *Variations* (published by Influx Press in June 2021) and do as much or as little journalism as I wanted, only taking on commissions I'd enjoy, using my spare time to train as a teacher, make a radio programme, and learn how to make films.

My PhD began in the same week that *Trans: A Memoir* was published. I wanted to step back from the front line of trans journalism, but didn't feel able to stay out of mainstream discourse for long. Since September 2015, things for trans and non-binary people across the world have deteriorated, in places as diverse as Brazil, Turkey, Hungary and Kyrgyzstan, and UK legacy media representation has taken a catastrophic turn for the worse. Before and especially after July 2018, when Theresa May announced a consultation to reform the Gender Recognition Act of 2004, potentially de-medicalising the process to allow trans people to obtain a certificate without the approval of two doctors, centrist and conservative journalists ramped up their attacks. They bombarded readers with op-eds about how trans adults were sexual predators who shouldn't be allowed into single-sex spaces, and about how giving hormone blockers to trans youths was 'child abuse'. 'Gender critical' groups became more vocal and organised, finding sympathy in the US from Donald Trump and the Republican far-right, and in the UK from Women and Equalities Minister Liz Truss, who suggested legislation to stop us from using single-sex services in summer 2020 – an idea eventually defeated by a vibrant protest movement. My response to this was to go to a big demonstration against Truss' proposals in London in June 2020, but also to write some articles that are featured here: an oppositional one for the *Guardian* insisting that 'Liberals Need to Stand Up for Trans Rights, Before It's Too Late', which took months to get past a sympathetic editor; and the long 'Towards a New Transgender Tipping Point' essay from 2019. (If you want more on this shift, I discussed it in an essay for *We Can Do Better Than This*, edited by Amelia Abraham and published by Penguin Random House in 2021, as well as an interview in *Vice* with Hannah Ewens, and a set of podcast interviews with young people called *Trans 20:20s*, made with Gendered Intelligence and Studio Voltaire.)

The schisms that had opened between the left and the centre around trans issues also became more intense after September 2015, with the election of Jeremy Corbyn as Labour leader. So much of what I now write deals with that four-year interregnum – the sense of hope his ascent sparked amongst the young, our constant frustration at the efforts of older people within the party and its supporting publications to wreck the 'project', the energy unleashed by the 2017 General Election and the hung parliament that resulted, and the historic defeat of December 2019. But at the time I was wary of putting my name to it: partly because so many people in British mainstream media seemed to suggest that any journalist who did so would regret it, but mainly because I didn't trust the Labour

Party to support trans people, even if Corbyn personally was unwavering on the subject. It was only during the 2017 campaign that I really got involved: this allowed for some separation between my journalism and my activism, which I channelled into canvassing and policy meetings. My writing didn't change all that much as a result, but my commitment to 'the project' inevitably came more into it as the 2019 election approached. Most of my writing on that is beyond the scope of this book, focusing as it does on my work on trans and non-binary issues, but my *New York Times* piece from March 2020, when Corbyn's potential successors came under scrutiny for their positioning on trans rights, is included.

If there's not quite a break in the pieces here from before and after September 2015, there's a definite sense of a change. About half of the Politics section is from 2010-14; there's a gap of four years where I tried to concentrate on my PhD while the media situation worsened, with all conversations circling back to the talking points of our opponents (on which I turned down numerous invitations to comment) but our political circumstances didn't drastically change. Watching the anti-trans movement become ever more aggressive, I worried that I – *we* – had done too much to provoke them, and maybe we should have kept quieter. But revisiting my earlier pieces in the Media section reminds me of just how bad it was before we got involved: the tone of the coverage was identical, even if they didn't need as much, in our relative absence, to say: 'You are not welcome here', and it's no surprise that these journalists' masks of objectivity slipped as soon as they were challenged. As I said in *Trans,* plenty of us had the same idea around the start of the 2010s – that the media was doing us immense damage, and as several key legal battles had been won during the previous decade, most notably the passing of the Gender Recognition Act, this should be our focus.

Most of the Media section also comes from before 2014, chronicling the (short-term, at least) failure of our attempts to change the British media by contributing to it, but includes a review of Paul B. Preciado's *An Apartment on Uranus,* published in *Tribune* – the only print magazine set up to support Corbyn's Labour, and which continues to provide a platform for left-wing writers – in spring 2020. Here, I offer thoughts on what a columnist should be: Preciado's approach to documenting the 2010s was unlike mine, but that's good. Growing up, I saw a range of gay and lesbian people on TV, so if I didn't like a particular figure, there was always another I might prefer, with each providing an increased sense that I could be my own person in the media. (This is what Laverne Cox meant in talking about *possibility models* rather than role models.) Despite the current backlash, more trans and non-binary people will emerge in writing, acting, music, film, sport and activism, inspired in part by what they read in newspapers and magazines during the 2010s, and they will encourage others to speak out. *Time* may yet be proved right about that 'tipping point', even if it didn't come as quickly or as smoothly as they – *we* – might have hoped. The final piece – a review of Shon Faye's *The Transgender Issue* – demonstrates how fiercely this battle is still being contested.

The bulk of the post-2015 pieces are in the Culture section, reflecting the fact that my social circles changed during this time, as I spent more time with artists and left-wing cultural critics (many of whom didn't identify as LGBT) and moved away from journalism. These pieces examine the past as much as the present, as I documented attempts to include trans and non-binary people within a history of queer art, and tried to create my own cultural canon. I wrote about literature, film, art and theatre – all long-term interests of mine – and although I'm now trying to focus on my creative work, criticism will remain the focus of my journalism for the foreseeable future, not least because what I've said about mainstream UK politics media since 2015 likely rules out a return to its publications, unless there are significant editorial changes and apologies for their previous positions.

After more than a decade as a transgender journalist, if not 'The Transgender Journalist', I feel I've managed to escape this typecasting. Partly, this has been through constant self-positioning, thinking years ahead to the kinds of projects I wanted to do and how I might use my journalism to open the paths towards them. But it has also been because of sustained, well-funded and co-ordinated efforts to push trans journalists back out of mainstream spaces. I wanted to escape the role because it was no longer necessary, not because it was *too* necessary for our opponents to handle. While we must not vacate the terrain to our enemies, I still feel it's worthwhile for trans writers to be covering a range of subjects and not just devoting ourselves to the arguments perpetuated by British legacy media – for the sake of our own mental health, and to offer more possibilities to younger trans and non-binary people who might otherwise look at the discourse and think it's not for them.

It's also worth noting that editorial gatekeepers can't stem the tide forever: the fierce arguments about, say, the *Guardian*'s attitude towards trans people notably split along generational lines, and as younger people finally reach positions of influence, the pendulum may well swing back towards us – not least because social media, new media and international broadcasters such as Netflix are full of trans and non-binary voices. In the UK and abroad, legislative attacks are a punishment for our progress in cultural battles, intended to impede us from further establishing ourselves in public life. Above all, activism is needed to fight this, with journalism to support it: there is no point in pretending to be objective in our work, as the stakes remain just as high as they were back in 2010, perhaps even higher after a decade of austerity and Tory rule. Those activists and journalists might find something of use in this collection, even if it's just to help them avoid the mistakes we made, in underestimating our antagonists in politics and media. It's far easier for people now to control not just the terms on which they speak, but the platforms through which they do it – and crowdfunding means there isn't always a big financial gap between these start-ups and legacy media. We're entering a new phase of collective struggle, with new fronts and new tactics needed: I hope this book can help to inform that.

A note on the selection

This anthology covers my non-fiction writing on trans and non-binary issues, published and unpublished, focusing on my essays and journalism. I wrote above that journalism can be repetitive. Looking through these pieces, that's reaffirmed by the number of times certain people, works and events come up: the Leveson Inquiry, *Time*'s 'Transgender Tipping Point' cover, and foundational trans theorists such as Kate Bornstein, Leslie Feinberg and especially Sandy Stone, whose essay 'The "Empire" Strikes Back: A Post-Transsexual Manifesto' is referenced so frequently due to the number of times I had to explain its premise to different audiences before I could continue my argument. I've left out all of my *Transgender Pieces,* as well as a few pieces from 2010-14 (such as my 'He to She' essay for *Aeon*) because they were incorporated into *Trans: A Memoir* – these are all detailed in the Bibliography. A couple of articles and essays were written in reference to photographs and wouldn't work without them, so are left out. I also excluded some of my early op-eds for *3Sixty* and *one80news* in Brighton as they were too topical, and perhaps too simple – the same goes for some early writing, especially blog posts and listicles, which would just have meant further repetition. The featured pieces are printed almost exactly as they were on their first publication: in a few cases, I have changed names and/or pronouns where the people concerned have publicly done so, or taken out references to articles that were hyperlinked, and corrected some typos that made it past their original editors, but that's it. Throughout the collection, readers can see how the vocabulary used by the British trans and non-binary community has changed over the last ten to fifteen years, and how the terminology I used shifted in accordance. In particular, there are several different acronyms – LGBT, LGBT+, LGBTQI and other variations – used throughout. This was usually a matter of what my editors thought their readers would recognise (and how much energy I had to argue about it) – LGBTQI+ is probably my preference at this point, but I have no doubt that our language will continue to evolve.

POLITICS

The articles in this section fall, broadly, into two periods: 2013-14, when I'd finished writing my *Transgender Journey* series for the *Guardian* and wanted to write more directly about the social and political problems facing trans people in the UK in particular; and 2018-20, when I was finishing my PhD (during which I wrote most of *Variations*) and returning to journalism, disgusted at how much airtime mainstream British media had given to anti-trans positions over the last few years.

I always saw the possibility of being an opinion journalist as a potential career rather than what I actually wanted to do with my writing, and I was reticent about it even as I secured platforms (in the *Guardian* and *New Statesman*) that might lead in that direction. I didn't want to be constantly defending my opinions, unpaid, in comment sections or on Twitter after my pieces went online under a deliberately inflammatory headline; I didn't want the logical next step of my career to be arguing with Tories and/or transphobes on TV or radio programmes. Uninspired, I struggled to come up with ideas for op-eds, and many of those featured here were suggested to me: 'Transsexual People and the Public Eye' by another journalist, intrigued to know my thoughts at the time; the pieces on global violence, football, and Kellie Maloney by editors. The Maloney commission was for the *Telegraph,* and I asked a select group of friends on Facebook whether they thought I should accept – they reasoned that 'from the point of view of our politics, it's no worse than the *Guardian*' or anywhere else I wrote. One piece, 'Travels of a Transsexual Football Fan', grew out of a Facebook post, when I was trying to work out how I felt about the encounter described – I worked the comments on my status update into a more refined version of the story, published on the *New Statesman* site.

The earliest pieces here are very matter-of-fact, basic if not naïve, reminding me of how much explaining of trans politics and history was needed for a mainstream audience before I could hope to explore these subjects in greater depth. This wasn't the kind of writing that most excited me, but they are interesting period pieces: it's amazing now to think that ten years ago, travel writer Jan Morris, then 85, remained Britain's best-known trans person, and that I could name so few examples of prominent US counterparts. (And it's sad to think that not just my take on the progress we were making in the media in general, but specifically my citing of Alexis Arquette as a possibility model, turned out to be so overly optimistic.) This section includes three pieces on two trips I made to Bishkek, the capital of Kyrgyzstan, in 2014 and 2018, and that, along with being asked to write for the *New York Times,* gave me a sense of building my reach beyond the UK. It was around this time that my writing moved up a level, as I went beyond having to convey the basics to readers, became more confident in my opinions and secured more length to develop my ideas.

The long essay, 'Towards a Transgender Tipping Point' was written for a book to accompany the Riga Biennial in 2020, with its publication long delayed due to the Covid-19 pandemic, but it was the first time I looked in detail at the transphobic backlash that built up during the mid-2010s in the UK, US and elsewhere. The essay – more academic in its approach than the other pieces here, having been written soon after I completed my PhD – looks at the bad faith use of 'debate' as a means to put transphobic ideas to the public, regardless of who 'wins', and around this time, I was turning down no end of broadcast media requests to argue with 'gender critical' feminists and hardline conservatives. I preferred to put my opinions into the public sphere whenever I felt it necessary, using platforms over which I had a little more control – the 'gender critical' writers, I thought, had enough space already, without letting them encroach further upon mine. (And, as an aside, I couldn't take the phrase 'gender critical' seriously, reminding me as it did of Alan Partridge calling himself a 'homo-sceptic'.)

The final pieces in this section deal with the amount of airtime those writers had been given by the ostensibly liberal press, and how that had influenced both Conservative government policy and the Labour Party in opposition. Plenty of people noted how the *New York Times* article about Labour's approach to trans issues would have been hard to place in any mainstream UK newspaper – although I must admit, I'd stopped trying – and the *Guardian* op-ed about how centrist transphobia was damaging our community and enabling the international far-right took months to get through a sympathetic editor. Like a lot of the British trans writers who briefly broke into the mainstream in the early 2010s, I had been boycotting the paper, but decided it was worth a one-off contribution to challenge the apparent editorial policy, something that, at present, doesn't seem to have worked. With these battles still raging in the *Guardian* and Labour – both of which police the left-wing limits of acceptable discourse, and contain people keen to redraw those limits to exclude the policies in Labour's 2019 election manifesto and people who supported them – I probably won't be contributing regularly to the paper any time soon, and since its publication, I have left the exhausting task of tackling widespread transphobia in these spaces to other people.

TRANSSEXUAL PEOPLE AND THE PUBLIC EYE

There are few openly transsexual people in British public life – and virtually none who have come out when already famous. The most notable exception remains acclaimed travel writer Jan Morris, who kept her gender reassignment secret until announcing its conclusion in 1972 and then published her autobiography, *Conundrum*, two years later. Since then, nobody approaching Morris' level of celebrity has publicly transitioned, with almost all of Britain's known transsexual people realising their identity before stepping into the spotlight.

By contrast, the hard work of post-war activists and the courage of openly gay, lesbian or bisexual people have created a climate where, slowly, public figures can discuss their sexual preferences without press intrusion – or pressure to act as advocates – ruining their lives. Since Thatcher's Conservatives passed the deplorable Section 28 in 1988, banning the 'promotion' of homosexuality in schools, progress has been remarkable: having apologised for this legislation, David Cameron's government now retains 13 openly gay Tory MPs, and there is now a diverse range of visible gay, lesbian or bisexual people in the arts, media and, gradually, sport.

The situation for noted people in any field who come out, or are outed as transsexual would almost certainly be less accommodating. (I focus on 'transsexual' rather than 'transgender' people, cross-dressers or transvestites, as the 'Real Life Experience' required to access medical treatment obliges full-time living in the chosen gender, making its public expression and resultant attention unavoidable.) As there have been so few test cases, I can only speculate on what may unfold, but the experiences of visible transsexual people in the USA offer some clues.

Recently, at least three Americans have publicly transitioned: Sonny and Cher's son Chaz Bono, actor Alexis Arquette and *LA Times* sports writer Mike Penner, briefly known as Christine Daniels. Chaz Bono transitioned from female to male, Arquette and Penner from male to female; their contrasting fortunes, including Penner's detransition and suicide, illustrate the challenges that a British counterpart might face.

The fundamental issues would be around privacy. There are many concerns for anyone whose transition is picked up by the print or broadcast media, but for our transsexual pioneer, these would be magnified by already being in the public eye.

Interest would be most intense at the point of disclosure, which could mean facing virtually every consequent social challenge simultaneously. If preparing to come out, a transsexual person would be best served telling family, friends and colleagues before the press – if secured, their support would be vital in dealing with inevitable 'curiosity'. If not, that person might think again about going public, although doing so would eventually become essential according to the gender reassignment pathway – and once made, the announcement may find its way into the public domain anyway, even if it is later retracted.

If outed by someone else, around the start of the process, that person would not have the reassurance that loved ones could be relied upon for backing – and may have no idea who to ask for help. (Anyone who did come out today might seek out Trans Media Watch as a first point of contact, as they provide support to people whose gender status is widely known.) Either way, the Real Life Experience would have to begin at some point – and the scrutiny of his or her appearance, if not entire life, would start.

'Before and after' pictures have long been a staple in media coverage of transsexual people, alongside undermining of the identity chosen. This is not to mention the possibility of speculation about personal and professional relationships or mental health, or intimate questions about sexuality, genitalia and surgery – something that activist Christine Burns, for example, had to manage in television appearances – all when this person would feel most vulnerable, striving on several fronts to assert his or her true self.

For those with little connection to other similar people or any grounding in trans politics or theory, some challenges may come as an unpleasant surprise. Chaz Bono and Alexis Arquette both spent plenty of time within LGBT circles before transition and probably knew what types of attack, and what support, could reasonably be anticipated not just from 'straight' conservatives, but from certain lesbian or gay critics, and the 'transgender' community (an increasingly fractious alliance, which, like many groups struggling for social change, has sometimes been susceptible to attacking its own). One of the saddest parts of Penner/Daniels' story was the breakdown in relations with trans support networks over how Daniels presented as a woman, and how unprepared she was for this kind of criticism. The crucial problems, however, involved her relationships with her family – not the media.

Given the continued lack of individuals who are able – or allowed – to offer a transsexual perspective to a large audience as a counterpoint to negative coverage, a public figure might feel pressure to 'represent' people, but this role could be declined relatively easily if he or she did not feel comfortable in assuming it. Bono and Arquette both became more famous as a consequence of transition, and have often seemed more comfortable performing an advocacy function, and their patient, articulate explanations of their histories and the support they have received from family, friends and the wider public bodes well for anyone in Britain who takes similar steps. But how much has changed here since Jan Morris's day remains to be seen.

New Statesman, 17 June 2011

CROSS-DRESSING IN VICTORIAN LONDON

With LGBT History Month taking place in February, it's an appropriate time to look back at one of Victorian London's biggest scandals – the arrest of Ernest 'Stella' Boulton and Frederick 'Fanny' Park in May 1870. After tracking the pair, known across Britain for their glamorous drag performances, the Metropolitan Police spectacularly accosted them outside the Strand Theatre for 'wearing women's clothes … for a supposed felonious purpose'. The arrest drew hundreds to Bow Street Police Court, desperate to glimpse the 'female personators': their trial promised the exposure not just of unnameable 'unnatural offences', but a homosexual ring that stretched from the lower middle class to the aristocracy – but their transgression of gender boundaries was not as new as the sensation-hungry crowd believed.

Anxieties over London's 'vice' grew throughout the 18th century, when 'buggery' was the only sexual practice outlawed. The capital's network of parish constables infiltrated several 'molly houses' – clandestine venues where men cross-dressed and slept with other men – and after the raid on Mother Clap's in Holborn in February 1726, three of the forty arrested were hanged.

Over the next hundred years, London's swift industrialisation allowed unprecedented numbers to flee their villages for the capital's anonymity. The population grew too fast for the law to keep up, and previously suppressed behaviours flourished: amidst concerns about rising divorce, prostitution, and cross-dressing, widely seen as the visible face of sodomy, the Metropolitan Police was established in 1829. The Met began controlling the borders of masculinity, frequently arresting men 'dressed in female attire'.

With female working rights limited, the few contemporary reports of women who presented as men suggest a belief that they did so to find work. Seeing no reason why men would dress as women, the Victorian authorities assumed sexual motives – particularly that they did it to trick men into sex with them.

The cases that ensued illustrate a problem for transgender historians: the concept did not exist in Victorian Britain, its development initiated by later sexologists who asked people why they cross-dressed and then coined terms such as 'transvestite' and 'transsexual' to describe them. To admit in court any innate need to cross-dress would have been to secure a prison sentence – the only safe defence was to deny it, with the occasion of arrest being a bet, an art project (as Luke Limner claimed in 1891) or, typically, "a lark".

With no specific laws against cross-dressing, defendants were often tried for solicitation. In March 1846, John Travers was charged with 'frequenting the public streets in female attire for an unlawful purpose' – according to *The Times,* 'the second or third case' heard at Bow Street 'within the past few weeks'. Constable C140 claimed to have seen Travers *en femme* more than twenty times, which made Travers' one-off "frolic" defence implausible, but the prosecution offered little evidence against Travers, who escaped with a fine.

In July 1854, George Campbell was charged with 'being disguised in female attire' – by now a public disorder offence, but no more – in an 'unlicensed dancing place'. Ex-Metropolitan officer Joseph Brundell said that, on reporting Campbell's "disgusting conduct", was told not to interfere "unless I saw such conduct take place on the public street". Campbell, a Reverend, claimed he'd wanted to see "vice in all its' enormity … to correct it from the pulpit". Judge Carden reluctantly discharged him, but only after the sitting magistrate, Alderman Carter, stated his "utter disgust at the prisoner's conduct in so attiring himself as a woman".

Boulton and Park's public appearances clearly went beyond "a lark" – so the Met subjected them to an examination to determine their sexual activity. Unsurprisingly, Victorian medical technology proved inconclusive: once Boulton and Park's lawyers contested the 'evidence' given by surgeon Dr Paul, the sodomy charge collapsed. A year after their arrest, during which time Boulton's aristocratic associate Lord Arthur Clinton died (officially of scarlet fever, but he more likely killed himself or fled the country), the pair were finally tried for 'conspiring to incite others to commit unnatural offences'.

The Society for the Suppression of Vice urged publications to withhold details, and London's *Pall Mall Gazette* refused to cover it. *The Times* capitalised on the scandal, but media speculation that the trial would expose a sodomite circle proved unfounded. Without evidence of sexual activity, just camp letters between the defendants and numerous photos of Boulton and Park in drag, the prosecution attempted to establish that Boulton and Park's cross-dressing was habitual, the defence that it was casual.

Astoundingly, Boulton and Park's lawyers successfully argued that their cross-dressing was an extension of their stage personas, and the case collapsed. Summing up, the judge attacked the Police's unwarranted 'examination', lamented the lack of laws against Boulton and Park's lifestyle and grudgingly freed them. On trial two decades later, Oscar Wilde – obsessed with Boulton and Park – attempted to place his own behaviour within an artistic context. Times had changed: under the 'gross indecency' law enacted in 1885, a broader legislation which regulated public and private behaviour, Wilde was convicted. The authorities ended the century in control over sexual and gender variants: sexologists would spend the next fighting for their greater understanding and acceptance.

Time Out, 16 February 2012

TRAVELS OF A TRANSSEXUAL FOOTBALL FAN

Saturday 9th November 2013. I've seen Norwich City beat West Ham United, and I'm on the train from Norwich to London. It's packed, so I end up without my friends from the Capital Canaries (Norwich's supporters club in London), who know my (male-to-female) gender history and happily take me as I come, and instead I'm in a carriage full of West Ham fans.

I think about listening to music, or writing, but the man opposite asks me about the game. He supports Rangers and the guy next to us supports West Ham, so we talk about our respective teams – Rangers' tax case and subsequent demotion to the Scottish Third Division, West Ham's inability to score and the pressure on Norwich manager Chris Hughton after a run of poor results – and it's all quite pleasant. I'm not wearing colours and I've put my Norwich scarf in my bag, which I think gives me the option of keeping out of post-football discussions if I don't feel like having them. We stop at Chelmsford and they leave, before three male West Ham fans, one in his early twenties, the others in their thirties, sit with me.

"Are you happy or sad?" asks the younger one, and it

takes a moment to realise he's asking which team I support. Not joining the conversation may well provoke an angry response, and anyway, they seem alright, like my friends from the Capital Canaries, so I say: "Happy."

I get good-natured questions about how long I've followed Norwich, and why. I explain that I'm from Surrey and have no good reason to support City. One says "I'm guessing you're 32? 33?" and I nod. As the other two say "No! You're 27, 28!" he says, "Norwich can't have been very good then – you had Robert Fleck up front, right?" He knows his football: instantly, he's put me in 1991-1992, when Norwich narrowly avoided relegation from the old First Division, after which they sold Fleck to Chelsea, and clearly differentiates it from the first Premier League campaign the next year, when City nearly won the title. This leads onto 'Disco' Dale Gordon, who left Norwich in 1991 and later joined West Ham, and we're getting on fine.

I say that as a child, my geography was terrible, joking that I liked yellow things, and that I'm glad I didn't choose my local team, Crystal Palace. As they laugh, I realise they already see me as a strange category error, a middle-class Canary from the Home Counties, and then that they're calling me "she", telling people not to swear in front of a lady, but occasionally calling me "he" – at least, I think they are.

Normally, once I'm comfortable with people I don't worry too much about 'passing'– that is, hiding my transsexual past – but I'm not sure how to play this. Are they reading and treating me as male or female? Why this mix of pronouns and gendered behaviour? The younger one asks where I'm going and I tell him it's an indie disco, and so they ask me about music. I realise this is going to be an extended conversation so think harder than usual about my voice, tone and gestures, and how my statements relate to masculine and feminine stereotypes: these three are alright, I reckon, and them realising I'm trans probably wouldn't be too problematic, but now lots of drunk West Ham fans are listening, and I'm not sure I want them all focusing on my gender identity.

The younger one says I should go for drinks with them instead, and I politely explain that I'm looking forward to seeing my friends at Scared to Dance. So they ask which bands I like, and I try not to be too obscure, naming The Smiths and New Order, Talking Heads and the Velvet Underground, and someone leans over, saying that he'd heard about Lou Reed's death, and I just nod. The younger one asks if I like Nickelback, and I say they're "not really my thing".

I decide to shift the conversation back to football, so they ask what I thought of West Ham's performance. "Not great," I said, "but you'll be alright."

"Nolan was shit, wasn't he?"

"He didn't do much," I laughed.

The younger one asks if I like West Ham: I say yes, and they enquire about my favourite West Ham players. Now there are some interesting gender stereotypes at work. In my late teens and early twenties, presenting as male in terrible jobs, football was my Get Out of Jail Free card when people thought I was irredeemably weird (as they often did). I didn't join many conversations but I'd ask who they supported and would ask a few questions: "£13m for Sylvain Wiltord – worth it?" "Should you have sold Beckham?" "Should Gérard Houllier have been sacked?" Even if we found nothing else to talk about, football usually provided enough conversation to get us through our days.

Here, I want to build enough of a rapport to ensure that they'll be cool if I'm 'read' as trans, and stick up for me if necessary, but as I think they're treating me as female, I don't want to look like a footy anorak as it's such a male archetype. How to answer? Discussing the merits of loyal utility man Steve Potts or the reasons for Romania star Florin Răducioiu's disastrous spell at Upton Park in 1996 probably wouldn't work – it would only invite follow-up questions about how I knew about them, but I don't want my interest to look too superficial either, because any suggestion that I'm only interested in football for the players' legs would really annoy me. I hit on current Irons player Winston Reid, a useful defender who plays regularly but isn't a household name, who'd missed the match through injury.

"Why Reid?" they ask, and I face the same dilemma.

"I used to have family in New Zealand." (I did, years ago, though I barely met them.)

They cheer and sing about Winston Reid, but I don't catch the words. I'm looking out of the window to see where we are, hoping it's near Stratford. We pass through Forest Gate: we're only a few minutes away, and as the train pulls up, we all wish each other a nice evening. As I walk to the Overground, I realise that I should have said Luděk Mikloško, West Ham's Czech goalkeeper from the Nineties – I know all the words to his song, and love the way they rhyme his surname with 'near Moscow', and I'm sure it would have been gone down well if I'd joined in.

New Statesman, 12 November 2013

REMEMBERING OUR DEAD: GLOBAL VIOLENCE AGAINST TRANS PEOPLE

In the past year, across the world, 238 transgender people have been murdered – 22 of whom were younger than 20 years old. Their names appear on the Transrespect vs. Transphobia Worldwide website, part of a total of 1,374 in sixty countries since 2008, found through online searches and co-operation with activist organisations.

78% of the reported deaths since 2008 have been in Latin America – a total of 1,074 people. There were more murders in Brazil (95 in 2013, and 539 since 2008) than any other country, some of whose ends, such as that of a 25-year-old 'shot' in Curitiba, and named only as Patricia, are recorded with a heart-breaking scarcity of detail. There is also a high prevalence in Mexico, and the US, particularly amongst African American trans women such as Kelly Young, aged 26, shot dead in Baltimore in March 2013, or 20-year-old Cernia 'Ce' Dove in Olmsted Township, who was stabbed repeatedly and thrown into a pond, naked from the waist down.

But proportionally, the higher rates for 2013 were in Central American nations with smaller populations, with 1.5

trans killings per million inhabitants in Honduras, and 0.71 in El Salvador. By contrast, there have been 117 recorded murders across Asia since 2008; 87 in North America and 84 in Europe; eight in Africa and four in Oceania.

This is almost certainly a fraction of the total number of trans people killed globally. The most recent Trans Murder Monitoring Project (TMM) press release notes that 'In most countries, data on murdered trans people are not systematically produced and it is impossible to estimate the number of unreported cases'. An additional problem is that in certain instances, victims may be misgendered by the press, especially in places that do not legally recognise their identities. TDoR's website notes on its entry for 32-year-old Jessica Rollon, strangled in Bergamo, Italy in 2011, that 'as with most cases, the local news continues to disrespect her by using male pronouns and a male name'. This coverage often mirrors official documentation.

Every year on 20 November, Transgender Day of Remembrance (TDoR) commemorates global victims of transphobic murder – killings which are thought to have been motivated by hostility to an individual's gender identity or presentation. Working to raise awareness of such violence, the Day of Remembrance website aims to record every such death of a trans person committed across the globe per calendar year. It gives the names of those killed, often alongside a distressingly high number of 'Unidentified' entries, along with the method of death, the date, and the location.

Now observed in 180 cities in twenty countries, The Day of Remembrance sprang from the murder of Rita Hester, an African-American trans woman, in Massachusetts on 28 November 1998. Hester's case, like many on the site's list of historical murders that goes back to the 1970s, remains unsolved.

Many of those remembered are sex workers, particularly in nations where there is no provision for hormone therapy or sex reassignment surgery and so many trans people, excluded from other employment, do this to raise money for medical treatment. At a social level, intersecting prejudices against sex workers, ethnic minorities and trans people account for the high rates; at an institutional level, they explain the lack of action. For example, the NGO Society Against Sexual Orientation Discrimination (SASOD) said of the killing of 19-year-old Tiffany Holder in Georgetown: "Violence against transgender sex workers is way too common in Guyana, underscoring that many incidents go unreported because the victims fear that no action will be taken against the perpetrators." They added that "laws which criminalise cross-dressing and same-sex intimacy provide institutional validation for the prejudices which fuel violence against sexual and gender minorities."

It is not that the challenges of social navigation for gender-variant individuals have never been raised. One of the strongest explorations is the 'Genderbashing' chapter in Viviane Namaste's *Invisible Lives: The Erasure of Transsexual and Transgendered People* (2000). Namaste suggests that visible gender transgression threatens heterosexual and cisgender (that is, crudely, people whose gender identities match those assigned to them at birth) male domination of public space, with entrance 'secured through the enactment of a sanctioned gender identity, preferably within the context of a heterosexual dyad'. She goes on to point out that this threat is often crushed with physical violence.

One issue which Namaste identifies is that this regulation means that trans people often have little choice but to exist within areas noted for their lesbian, gay and bisexual nightlife or meeting spaces, or are known to play host to trans sex workers, and so may provide some safety in numbers. Consequently, they become targets for attacks which are recorded as homophobic, which they often are, but not as transphobic, which denies the fact that they have been killed because of their gender presentation rather than, or as well as, because of their sexual orientation.

The involvement of sexual activity, whether or not money is involved, in such killings complicates this still further: Namaste writes about how rape is often a routine part of violence perpetrated against trans men, telling them, 'through the act of sexual assault, that they are "really" women, and they will be treated as such' – the murder of Brandon Teena in Nebraska in 1993 remains the most famous instance, mainly due to Hilary Swank's portrayal of Teena in the film *Boys Don't Cry*. The extent of this kind of violence remains difficult to ascertain but a study of the corrective rape in South Africa, which interviewed 121 people of colour and was published in 2011, looked at how trans men were just as likely as lesbian women to suffer such attacks, and just as unlikely to report them to the police for fear that they would be ignored, or endure further violence.

A glance at TDoR's lists for the last few years shows a number of harrowing, almost ritualistic murders of trans women, too, but knowing that such a problem exists is one thing; gathering statistical evidence to form the basis for arguing that transphobia should be included in hate crime policy is quite another. Meaningful research requires government backing, but the lack of recognition, through ignorance or malice, for trans people and their issues remains a massive barrier to its commission. Any study would most likely be conducted through activist and support groups, from which some trans people are isolated, or do not wish to be involved as they prefer not to disclose their gender history.

All told, the scale of the matter is huge, but trans-gender people worldwide will continue to do all they can to organise against transphobic violence, and the causes are gradually becoming better understood. As communications between activists and governments slowly improve, the Day of Remembrance remains an important way of keeping the issue in the spotlight, reminding everyone that violence against transgender people is a serious concern across the world, throughout the year.

Open Democracy, 26 November 2013

KINDNESS WILL HELP KELLIE MALONEY IN HER COMING OUT, AS IT DID ME

"Living with the burden any longer would have killed me," said Kellie Maloney, talking to the *Daily Mail* about her decision to undergo gender reassignment – and retire from a 30-year career as a boxing promoter, during which she was known as Frank, managed Lennox Lewis and took four other fighters to world titles.

Maloney came out as transsexual in a *Sunday Mirror* exclusive, and you might have expected that this revelation from one of the toughest figures in a notoriously macho sport would have provoked derision and hostility. But Lewis, whom she managed from 1989 to 2001, didn't see her transition as a challenge to his masculinity, but as an honest admission from a friend and loyal supporter, saying that: "[Now] I understand better what she, and others in similar situations are going through. I think all people should be allowed to live in a way that brings them harmony and inner peace."

The fear of "walking into a boxing hall dressed as a woman" put Maloney off transition for years, and beginning in her early 60s must be incredibly difficult. When I began the process, terrified about telling family, friends and colleagues – let alone what abuse I might take on the street – I went to a support group in Brighton. Aged 27, I was amongst the youngest there, and seeing the older transsexual women in tears because their children had rejected them, or because their elderly parents had disowned them after a lifetime of fear about their response, or because their friends felt their identities were false after so long living a lie, was heart-breaking.

"With this, you get over one hurdle and hit another one," Maloney said in the *Mirror*, worried that she would not be allowed to see one of her three daughters get married. Fear has dominated her life: she threw away women's clothes after trying them on, furtively going to underground 'dressing services' and telling no one, blaming the break-up of the first of two marriages on the pressure of resisting her gender identity through her flight into hyper-masculinity. But pleasant surprises didn't just come from Lewis and other boxing figures: Maloney's mother just joked: "Why didn't you come to me when you were younger? All we had to do was change the 'I' to an 'E' in your name, Francis."

My mother grew up in a Conservative household in the Seventies, braving the club's notorious hooligan firm to watch Chelsea with my grandfather. When I came out to her, she asked: "Who will I talk to about football?" thinking that transition would change my personality. "Me!" I said. "You're a woman, you like it – why wouldn't I?" From there, we reached an understanding that led to her nursing me through recovery from sex reassignment surgery – the end of a three-year journey in which I was constantly surprised by who proved the most accepting: after I emailed everyone I worked with at the PCT, the rugged Head of Security who sat next to me, and always called me "chap", just said: "Good for you, Juliet!"

Several male athletes have recently come out as gay: Jason Collins in basketball, Robbie Rogers and Thomas Hitzlsperger in football. Like Maloney and me, they met a largely positive reaction, but they all emphasised their masculinity, feeling held back by the perception that gay men are effeminate. Before transition, Maloney stood as a UKIP candidate in Barking in 2010, and it's disappointing that, perhaps trying to cover her own issues, she declined Camden as it had "too many gays". I hope the generosity of Lewis and others helps her become kinder: at their core, misogyny, homophobia and transphobia all share contempt for behaviour considered feminine, whether it's being female-bodied, sleeping with men or wearing women's clothes. We're all on complicated paths in a challenging world, but whatever her faults, Maloney's decision is a brave human act, and may generate a little more compassion.

The Daily Telegraph, 12 August 2014

IN BISHKEK

The PEN International Congress in Bishkek, the capital of Kyrgyzstan, last week was the first to be held in Central Asia. It was also the first at which the organisation resolved to oppose 'anti-LGBTQI (Lesbian, Gay, Bisexual, Transgender, Queer and Intersex) legislation which restricts the right to freedom of expression', having never before campaigned on sexuality or gender identity.

John Ralston Saul, PEN International's president, opened the Congress by saying that Bishkek was the only city in Central Asia that could host it. Two revolutions in the last decade have produced a democratic government committed to freedom of assembly, and domestic and international human rights organisations are allowed to operate there. PEN has expressed concerns, however, about police killings, torture in custody and the jailing of Azimjon Askarov, an ethnic Uzbek journalist, on charges of complicity in a Kyrgyz policeman's murder during inter-ethnic clashes in South Kyrgyzstan in June 2010, shortly after Kurmanbek Bakiev was ousted.

PEN also questioned Russia's growing influence over the former Soviet republic. The Kyrgyz parliament introduced a draft bill in March 2014 that copied Russia's legislation to outlaw 'gay propaganda'. I was invited to help

PEN finalise their position on this, but told not to mention it publicly until I returned to London for fear that the government would shut down the congress.

The draft resolution demanded that laws or bills banning the dissemination of information about LGBTQI people be repealed or rejected. There was a meeting at the congress to discuss it; I was on the panel along with Masha Gessen and Syinat Sultanalieva, a Kyrgyz activist. Marian Botsford Fraser was in the chair.

Gessen described the effects of the selective enforcement of the Russian 'propaganda' law, which not only prevented LGBTQI people from challenging hate speech or physical attacks, but also blocked discussion of domestic violence or child abuse by banning criticism of the 'traditional family'.

Syinat said that the Kyrgyz government hoped to secure Russian political and financial support by mimicking its legislation, with two crucial differences. The first was that Russia outlawed 'propaganda' directed at minors, while the Kyrgyz version had no age limits. The second was that in trying to justify itself, the bill mentioned not only Russia law but also the United Kingdom, pretending that Section 28 was still in force.

I talked about growing up under Section 28, which didn't only make it impossible for my school to help me to understand my gender identity or sexuality, but also prevented my English teacher from intervening when I was on the receiving end of homophobic abuse because liking poetry was 'gay'.

A delegate from Macedonia asked why PEN should address this issue, when there were no writers in prison because of their gender or sexuality, and more important matters of linguistic repression to consider. I'd been expecting the line of questioning, but not the wave of applause it received. Botsford Fraser explained that PEN had in fact fought to get LGBTQI writers released from jail.

Gessen grabbed the microphone: 'It is true that there are no writers in prison because of the anti-propaganda laws, but I had to go into exile with my family because of this anti-gay campaign.' (She now lives in New York.) 'We are not actually discussing LGBTQI rights, though I think that would be appropriate; we are discussing laws that limit the rights to free expression and access to information, which are classic PEN issues.'

When the resolution was put to a vote the next morning, it was approved with no objections and only three abstentions.

London Review of Books, 8 October 2014

ONE AFTERNOON IN BISHKEK

To my surprise, as I couldn't see any buildings besides a few high-rise blocks on the horizon, Syinat told the taxi driver to stop on a busy main road. I trusted her: we'd only just met but we were already friends, having spoken together on a panel about LGBTQI freedom of expression at the PEN International Congress, held in her home city of Bishkek, in the former Soviet Socialist Republic of Kyrgyzstan, for the first time. We'd spent the journey discussing how the Kyrgyz parliament were voting to adopt Russia's law against 'propaganda' in support of 'non-traditional sexual relationships' to 'protect the traditional family', applying sanctions across society rather than just in schools, effectively making Labrys, the support centre that we were visiting, illegal.

"We have to stop here because I can't tell the driver where our organisation is," she explained in English. The pavement, like most in Bishkek, was broken: even in the capital, there isn't money to maintain them, and the roads take priority. During our ten-minute walk down a dirt track, Syinat said that because they kept getting kicked out of places they rented, Labrys had to buy a house. They're in a religious area on the outskirts, where the locals have taken exception to them looking 'different', she told me, often abusing or threatening them.

Syinat pressed the buzzer; Masha verified her, and we entered. Having left my suburban, conservative home town aged 18 for England's most queer-friendly cities – Manchester, Brighton and then London – this level of secrecy felt jarring, especially as it's not illegal to be lesbian, gay, bisexual, trans, queer and/or intersex in Kyrgyzstan. But there is still plenty of prejudice within families, employers and the wider public (as in Britain); with the propaganda bill likely to pass, it's becoming harder for them not just to challenge violence and discrimination, or simply to exist. Without the international support given to LGBTQI people in Russia, Uganda, Nigeria and Iran – societies better understood in the West – the people at Labrys feel isolated, and they're surprised when they have any visitors.

Inside, it wasn't unlike the radical queer spaces I've visited in Britain or the Balkans – there were posters and pamphlets with slogans, some familiar in English but most in Russian. (Or so I assumed: I can't read Cyrillic, which Kyrgyz also uses, but the native tongue is not widely spoken outside official circles.) Ten people listened patiently as Syinat explained in both languages that I was a transgender writer from London: "she wants to talk about the propaganda law but she's happy to answer questions." Gulnara, a lively 19-year-old trans woman in jeans and a sequinned top, spoke first – in Russian, so I looked to Syinat for translation.

"She asked how she can get asylum in Britain."

I paused, stunned. Then I said that it was difficult, but not impossible, as discrimination against gender identity or sexuality could be grounds for asylum, and that I'd send more information when I got home. Then she asked about getting sex reassignment surgery on Britain's National Health Service as she thought she'd need it to change her documents, and it is prohibitively expensive in Kyrgyzstan. "It took me three years, starting in 2009," I said, "and it's harder now: the government wants to abolish the NHS, which they'll start by charging non-EU nationals to use it, and scrapping unpopular treatments."

Gulnara asked if she'd be socially accepted in Britain. "You're a Russian-speaking, transgender asylum seeker from a Muslim country", I replied. "I think you'd find it tough." I watched her face drop as Syinat (who studied in York and worked for the British Embassy in Bishkek) translated, adding details about the British media's anti-asylum rhetoric and the related rise of the ultra-conservative, anti-immigrant UK Independence Party. Crestfallen, Gulnara said she'd been told that Britain was very liberal – was it really so bad? "If you're white, English, middle class and prepared to play the Conservative Party's game, then it's not impossible" to be LGB or T (more than Q or I), I suggested, but otherwise, dealing with family, employers or public services could be a struggle.

I asked about the propaganda law. Uzalia, who like the other trans woman in the room had been disowned by her family, told me she'd leave Kyrgyzstan if it passed; another woman said she thought she'd be alright but worried for her friends, at Labrys and the Feminist Collective, both of which the Kyrgyz parliament has talked about shutting down. Then we talked a little more optimistically – they asked about my transition and surgery, and I gladly said it had gone well, socially and physically, promising to keep in touch after I returned to London, saddened by their circumstances but touched by their intelligence, solidarity and irrepressible humour.

The climate is getting worse, they tell me now: one MP criticised the bill and got called 'gay' by other politicians, despite his 'traditional' family, and the community have no other support. The media portray gender and sexual diversity as alien to Kyrgyzstan, despite the evidence at Labrys, and the bill is being introduced with a copy of Russia's Foreign Agents legislation, banning organisations from receiving *any* external donations. Lesbians and trans men already face corrective rape, with gay men and trans women often beaten and sometimes killed – the ambiguously worded propaganda law will censor journalists and enable the police to blackmail people, with the accompanying one making human rights groups reluctant to back them.

Their main hope is that President Atambayev will decline to pass the law, which may not stop it but will allow them to challenge it in the Supreme Court. However, the bill passed its first reading by 79 votes to seven, and Atambayev is firmly aligned with Vladimir Putin – any action needs to be taken in dialogue with the activists in Kyrgyzstan, to avoid making their situation any worse, but clearly, the time has come for international support.

Dissident blog, 16 December 2014

FOOTBALL TOLD ME I WASN'T WELCOME. WHEN WILL I BE?

My love of football has always placed me in a difficult position.

On one hand, there's an environment of conflict, oppression and political injustice around the sport. On the other, there are football's simple, scintillating pleasures. This tension – between the ugliness of the game's culture and its aesthetic beauty – has always been acute for LGBT fans, even more so for activists from our community. And at this World Cup, where President Vladimir Putin has presided over a hugely successful global spectacle while jailing and torturing dissidents (notably the Ukrainian filmmaker Oleg Sentsov), the contradiction between the joy of football and the misery of its culture and politics has been especially sharp.

But contradictions can be combated. And in the eight years since FIFA awarded the World Cup to Putin's Russia, LGBT activists have made great strides in their efforts to make the sport more accessible, more welcoming, more truly beautiful.

My own fight against homophobia, biphobia and transphobia in football goes back a long way. I joined my local club, Horley Town, when I was 11. I soon found I couldn't bond with my teammates, an experience replicated when I played, once, for my school. I didn't play competitively again until I joined the Brighton Bandits, a team on the English South Coast who were part of the world's only national LGBT football league, the Gay Football Supporters' Network League.

At the time, some friends asked why such segregation was necessary. I told them the truth, which was that LGBT people were unlikely to socialise in the same places as straight teammates and would feel nervous about disclosing same-sex relationships. They had good reason to: managers such as the English legend Brian Clough and the former Croatia boss Otto Barić publicly denounced gay players. Homophobic chants remain the norm.

After my first Bandits match in 2008, I talked to a teammate about Justin Fashanu, who in 1990 became the first (and at the time only) professional player to come out as gay. As the 10th anniversary of Fashanu's death approached, nobody was discussing it. In part this was because his life was so complicated, and his death – he committed suicide after being accused of sexual assault – so traumatic. But it felt like an impediment to a wider conversation about the gulf between LGBT fans and professional football.

It was not Fashanu's only problem, but he suffered from prejudice before and after coming out, so we adopted his name for The Justin Campaign against homophobia in football.

Later, the campaign rebranded as Football v. Homophobia and became an important agent in anti-discrimination initiatives, running workshops for clubs and organisations across Europe about how to create an environment where a professional player might feel able to come out and where fans might be able to challenge the perception that LGBT people weren't harmed by homophobic behaviour. Though

I had left the campaign to begin my gender transition – I had a lot to sort out – its work was vital in spreading the tenets and techniques of inclusion.

But there's so far to go. Issues like how to include trans players in men's or women's divisions have been left to national associations, even though, as the International Olympic Committee urges, they should be allowed to compete without restriction. And despite FIFA's heartening willingness to engage with activist groups, most of its initiatives have focused on "diversity" rather than concrete actions on LGBT inclusion.

And then there's the World Cup. Awarded to Russia – a country ranked second bottom of European countries for LGBT rights in 2016 – the tournament has been full of contradiction and frustration. FIFA supported Diversity House in Russia, a place for discussions, meetings and, most important, ardent game-watching, but was slow to act on Mexico fans' homophobic chants during their country's 1-0 win over Germany.

The organisation has, however, allowed fans to take rainbow flags into the stadiums. One supporter to do so, Di Cunningham, experienced a few frosty exchanges with Russian and English fans (including an England supporter who told her to "keep politics out of football"), but plenty of support and exposure, too. Cunningham hopes her example will prompt LGBT fans from other countries to ask, "Why can't we do this?"

When I stepped, tentatively, back onto the football field a decade ago, nobody paid much attention to the systematic marginalisation of LGBT fans and players. Our concerns were far from the mainstream. Now the game's governing bodies interact with LGBT activists, and top-level clubs have established links with "gay-friendly" amateur teams and LGBT supporters' groups.

This progress proves an activists' axiom: Changes in public opinion are almost always led by the grass roots, with institutions slowly (and often grudgingly) catching up.

At least at Norwich City – the team I follow devotedly, based in the east of England – the supporters and the club have reached the same place. A month before the World Cup began, I played in a tournament for LGBT teams, hosted by Norwich City, with Justin Fashanu's niece Amal as the guest of honour. I realised my childhood dream of scoring at Carrow Road, Norwich's home ground, where I have spent countless Saturdays. After it finished, I was presented with a pink World Cup trophy, last seen at a small Justin Campaign event back in 2010.

It felt like the perfect reward for persevering with a sport, or more accurately a sporting culture, which had told me so many times that I wasn't welcome.

Football Told Me I Wasn't Welcome. When Will I Be?
by Juliet Jacques originally appeared in
The New York Times on 12 July 2018

FEAR AND LOATHING IN KYRGYZSTAN

In September 2014, I visited Kyrgyzstan for the first time, to speak at the PEN International Congress in the capital, Bishkek. We had to keep our panel, which argued for the repeal of "anti-LGBTQI" (Lesbian, Gay, Bisexual, Transgender, Queer and Intersex) legislation that restricts the right to freedom of expression, secret. A few months earlier, the Kyrgyz parliament had introduced a bill that copied Russia's legislation against "gay propaganda", with additional jail sentences for people who "promote homosexual relations" through the media, so we feared that the entire Congress could be shut down if the authorities found out about it.

International concern grew after the bill passed its first reading by 79 votes to seven. The only MP who publicly criticised it was called "gay" by other politicians and newspapers, despite his "traditional" family. The bill had a second reading in June 2015 with little discussion, no questions asked of the 28 MPs who sponsored it, and 90 votes in favour. However, it then went no further, and in May 2016, a parliamentary subcommittee proposed another second reading rather than a third and final review. Their official reason was that the bill's initial proponents were not re-elected in the October 2015 parliamentary elections, and that the new government should discuss this contentious issue. This has not yet happened.

Unofficially, pressure from the UN Human Rights Council, the EU Parliament and the Coalition for Justice and Non-Discrimination – a body of NGOs and activists that lobbies for anti-discrimination legislation in Kyrgyzstan – may have influenced the subcommittee, as well as the parliamentary rejection of a bill, inspired by similar legislation in Russia, requiring any NGO receiving foreign funding to register as a "foreign agent". It is emblematic of Kyrgyzstan's struggle to remain open towards Europe whilst sustaining ties with Russia and their central Asian neighbours that the bill seems to have been quietly dropped, but it is still on the books. Politically, this may be the only way to appease the European Union, the Russian Federation and Kyrgyz nationalist groups, who, like their post-Soviet counterparts, notably in Ukraine, where far-right groups routinely attack Pride events, are virulently opposed to LGBTQI people.

Such laws, however, do not have to pass to have a chilling effect. In 2014, I met Kyrgyz LGBTQI organisation Labrys, who said that lesbians and trans men already faced 'corrective' rape, and gay men and trans women were often beaten and sometimes killed. Such attacks have since intensified. Soon after I went back to London, Labrys shut down their Facebook page, and had to sell the house where I first met them after it was subjected to an arson attack in 2015. They resurfaced last year, and in March I returned to Bishkek to meet a new generation of activists who, amidst the confusion and hostility, are fighting to make Kyrgyzstan more open to diversity of gender and sexuality.

"In 2017, we wrote to the Committee [on Law and Order] about the status of the bill, but never received a reply. It's still unclear what will happen – every month it's updated on the parliament website," one of the activists, Aizhan, told me. There are still legal issues: this impasse meant Labrys' National Action Plan recommendations – for LGBTQI groups, sex workers, drug users and HIV-positive people – were rejected after two years, as the Kyrgyz parliament said it refused to be ordered to withdraw the bill and called off the negotiations. A December 2016 referendum on the constitution included an amendment to define the family as "created upon the voluntary union of a man and a woman", and gave precedence to Kyrgyz law, making it harder for Labrys and other human rights groups to cite international legislation in their opposition to institutional discrimination.

No law (yet), but more attacks

The lack of statistics about crimes against LGBTQI people in Kyrgyzstan remains a concern, so last year Labrys started monitoring and published a report on their website in 2017. Anecdotally, the activists agree that attacks have become more frequent, and organised, since 2014.

"After the draft law, far-right groups started working to promote family values. Two years ago, [US preacher] Scott Lively, who promoted the anti-gay law in Uganda, visited Bishkek. He met anti-LGBTQI groups, who put photos on Facebook," one of the activists recalled as we met in their office in central Bishkek. "In 2015, we launched proceedings against nationalists who attacked our 17 May [the International Day Against Homophobia, Biphobia and Transphobia] event, which was the first-ever case concerning violence against a Kyrgyz LGBTQI organisation." After two years, the court sent it for re-investigation; the police said there was not enough evidence, and that they couldn't contact witnesses. The main victim declined to proceed because of security issues.

"In September 2017, we tried to organise a march for Bisexual Visibility Day," said Labrys' executive director, Sanjar. "We didn't have to get permission from the mayor's office, but we informed them, so we could say we did if anything happened. We still weren't allowed to march, as the district court had ruled against it because the government were preparing for [presidential] elections [in October]. Then we got a call saying a taxi driver had a foreigner wanting to visit us, asking for our address. We told them to come to TSUM [a shopping centre in Bishkek]. It was someone from the national security office, saying we shouldn't go on our march. People came three times, threatening us. Then, a nationalist group leader called, telling us we would regret going ahead."

"The police often undress trans women, and so do trans-phobic people," says Sanjar. Indeed, this nearly happened to me on the Kyrgyz-Kazakh border: a passport control clerk took exception to me, and soon I had five security guards yelling at me. They didn't strip me, or order me to undress, but made it obvious that they could. "People get outed online, and there is a lot of hate speech. The winner of Miss Kyrgyzstan said we should burn all LGBTQI people. We asked the national security office to investigate this as incitement to violence, but nothing happened."

With the propaganda law lurking in the background, and no law against hate speech or crimes – in legal terms, only murder can be based on discrimination, with religion, ethnicity, and nationality as the only criteria – LGBTQI people remain easy targets in Kyrgyzstan, with nowhere to turn for recourse. "A [Kyrgyz] journalist went with the police on a raid and started filming trans women; she then posted on Facebook about how they beat her up, which wasn't true. She provokes trans women, films them and then asks for 400 soms [about £5] to keep it off social media," said Mohira, an activist who has also been involved with queer leftist collective ShTAB – the School of Theory and Activism in Bishkek, adding that the same journalist had leaked information about the International Day Against Homophobia, Biphobia and Transphobia, a closed event, to Kyrgyz nationalists, and wrote a slanderous article about a film screening hosted by ShTAB. "She's a long-term enemy," Mohira stated.

However, Labrys have had some successes. In January, they secured the right for trans people to change their documents with just a diagnosis of gender dysphoria from a medical professional, having previously required surgery; the health ministry also approved their guidelines on endocrinological and psychiatric support. On a wider level, Labrys have organised events to empower and mobilise communities, such as round tables in Bishkek and Osh, Kyrgyzstan's second-largest city, to create dialogue between trans people, medical specialists and the health ministry. They are also planning for a delegation to talk to the police about how to treat the LGBTQI community with greater respect.

Internationally, Labrys are part of a coalition of trans people in post-Soviet countries, and in touch with an association of Russian-speaking intersex people and LGBTQI groups in Kazakhstan and Tajikistan. They are also part of IGLA (International Gay & Lesbian Association) Europe, but Mohira stresses the importance of Kyrgyzstan and Central Asia being grouped with Eastern Europe, as their recent history has more in common with Ukraine or Belarus, and especially Russia, than India or Bangladesh. This might be a step towards the social issues affecting the LGBTQI community in Kyrgyzstan, and the wider region, being better understood in the West and, it is hoped, receiving greater international support.

Open Democracy, 20 September 2018

MARIO MIELI'S
GAY COMMUNISM

Mario Mieli's *Elements of a Homosexual Critique* was first published in Italy in 1977, amid the country's tumultuous 'Years of Lead' and post-1968 sexual radicalism. Though Gay Men's Press translated the text as *Homosexuality and Liberation* in 1980, Mieli was eclipsed by his French contemporaries – notably Michel Foucault but also Guy Hocquenghem and Leo Bersani, who worked within a larger and more visible queer movement, and did not share Mieli's interest in finding a way to combine the ideas of Marx and Freud. This was his only theoretical work. Mieli killed himself in 1983, aged 30, and did not live to see the HIV/AIDS crisis kill Foucault, Hocquenghem, and millions of others, and irrevocably change queer politics.

Pluto Press' recent edition, re-translated by David Fernbach and Evan Calder Williams as the more eye-catching *Towards a Gay Communism* (with a shocking-pink cover that captures Mieli's confrontational, camp persona) appears as many Western activists question the compromises of respectability politics. Like Matthew Warchus' 2014 film *Pride*, about the Lesbians and Gays Support the Miners movement, this publication asks what can be recuperated from the period between May '68 and Stonewall. Unlike *Pride*, however, it refuses to play down Mieli's ideology – Warchus' film never mentions that its protagonist Mark Ashton was the general secretary of the Young Communist League from 1985 until his AIDS-related death two years later.

As with many queer texts of its time, not every premise of *Towards a Gay Communism* feels reconcilable now. In France, the gay liberation movement split from the lesbian movement over issues of consent. Mieli's aim to replace identity with a world of erotic abundance suggests a lack of boundaries, and his openness to a range of behaviours – including coprophilia and necrophilia – has aged badly. Likewise with his discussion of children's sexuality, which was written in an era of harsh repression for young LGBT people, but is nonetheless dangerous. However, his writing in this area does have merit. As states from Russia to Turkey adopt Section 28-style laws that criminalise not LGBT behaviour but 'propaganda', Mieli's critique of an 'educastration' process that aims to dissuade children from growing into an openness about the endless possibilities of sex and gender still feels revolutionary.

The homo-masculinity of the French movement, and Hocquenghem in particular, was also an issue. Mieli chimes more with the present in his embrace of 'transsexuality', which he uses to mean a polymorphic drive that breaks down boundaries between masculine and feminine, male and female, as well as homosexual and heterosexual. Mieli appreciated that gender norms were a vital means of upholding capitalist hierarchies, and that their reproduction within homosexual subcultures meant the reproduction not just of the suppression of femininity, but of conservative divisions of labour.

Had he lived another decade, Mieli may not have placed the idea that nothing horrifies 'the policeman of capitalism' more than the thought of 'being fucked in the arse' (even if this became even more true during the HIV/AIDS crisis), or that anal sex is 'itself a significant revolutionary force' at the heart of his thesis. But his awareness that gay identity could easily be co-opted, especially when revolutionary ideas are channelled towards the 'respectable' classes, and that legal rights do not mean an end to oppression, seems visionary. His conclusion that the most radical way to reject marginality was to assert a collective refusal of majority viewpoints remains relevant today.

Tribune Issue 1, Autumn 2018

TOWARDS A NEW
TRANSGENDER TIPPING POINT

In May 2014, *Time* magazine announced the 'Transgender Tipping Point' – the moment when, after decades of writing and organising, trans and non-binary people could no longer be kept out of mainstream culture, nor our rights excluded from progressive political movements. *Time* had its first trans cover star: Laverne Cox, star of the Netflix series *Orange is the New Black,* who was interviewed for a feature on 'America's next civil rights frontier'. What many people, including myself, did not anticipate was that rather than being carried forward by its apparently unstoppable momentum, the trans liberation movement might instead be tipped *back* by a constellation of reactionary forces.

In the five years since that 'Tipping Point' was declared, we have seen nominally liberal UK publications such as *The Guardian* and *The New Statesman* – for whom I wrote extensively on trans politics and culture between 2010 and 2014 – build up a long-standing conflict between trans-exclusionary feminists and trans 'activists' (mostly just trans people asserting their right to exist) and then side with the exclusionists. Worse, we have seen the Trump administration's efforts to ban trans people from the US military (partly in response to the attention paid to Chelsea Manning, but also as part of a wider attack on LGBT rights) and to (re)define gender as being just 'male or female based on immutable biological traits identifiable by or before birth'. We have seen Viktor Orbán ban Gender Studies from Hungarian universities, and efforts to outlaw the very word 'gender' from the Polish language; attacks on LGBTQI+ communities led by president Bolsonaro in Brazil (with Judith Butler in particular becoming a hate figure for their apparent influence on changes to gender roles) and president Erdoğan in Turkey; attempts to outlaw 'gay propaganda' in Kyrgyzstan, following the example set in Russia in 2013; and trans people in the global south suffering from ongoing poverty, violence and murder.

One way that this backlash has been orchestrated through British mainstream media has been through bad faith use of 'debate' – a tactic that has been widely adopted by the far-right in the UK and USA. During the 1970s, arguments about whether to admit trans women into women-only spaces crystallised a transphobic feminism that, by the 1990s, had become hegemonic in British liberal newspapers, which would frequently publish op-eds that questioned an apparent politically-correct consensus that made it obligatory to accept trans people's stated identities – a consensus that many trans people, having been disowned by their family and/or friends, dumped by their lovers, denied medical treatment, sacked from their jobs or attacked in the street would say did not exist. My approach, in my writing, was to try to shift the discourse: rather than argue on someone else's terms over our right to exist, I tried to speak about problems with the medical process of transition, issues trans people had finding safe housing or secure employment, the psychological effects of transphobia and how the media fuelled it, and so on.

In May 2014, this tactic, widely used by trans people in the press, seemed to be working. Since then, there has been a co-ordinated effort by conservatives and anti-trans feminists to push the conversation back onto the least favourable terms and paint trans people who boycott such discussions as enemies of free speech. Paradoxically, this has served to drive us out of mainstream discourse by making it ethically unjustifiable for us to participate in its institutions – whilst the perpetrators continue to use their national newspaper columns to complain about how the 'trans lobby' are silencing them.

The tactic of denying basic humanity to trans people has been around since the first sexological studies of gender variance were carried out in the early twentieth century, and has manifested itself in everything from micro-aggressions such as individuals pointedly using 'it' rather than our preferred pronouns, to laws to prevent us from accessing hormones or surgeries, or mandate us out of existence. Radical history teaches us that liberal notions of slowly unfolding progress do not hold water, and that we will have to fight such behaviours repeatedly, in different settings and in different ways. In taking on transphobes in mainstream media, my generation has replicated the struggles in late 20th century activist and academic circles; I borrowed my tactics from Sandy Stone, the trans writer, artist and sound engineer whose influential text 'The "Empire" Strikes Back: A Post-Transsexual Manifesto' ([1987] 1992) kickstarted the first wave of (North American) trans theory. Stone's demand for us to explore the space between 'male' and 'female' in our work had a huge impact on trans authors who emerged in the 1990s such as Kate Bornstein and Leslie Feinberg, as well as on the generation of journalist-activists such as myself who became prominent before 2014 (Jacques 2018). For now, we may be going back underground, but we are definitely *not* going away; at this point, though, we need to reassess our theories and strategies.

In 'Normalized Transgressions: Legitimizing the Transsexual Body as Productive', Dan Irving argued that the 'Real Life Test', which gender identity clinics use to see how transsexual people will adapt to living full-time in their preferred gender before prescribing hormones or surgery, specifically demands they fit into heteronormative, bourgeois society. Irving wrote that 'Embodied identities, such as transsexuality, are the result of complex amalgamating relations of domination, exploitation and agency' (2008, p.17), and suggested that in seeking to justify themselves in a transphobic world, trans people reproduced capitalistic norms not just in satisfying clinicians, but also in emphasising their capabilities as 'productive' citizens within a neoliberal economy, and in forms of activism that sought trans assimilation into oppressive social structures. Irving's essay was first published in 2008 – the point at which the façade of the post-Cold War neoliberal consensus collapsed – and in the ten years since, the disaster mode of capitalism that brought bank bailouts, brutal austerity, and the international rise of the far right has made such assimilationism untenable. (Speaking personally, on starting my transition via the National Health Service in 2009, I was surprised to learn that I was obliged to be in full-time employment, education or voluntary work despite not having to pay for treatment, at a time when numerous public sector jobs like the one I had were being cut.) The line of theorists who followed Stone largely rejected liberal approaches to trans activism, preferring instead to ground their work in radical politics, media criticism or considerations of how our bodies intersected with scientific technology, or the pharmaceutical industry. What else, at this point, might we pick up from them?

Trans people have always had a complex relationship with ideas of the 'natural'. Sexologists constituted our identities in the twentieth century, categorising us as 'transvestite' or 'transsexual' depending on how they diagnosed our relationships with our bodies and social presentations, and then worked towards the development of gender confirmation surgeries. In a transphobic society, some trans writers have concentrated on promoting greater understanding of these identities, both within our 'community' and outside it. Many, but not all, of the anti-capitalist theorists who followed Stone grounded their work within the material realities of contemporary Western life, for obvious political reasons. It's worth noting, however, that one of the major influences on Stone was Donna Haraway, whose *Cyborg Manifesto: Science, Technology, and Socialist-Feminism in the Late Twentieth Century* (1984) raised questions about what it meant to be conscious and embodied in a world where things such as organ transplants (and, indeed, reassignment surgeries, although Haraway did not discuss them) were possible. Arguing that boundaries between the organic and the technological, human and animal, and human and machine were breaking down, and that 'cyborg imagery can suggest a way out of the maze of dualisms in which we have explained our bodies and our tools to ourselves' (1984, p. 116) Haraway speculated about a post-gender space in which marginalised subjects might move beyond dehumanising discourses about what their bodies meant, and think more creatively about what their bodies *could be.*

Haraway's ideas strongly influenced trans historian, filmmaker and activist Susan Stryker, who co-edited two *Transgender Studies Readers* and co-founded *Transgender Studies Quarterly* in 2014. In her essay *My Words to Victor Frankenstein above the Village of Chamounix,* subtitled 'Performing Transgender Rage', Stryker notes that 'Like the monster, I am too often perceived as less than fully human to the means of my embodiment' (1994, p. 245). Stryker's inner monologue about her feelings towards her body shows her dealing with internalised transphobia in a way familiar to me and (I suspect) countless other trans people: *'I am alienating from Being. I'm a self-mutilated deformity, a pervert, a mutant, trapped in monstrous flesh. God, I never wanted to be trapped again. I've destroyed myself. I'm falling into darkness I am falling apart'* (1994, p. 251, emphasis in original). Stryker concludes that 'transgender rage furnishes a means for disidentification with compulsorily assigned subject positions' and turns 'the stigma [into a] source of transformative power' (p. 253). By embracing the role of the outsider whose existence reveals the artificiality of assigned sex and associated gender norms, Stryker argues, we could not just reclaim our agency but also, turning Haraway's conclusion on its head, assert our humanity.

There is much to be said for this tactic, which has been central to the line of transgender studies that has followed Stone's manifesto, and Stryker's work – especially her pioneering *Transgender History* (2008) – has been inspirational to me and many of my contemporaries. The idea that there is radicalism to our very *being* is seductive, allowing us to neutralise the conservative characterisation of us as freaks, and challenge the anti-trans feminist depiction of us as conformists. But the tension between this position and one that seeks to find ways for us to better fit into mainstream society persists: the best way around it would be to use trans perspectives as a basis to reshape society, rather than seek to assimilate or decide to shun that society as it is. In her 2003 speech 'Tracing This Body: Transsexuality, Pharmaceuticals, and Capitalism', which was transcribed and distributed between friends via email in the true manner of an 'underground' publication,

Michelle O'Brien examined how her very existence relied upon 'health insurance corporations [who] are defining what medical care they consider to be appropriate, and which they do not', obliging her to spend a third of her income on basic prescriptions (2003, p. 57). This was 'the bureaucratic expression of the brutal violence trans people often face out in the streets – the devaluation of our bodies as worthless (p. 58). Like many other trans writers, O'Brien identified potential in Haraway's manifesto, writing that 'The cyborg is the bastard child of the patriarchal realms of capitalism, nature, and technoscience [...] Like the cyborg, [trans people] are both complicit in and a challenge to the biomedical industries [...] Far from the dupes of doctors or the crude escapists of eco-primitivism, we are living amidst the systems we are always subverting' (p. 64). Ultimately, this assimilation of medical technology into our bodies does not make us any less (or more) human: the point is that our struggles to secure medication and healthcare, for our bodies to be treated with respect, for our identities to be understood and acknowledged, and for better cultural representation are all linked to the wider struggle against capitalist domination. This is becoming ever more relevant as far-right movements, aided by sympathetic and divisive media outlets, are making gains in reaction to the brutal austerity programmes pursued across Europe since 2008. Our experiences at the sharp end of violence, funding cuts and censorship ought to make us an integral part of feminist movements, which should be central to any anti-capitalist politics, given how much women more widely suffer from this structural oppression.

For this to happen, I feel there needs to be a slightly different way of understanding us and how we exist in the world as trans and/or non-binary people. There has been considerable resistance to the idea that we can self-identify our genders – our tactic for escaping the medical industry's control over our identities, and more widespread dehumanisation – and a demand that we spend all our energy meeting outsiders' questions about *why* we are trans. I have written so much (a newspaper series and a memoir, a volume of short stories, and numerous articles and essays) about my experiences of being trans and how they fit into a longer history of gender variance, and the fundamental question of *why* continues to elude me – as it has everyone else. In truth, it is a question that interests me less and less: it has served its purpose to helping sexologists to understand our needs, categorise us and help us accordingly, and now functions more as an instrument of aggression, humiliation, and enervation. I can no more explain the fundamental impulse that 'makes' me trans (and made me transition) any more than I can explain why I am left-handed. To be able to explain this impulse may either be to kill it – in the way that finding the source of emotional patterns or behaviours through psychotherapy is to begin to change them – or to convey it so perfectly to others that they feel the same visceral sense of gender dysphoria that I and others have felt, and need to act on it in a similar fashion. (As far as I am aware, my writing has helped some people to deal with their own gender dysphoria, and others to understand the situation of friends, family, or lovers, but no-one has ever told me that my work has 'turned' them trans. Perhaps that qualifies as a failure on my part.)

Far more interesting to me is how my (trans) consciousness has been formed in relation to other people, in a transphobic society. An intriguing shift in feminist–transphobic discourse is that it has moved from being dominated by lesbians who opposed the entry of trans women into women-only spaces in the 1970s and 1980s to being led, at least in the UK's mainstream media, by heterosexual mothers (questions have been asked about how much the Mumsnet website, in particular, has incubated anti-trans organising). Recalling Haraway's *Cyborg Manifesto,* and the idea – expressed by *Testo Junkie* author Paul Preciado and others – that in the twenty-first century, *everyone* is reliant on medical technology in some way, it's worth noting that abortion rights and access to sex reassignment surgeries attract far more opprobrium from conservatives than organ transplants or test tube babies. The survival and procreation of the species, and attendant preservation of traditional gender roles, is central to their political project, and both cisgender and trans women, as well as trans men and non-binary people, should unite against them in order to protect our bodily autonomy. It is also useful, politically, to acknowledge that while trans people are authorities on the specific gender dysphoria that leads us to transition, many people have some level of discord with their own bodies in a society that encourages such feelings in order to sell things to us – increasingly so, given the prevalence of self-curation on social media.

That social media has given trans people a louder voice and made it easier for us to organise, countering the ways in which the gender identity clinics 'programmed [transsexual people] to disappear' in Stone's time (1987, p. 230). For all the reactionary backlash, such organisation cannot be entirely undone, and it may be useful for us to assert ourselves through culture – disseminating our stories and ideas through art, literature, film, and music, but also by making ourselves prominent for things that are not directly related to our trans-ness. This would also allow us not just to get beyond the established romantic-heroic trans narratives that talk about how successfully we integrate into wider society, but also to become a more effective part of movements that aim to change that society. It might even encourage outsiders to see the world from a trans perspective, rather than simply 'tolerating' us: that would engineer a 'tipping point' that would be far harder to reverse.

References

Haraway, D. (1984) 'A Cyborg Manifesto: Science, Technology, and Socialist-Feminism in the Late Twentieth Century'. In: Stryker, S. & Whittle, S. (eds.) (2006) *The Transgender Studies Reader.* London/New York: Routledge, pp. 103–118.

Irving, D. (2008) 'Normalized Transgressions: Legitimizing the Transsexual Body as Productive.' In: Aizura, A. Z. & Stryker, S. (eds.) (2013) *The Transgender Studies Reader 2.* London/New York: Routledge, pp. 15–29.

Jacques, J. (2018) 'Écriture trans-féminine?', *Mal*, October. Available online: https://maljournal.com/1/that-ob-scure-object/juliet-jacques/ecriture-trans-feminine (accessed 9 April 2019).

O'Brien, M. (2003) 'Tracing This Body: Transsexuality, Pharmaceuticals, and Capitalism.' In: Aizura, A. Z. & Stryker, S. (eds.) (2013) *The Transgender Studies Reader 2.* London/New York: Routledge, pp. 56–65.

Stone, S (1987) 'The Empire Strikes Back: A Post-Transsexual Manifesto'. In: Aizura, A. Z. & Stryker, S. (eds.) (2013) *The Transgender Studies Reader 2.* London/New York: Routledge, pp. 221–235.

Stryker, S. (1984) 'My Words to Victor Frankenstein above the Village of Chamounix: Performing Transgender Rage'. In: Stryker & Whittle (eds.) (2006) *The Transgender Studies Reader.* London/New York: Routledge, pp. 244–256.

Published in *Becoming Human: Riga International Biennial of Contemporary Art Reader 1* (edited by Katerina Gregos), 2022.

First published in the RIBOCA Text Book: *Becoming Human*, edited by Katerina Gregos, Zane Ozola commissioned by the Riga International Biennial of Contemporary Art

TRANSPHOBIA IS EVERYWHERE IN BRITAIN

It must look odd to an outsider.

The race to replace Jeremy Corbyn as leader of the Labour Party, after its traumatic defeat in December's general election, has largely been conducted in the spirit of bury-the-hatchet pragmatism, to the point of tedium. The three candidates have promised, however sincerely, to maintain the general thrust of the party's policy platform; divisions have mostly been a matter of tone, style and subtle implication. Rancour and controversy have been restrained among the candidates as well as the 500,000-strong membership. Except in one area: trans rights.

A contentious row began last month, when the Labour Campaign for Trans Rights announced itself with 12 pledges, which ranged from recognising trans people's oppression – at risk of hate crime and denied equal access to public services, health care, housing and employment – to supporting the expulsion of members who express transphobic views. Rebecca Long-Bailey, the candidate closest to Corbyn's politics, and Lisa Nandy, the one farthest away, supported the campaign. The outcry was immediate:

people started the hashtag #expelme on Twitter, hecklers disrupted leadership hustings, and Tony Blair warned of "the cul-de-sac of identity politics."

To many, the sight of a centre-left party failing to support trans rights without equivocation must be baffling – not least to American Democrats, whose party, divided in many ways, is more firmly united in its support for trans and non-binary people. But really, it's no surprise. Transphobia, constantly amplified by the country's mainstream media, is a respectable bigotry in Britain, shared by parts of the left as well as the right.

There are two main types of British transphobia. One, employed most frequently but not exclusively by right-wing men, rejects outright the idea that gender might not be determined only by biological traits identifiable at birth. This viewpoint can often be found in publications aligned with the Conservative Party, such as *The Spectator, The Times* and *The Telegraph*, all of which are looking for a new "culture war" to pursue now that the long, exhausting battle over Brexit has finally been resolved in favour of Leavers.

The other type, from a so-called radical feminist tradition, argues that trans women's requests for gender recognition are incompatible with cis women's rights to single-sex spaces. At its core, such an argument is not at odds with the first type – both rely on the conceit that trans and non-binary people should not determine their own gender identities – but it is this second strain that is often expressed on the British left, from the socialist *Morning Star* to the liberal *New Statesman* and *The Guardian*. Imported from American feminist circles during the 1970s, the argument is largely disowned in the United States. But it remains stubbornly persistent in Britain.

That is has done so owes much to the longevity of a generation of journalists who established themselves when the argument was orthodox. Many still hold influential roles as columnists or editors and have used their positions to keep the argument in the mainstream, while favouring a younger generation of writers who share their antipathy to trans people.

Younger trans and non-binary people and their feminist allies have tried to shift the discussion onto the challenges we face in a transphobic society – with some success, especially in the early 2010s, when Trans Media Watch submitted a report to the Leveson inquiry into abuses of power by the British press. But that provoked an avalanche of commentary insisting that any discussion be returned to the intractable "debate" about whether trans and non-binary identities (and especially those of trans women) were valid. Trans "activists" – anyone who questioned the terms of this "debate" – were characterised as an abusive mob and accused of silencing their critics, despite the fact that these critics could be heard advancing the same views in all major newspapers, every day, throughout the decade.

This counteroffensive reached its height in autumn 2018, as the Conservative government held consultations on reforms to the Gender Recognition Act, which had been passed in 2004. In response to demands for the bill to allow self-determination of trans and non-binary identities, *The Guardian* – which, as the country's only centre-left broadsheet newspaper, plays an outsize role in political debate – published an editorial that attempted to find a centre ground. But to do so, it took its framing and talking points from organisations implacably opposed to trans rights, as the writer Jules Gleeson noted in the *New Socialist*. Many British trans writers, including me, have since declined to contribute to *The Guardian*, repeating a pattern played out in the *New Statesman* several years earlier.

The reforms to the Gender Recognition Act were shelved, topping off a dispiriting few years: The Leveson inquiry changed nothing, and none of the recommendations in a 2016 parliamentary report on transgender equality were brought in. Effectively excluded from mainstream liberal-left discourse and despairing of the possibilities for change under any Conservative government, trans and non-binary people turned back to Labour as the only political institution potentially able to change both the conversation and legislation. That seemed especially possible after the narrow electoral defeat in 2017 offered hope that the party could soon take power on a platform of social democratic reform – led by someone who offered vocal, unwavering support for trans rights.

But John McDonnell, Corbyn's long-term ally, was far more equivocal. And Labour's 2019 manifesto, mostly more radical than two years earlier, included just a few lines on trans issues and hedged its bets about single-sex spaces and gender recognition. Such division and ambivalence isn't confined to an older, outgoing generation: Laura Pidcock, regarded as a potential successor to Corbyn until she lost her seat in December, recently caused consternation by calling for "the space to talk about sex and gender, without fear of being 'no platformed'" – language that put her in line with older, 'gender-critical' commentators.

The intervention did not go without challenge: many of Labour's younger, more left-leaning members rejected the suggestion that trans rights were up for debate. So does much of the left. But the party – and the centre-left coalition it contains – is far from united. Keir Starmer, the overwhelming favourite to win the leadership race who has based his campaign around "unity" above all else, tellingly attempted to bridge the divide: he offered rhetorical support for trans and non-binary people while declining to sign on to the pledges.

But in the face of Britain's unreformed and unrepentantly hostile media, and the virulent transphobia it endlessly churns out, calls for unity won't be enough. Starmer – and the Labour Party – will have to decide whose support is worth keeping, and pick a side.

Transphobia is Everywhere in Britain by Juliet Jacques originally appeared in *The New York Times* on 9 March 2020

LIBERALS NEED TO STAND UP FOR TRANS RIGHTS, BEFORE IT'S TOO LATE

Ten years ago, I began writing a series for the *Guardian* called *A Transgender Journey*, documenting my gender reassignment process. At the time, some trans people felt it was backward-looking to use this autobiographical framing; they believed we had passed the point when we had to write memoirs to counter hostile coverage, especially as this seemed to encourage journalists to focus on our personal stories instead of our political concerns. I agreed, but I wrote it nonetheless. It eventually ran for thirty instalments and formed the basis of my book, *Trans: A Memoir*.

Growing up under Section 28, before mass adoption of the internet, I found nothing in schools or public libraries that could help me understand my gender identity, with disastrous effects on my mental health. But by 2010, there were so many blogs and forums talking about trans healthcare and wellbeing, and trans politics and culture, that a young person looking for answers, let alone a sympathetic outsider, might not know where to begin. I thought my *Guardian* series could provide an accessible place to start.

There was little point, I felt, arguing with people who questioned the validity of our identities – which reduced any discussion of our lives to the question of our existence. Instead, I hoped to persuade people – including cultural gatekeepers – that it was fairer, and more interesting, to let us describe our own lives. I thought that if I compromised and convinced an editor by using my transition as a hook, my series could introduce a large, diverse readership to the realities of living in a transphobic society – which I hoped might be a means to shift the conversation toward the challenges we faced in securing adequate healthcare, safe housing, and protection from abuse and assault.

Around this time, many other trans writers and organisations had the same idea – focusing on visibility and recognition in the media. By 2010, trans people had the right to hormones and surgery via the NHS, along with protection from being sacked from work, and the right to legally change gender, enshrined in the Gender Recognition Act of 2004. But there was still a belief that the negative stereotypes dominant in the media did us considerable damage – not only legitimising attacks on our rights, but also social exclusion, street harassment and worse. In 2012, Lord Justice Leveson agreed, concluding that "there is a marked tendency in a section of the press to fail to treat members of the transgender and intersex communities with sufficient dignity and respect".

The very fact of these issues being raised at the Leveson inquiry contributed to a sense that things were slowly improving in the early 2010s, as a wave of trans and non-binary people had their voices heard in mainstream newspapers and magazines, TV shows and films like never before, in both the UK and US. This led to *Time*'s famous 'Transgender Tipping Point' cover story of 2014, featuring *Orange is the New Black* star Laverne Cox.

This 'tipping point' – declared in the wake of the US supreme court's decision to legalise gay marriage – was meant to suggest the trans rights movement could no longer be suppressed. But it turned out that the advancing wave of cultural liberalism was far from unstoppable. In the US, the forces and attitudes that would propel Donald Trump to the White House were coalescing, visible in the Gamergate controversy and on 4chan, as well as on Fox News and in the Tea Party movement. In the UK, the tabloid press were relentlessly portraying trans people as violent criminals stealing from the taxpayer – peaking in 2017 with a false story about Ian Huntley transitioning in prison.

A backlash against trans rights and increasing visibility began to grow online, on Twitter and internet forums. The radicalisation that took place in these spaces soon prompted a dramatic increase in sober broadsheet pieces "debating" whether trans identities were real, depicting trans people as unreasonably angry, and dismissing anyone protesting the imbalance in these debates as an opponent of free speech. But the endless restaging of the same argument about trans identity suggested that the point of these interventions was not to have a debate. A debate contains the possibility of resolution on both sides; this felt more like a campaign to push us out of the public discourse by making it as unfavourable to us as possible, while claiming that it was trans people who would not let the matter rest.

This unending argument over the rights of trans people, which had been simmering in liberal and feminist spaces for nearly a decade, became front-page news in 2018, when Theresa May's government proposed the Gender Recognition Act might be reformed to allow trans people to define their own identities more easily. At a time when the Trump administration was, in the words of the *New York Times*, planning to define transgender people out of existence, such a step would have simply brought England into line with Argentina, Ireland and Portugal, among others. But it became a rallying point for a minority of feminists strongly opposed to trans rights, and occasioned hundreds of stories about the same old "debate", narrowly framed as a zero-sum conflict between women and trans rights. In the *Guardian*, a leader referred to "both extremes of this argument" (for and against self-definition) making for "a toxic debate" – a framing usually associated with anti-trans groups opposed to "gender ideology" that had formed after 2010.

One reason why I had chosen to write *A Transgender Journey* for the *Guardian* was that the paper, like other liberal outlets, had typically started conversations about trans issues with dismissive pieces by prominent 'gender-critical' feminists, to which openly trans writers would then be invited to respond. (When Germaine Greer called trans women 'a ghastly parody' in a 2009 comment piece about the South African athlete Caster Semenya, the "other side" was presented one day later by the trans writer CL Minou.)

The absence of trans voices from liberal spaces has meant there has been little serious opposition in the UK to our domestic contribution to a global campaign against LGBTQ+ rights. This campaign includes Viktor Orbán's government in Hungary – allies of the Tories – unilaterally revoking gender recognition, placing the nation's trans community in great danger. But it is part of a wider attack on the LGBTQ+ community, following those in Poland, Russia, Kyrgyzstan, the US, Turkey, Brazil and elsewhere. Earlier this year, leaked proposals from Liz Truss, the minister for women and equalities, suggested that the government would not just ignore public opinion on the Gender Recognition Act reforms, but might attempt a more thoroughgoing bar on trans people accessing single-sex spaces, potentially making *anyone* the legal arbiters of our identities.

The GRA reforms have now been shelved; the only likely effect of the part about exclusion from single-sex spaces would be to make Britain's trans community feel more insecure and embattled, given how difficult it would be to enforce. But if it does make it into a bill – which has still not been ruled out – it would likely make it through the Commons, given the Conservative majority. If so, it would be the first ever piece of legislation to actively revoke our rights, and would come after a sustained media campaign against us, during which the Labour leadership has often been reluctant to take a side. With the party's increasingly marginalised left being the most vocal about the need to protect trans rights, it has been reminiscent of the path to Section 28.

And in a time of rising far-right reaction in the UK and worldwide, it might not stop there. Such an assault on non-conformity will have ramifications not just for trans people, but ultimately anyone who fails to meet gender norms, or whose bodily autonomy lies in the hands of the state. Such regressive legislation now seems less likely, given that the government tempered its refusal of self-identification with confirmation that it will create three new gender identity clinics and simplify the existing gender recognition process. But the Tories' leaked proposals should still serve as a clarifying moment, showing what can happen when liberals and centrists refuse to stand against, or even join in with, a right-wing moral panic, and serve as a warning to change course before it's too late.

The Guardian, 24 September 2020

TRANSGENDER ATHLETES DO NOT THREATEN WOMEN'S SPORTS

As a transsexual woman and fervent soccer player (and fan), the idea that someone would transition just to succeed in women's sports because they couldn't do so in men's sports is absurd. It does female athletes a massive disservice, assuming the inherent inferiority of any cis woman to any trans woman or cis man. And it pays no attention to the fact that transitioning is long, physically and psychologically gruelling. Gender dysphoria may not have any indisputable or immutable criteria, but no one begins reassignment on a whim – in fact, gender identity clinics rigorously screen against this.

I kept playing soccer after transition, but once I reached the point of two years after surgery, aged 32, having had HRT to put my testosterone and oestrogen levels within a "normal female range," I decided to carry on with a men's team (admittedly in an LGBT+ league), preferring that discord to the inevitable attention and abuse that would come with playing for a women's club. When I did play, casually, with cis women, I found my advantages were not hormonal – I was less quick and less strong than many of my new teammates – but cultural. Having been raised male, I'd had far more coaching, having not been discouraged or excluded from soccer at a young age like some of them. Consequently, I had advantages in its less physical and more teachable aspects: passing, moving off the ball, and shooting.

The question of whether transgender athletes threaten women's sports comes up periodically – specifically, whenever a trans woman has any modicum of success. It persists even though none of the few transsexual women who have been allowed to participate in women's competitions over the last fifty years, and especially since the International Olympic Committee (IOC) first published guidelines on the subject in 2004, have ever gone on to dominate them; and even though, as in the case of South African middle-distance runner Caster Semenya, the ferocity of demands for the exclusion of women – trans or not – with high testosterone levels has worrying implications for anyone who does not meet conventional, conservative standards of femininity.

The separation between men and women's sports is deeply linked to our society's other ways of regimenting gender; it can be traced back to Victorian Britain's preconceptions about the need for male and female spheres with associated gender stereotypes, which led (for example) to the English Football Association declaring soccer "unsuitable for women" in 1921 and banning it for what ended up being half a century.

But the particular issue of transgender athletes has occupied sports leagues for only about 40 years, ever since the U.S. Tennis Association barred transsexual player Renée Richards from the US Open in 1976, citing a hitherto unprecedented woman-at-birth policy. They borrowed this terminology from second-wave feminist circles, which were then embroiled in fierce debates about whether to allow transsexual women into women-only spaces, and about how to border and police the category of "woman." In Richards' case, anxieties that she would be "naturally" stronger, fitter or better than cisgender women were unfounded: She won a New York Supreme Court case in 1977, allowing her to compete, and lost in straight sets in the first round of the ensuing tournament. Despite this, Richards' was one case that influenced the IOC guidelines, which state that "transsexual and transgender" athletes must have legal gender recognition – ruling out anyone from countries that do not allow this – as well as hormone therapy in order to "minimize gender-related advantages," as well as proof of living two years in their "newly-assigned gender" after surgery.

Notable subsequent developments included Mianne Bagger competing on the Ladies European Tour (highest finish: 35th in 2005) and 47-year-old Martine Delaney playing for Claremont United in an Australian women's soccer league. After Delaney scored six goals at a low level, opponents put in complaints to Soccer Tasmania and the Football Federation of Australia. The governing bodies, which had adopted the IOC guidelines, allowed Delaney to play on, but she continued against a backdrop of player, supporter and media hostility that was wildly disproportionate to the low level at which she was competing.

Delaney's experiences provoke further thought. Sports such as soccer, golf or tennis obviously differ from track and field events, which are mostly a simple test of physical attributes like pace and strength. However, while physical variations within the men's and women's categories, and the matter of how athletes utilize them, have always been integral to their appeal, two specific things have raised anxieties over the last 16 years. One is the revision of the IOC guidelines to remove the surgical requirement, acknowledging that HRT is sufficient to level out any hormonal differences between cis and trans people at an adult level. The other is the emergence of Caster Semenya, who won the 800 metres at the World Championship in 2009 but was then suspended while her testosterone levels were investigated.

The responses to Semenya, then and since, have been astonishingly cruel – and have sometimes spilled into more overt transphobia, even though she does not identify as trans but has hyperandrogenism, which entails an overproduction of male hormones. To limit these conversations – about Semenya and trans women – to sport and its governing bodies' laws is important, but it's important to recognize that they take place within a transphobic society and a media culture that endlessly undermines the validity of trans identities and people. The recent Swiss court ruling against Semenya, stating she *must* lower her testosterone level "through medication or surgery" if she wishes to compete at next year's rescheduled Tokyo Olympics, could not have happened without this loud, relentless hostility toward trans people and those who do not conform to gender stereotypes.

So, what is to be done? More so than in the past, women are being encouraged to take up a wider range of sports from a younger age, with more investment and television coverage. This will continue to improve standards and change perceptions, gradually levelling out the inequalities that lead some commentators to identify trans women as a threat. The IOC, and other sporting bodies that take the IOC's lead, should continue to assess on a case-by-case basis – and perhaps draw up firmer guidelines where necessary, working with endocrinologists and other experts. But there is a bigger picture, a deeper ethos to consider in all this.

The decade-long shift from pundits insisting that Semenya wasn't really a woman to the legal demand for her to adjust her hormone levels is the result not just of an overblown moral panic, but also the rise of an international Far Right that is, among other things, making efforts to rehabilitate eugenics. Even as "gender-critical" pundits fulminate against trans bodies as "unnatural" (while remaining quite happy to, say, drive a car rather than a horse), some, such as Toby Young, talk about "progressive eugenics" – with its extreme but predictable conclusion that there are objective qualitative standards for how human bodies should look and behave, and deviations should be suppressed. In this context, allowing the issue of a tiny number of trans woman athletes to become a vector for such ideas re-entering the political mainstream seems far more threatening, to me, than the limited progress of the likes of Mianne Bagger, Martine Delaney or Renée Richards.

Newsweek, 20 October 2020

MEDIA

Whenever the subject comes up, you'll often hear journalists say that "the public", whoever that may be, don't want to read them writing about the media, claiming that it comes across as self-indulgent (a fear that rarely seems to inhibit them in any other context). Generally, if journalists say, "the public don't want to read about X", that means "the public may well be interested in X, but we don't want them to think about it". This was true of trans politics, history and culture, as writers in the early 2010s proved there absolutely was a keen audience for these subjects, after years of being told otherwise, and it's true of reflections of the nature of the media too: its impact and influence; its role in upholding existing structures of power; and how and why those who unquestioningly reinforce those structures tend to advance within the industry while those who challenge them tend to come up against hard limits (especially if they weren't privately educated).

It might seem strange to have separate sections for the two, given the importance of the media to British politics – highlighted in the Leveson Inquiry of 2011-12 that followed the phone hacking scandal, which could have led to widespread change if not for the great effort taken to ensure that just a handful of careers were ended, no stricter regulation was brought in, and the fact there was no second part investigating the relations between journalists and the police. But besides being an interesting bridge between politics and the arts, I've always thought the media worthy of consideration in its own right (ignoring those voices in journalism who would tell you Media Studies is a waste of time). Trans people spend a lot of time thinking about its role, mainly because when closeted, we mostly encountered people like ourselves through the media, and the hostility of that coverage often prevented us from coming out, perpetuating a cycle that made it harder for us to challenge systemic transphobia. Working in the mainstream of British political journalism, I tried to think about the privilege of having a platform and the possibilities – and responsibilities – that came with it, being open about *why* I was doing what I did, why I did it *where* I did, the compromises I made, and the effect all this had on me. I did this more in my public speaking than in writing, but 'Liz Jones and Me' (one of my favourite things I've written) explores the psychological impact of 'confessional' journalism.

Once a year, I did a stock-take of the behaviour of the media and its relationship with the British trans community for the *New Statesman,* first in 2012 with 'The Turning of the Tide?' and then in 2013 with 'Compromise is Neither Desirable Nor Possible', which I wrote in the wake of the death of transsexual teacher Lucy Meadows, who came out at her primary school in Accrington and was consequently hounded by the press, being the subject of two *Daily Mail* editorials. The pieces got angrier every year as the reaction against trans visibility became more intense: I stood down after writing an 8,500-word essay about the 'debate' between trans people and anti-trans feminists, which I got through the editor by initially pitching an 800-word piece and then emailing to say I had more to say (this wasn't planned). As mentioned above, this piece went viral, being the most-read thing on the *Statesman* website for days, and became the basis for *Trans: A Memoir*.

The other pieces here are interviews with, or reviews of books by, trans people who worked in the media (such as Paul B. Preciado's collection of columns) or advocates such as Janet Mock or intersex activist Hida Viloria, as they seemed like a better fit here than in the Culture section. That my focus changed after 2014, when I quit the *Statesman* (without making a shameless fuss about being "cancelled"), reflected my exhaustion with battling the entrenched transphobia within the British media establishment, and my sense that it was more constructive to advocate for trans and non-binary art and culture instead.

CHAZ BONO AND TRANSGENDERISM'S RICH HISTORY

'The transgender experience is one of the few human condi-
tions almost completely without cultural, literary or artistic
landmarks ... Transgenderism remains so foreign a concept to
those who have not experienced it that its explanation falls
totally to those who have.'

These are two of the more eye-catching statements in
Mary McNamara's *LA Times* review of American TV
documentary *Becoming Chaz*, on Chaz Bono's transition
from female to male. The assertions may sound accurate,
but they belie a more complex reality than some cisgender
(crudely, non-transgender) critics realise.

McNamara suggests that "the idea that a person could
be born into a body at odds with his or her sense of gender
has only recently entered the public conversation" via films
such as *Boys Don't Cry* (starring Hilary Swank as murdered
trans man Brandon Teena) and *The Oprah Winfrey Show*.

Historically, trans individuals have been denied control
of their stories within the mainstream, having them framed

by cisgender journalists, filmmakers and editors in ways that are frequently sensationalist or deliberately transphobic, or that cast people as passive victims. From both necessity and choice, trans people's creative reflections have often been produced out of the spotlight, and their relationship with the media has been fractious – hence the casual observer's perception that we have scant heritage.

For those willing to look, there exists a century of cultural landmarks, often intertwined with, and sometimes overshadowed by gay and lesbian history. This begins with the gay German sexologist Magnus Hirschfeld. Aware that what later became understood as transgender behaviour had existed across a variety of cultures for centuries, he published the first specific investigation into the subject in 1910 – *The Transvestites: The Erotic Drive to Cross-Dress*. Hirschfeld coined the first trans-related term, "transvestite". It held a broader meaning than today, as other words have since evolved to represent differing positions on the gender-variant spectrum.

Hirschfeld also devised the term "transsexualismus" (but did not popularise "transsexual") before overseeing the first sex reassignment surgery in 1930, on the Danish painter Lili Elbe. Elbe died a year later, but her collated memoirs were published as *Man into Woman* in 1933. This was the first transsexual autobiographical text, initiating what became the dominant means for people to explain their transitions.

Hirschfeld and Elbe attracted little attention beyond Germany. Roberta Cowell and Michael Dillon, the UK's first male-to-female (MtF) and female-to-male (FtM) transsexual people hit the British headlines. But the first internationally famous transsexual woman was Christine Jorgensen, who appeared on the *New York Times'* front page in December 1952. Like Cowell, Jorgensen wrote an autobi-ography, and a biopic was later produced. Subsequently, transsexual issues found their main expression in queer American counter-culture – particularly underground film.

During the Sixties, avant-garde US directors including Jack Smith and Ron Rice cast drag queens and trans women in provocative movies such as *Flaming Creatures*, which presented a loose set of highly sensual scenes in which participants did not need to define their gender. Works produced around Warhol's Factory, particularly *Women in Revolt*, created trans icons in Candy Darling, Holly Woodlawn and Jackie Curtis. Darling and Curtis later became documentary subjects, as did the trans women who fought police oppression at Compton's in San Francisco in 1966, three years before Sylvia Rivera and others struggled alongside gay and lesbian people at New York's Stonewall Inn.

By the mid-Seventies, there existed a trend for Hollywood films to show trans people as psychotic, seen in *Psycho, Dressed to Kill* and others. Cultural portrayals focused almost exclusively on male-to-female identities. So too did the "radical" lesbian feminist Janice Raymond's assault, *The Transsexual Empire* (1979), which accused Gender Identity Clinics and their patients of propagating misogynistic models of femininity.

Raymond's tract galvanised transsexual women and men into reasserting and reassessing their personal histories and cultural traditions. Sandy Stone's response, 'The "Empire" Strikes Back: A Post-Transsexual Manifesto', questioned the portrayal of the effects of gender reassignment in several autobiographies. She suggested that people go beyond "passing" in their acquired genders to form a strong, specifically transsexual identity that could withstand transphobic stereotyping.

Stone inspired a generation of writers who thought past traditional gender conventions, trying to unify disparate people under the transgender banner to fight shared oppression. The trans man Leslie Feinberg argued for "transgender liberation" and collected a history of gender variance "from Joan of Arc to Dennis Rodman". Kate Bornstein and Riki Ann Wilchins, meanwhile, pushed for greater recognition of the grey areas within the recognised binary.

In Britain, Press For Change, founded in 1992, strove for legal reforms for trans people, their greatest triumph being the Gender Recognition Act (2004) which won official acknowledgement for transsexual people. Throughout the 1990s, screen portrayals of trans people increased, for example in the European arthouse films of Pedro Almodóvar and Rosa von Praunheim. In more mainstream productions, trans actors rarely played trans parts, but docu-soap and reality TV formats allowed certain trans individuals greater self-expression – and showed producers that the public was prepared to listen.

Building on the sense of identity formulated by activists and academics, and aware that the mass media is becoming more ready to let them represent themselves, trans people – and particularly trans men – are finally being allowed to document their own experiences in more visible contexts, in greater depth and with less editorial intervention. With heightened consciousness of the effects of negative print and screen portrayals, a plurality of voices that express the diversity of transgenderism is slowly emerging from the margins. It could not have happened without this rich cultural history; one from which transgender people of all shades continue to draw confidence.

New Statesman, 26 May 2011

LAUGHING MATTERS?

Growing up in the Nineties with plenty of 'alternative' humour on television, including Chris Morris, Lee and Herring and *The Friday Night Armistice*, I was told that predictability is the enemy of laughter. The narrative behind their growing popularity ran that the Bad Old Comedy (stand-ups like Bernard Manning and Jim Davidson, and sitcoms such as *Love Thy Neighbour*) used cheap stereotypes to pick on easy targets, especially ethnic minorities, women and gay men, before rightly being side-lined by a new wave, more adventurous in form and content.

As it transpired – and as Stewart Lee has expertly depicted via a range of television and stand-up shows – the Nineties represented the mid-point between the old guard's overthrow and the rise of comics who similarly exploited populist prejudices to become the new orthodoxy. Unlike their predecessors, they may justify their acts by claiming irony or opposition to their straw man conception of political correctness but in practice, their apparent stretching of liberal boundaries is sometimes barely distinguishable from the retrograde bullying of the Seventies, even if the butts of their jokes are slightly different.

Britain's trans community is increasingly concerned with how media representation affects our lives, and frustrated at how regularly comedians reduce our bodies and social challenges to objects of derision. Whilst being far from the only minority group in this position, it's especially damaging as the number of 'out' trans people remains relatively small, and so for many people, the clichés in *Little Britain* or Littlejohn cartoons (for example) go unquestioned, and continue to be used against any trans person who dares to be visible.

As an openly trans woman in a (still) frequently transphobic society, I deal with a certain amount of street harassment. The most stressful encounters nearly always start with being laughed at, sometimes with aspects of my dress or demeanour singled out. This usually comes when I am alone, from a group of people, or a passing car (an act of cowardice just one rung above calling someone a cunt via the internet). Violence, threatened or realised, is rarely their first weapon, but I know that if I object to the taunts, or incidents where my basic existence serves as a comic foil, then I can expect them to assert their power with more aggression than passivity. If I or anyone else reasons with them - it's just "banter".

Often, the insults are generic, and I cannot identify their main cultural influence. However, if some slack-jawed wazzock hollers "I'm a lady!" at me, I know exactly where it came from. At times, it felt that *Little Britain* and its successor *Come Fly with Me* served as an index of those which contemporary comedy deems legitimate to ridicule, its "rubbish transvestites" appealing to as low a denominator as its attacks on the white working class or isolated gay men striving to define their identities.

The trend epitomised by Lucas and Walliams' hit series has not been discontinued. Christine Burns and Paris Lees both discussed Russell Howard's recent *Good News* sketch, made in response to reports of a Thai airline allowing trans women (who struggle to find safe employment elsewhere) to work as cabin crew, which relied upon depictions of trans people that could have been lifted from the *Daily Mail*. Clearly, some viewers find these images funny – that is their right – and not all trans people find this particular skit offensive, but it raises questions about when and how it is fair for performers to use stereotypes, and the extent of their responsibility to interrogate their origins rather than merely reiterating them.

When we complain about such comedy, the accusation that we are humourless is often used as a counter, as it was against feminist critiques in the pre-alternative days. The truth that this allegation (which has itself become something of a cliché) ignores, or serves to mask, is that gifted comedians can and often do empower marginalised groups. During my teens, Eddie Izzard's laudable wit in discussing his transvestism, and particularly in exploding the media trope of the psychotic cross-dresser, proved immensely useful, helping me relax about my gender difference and setting favourable terms for me to disclose it to friends.

Despite Izzard's breakthrough, the dialogue remained notably one-sided - until recently. As trans issues gradually become more mainstream, a wave of distinctive, intelligent stand-ups are offering humorous perspectives on them, even if they are not (yet) darlings of the ubiquitous panel shows. This new generation includes transvestite Andrew O'Neill, transsexual women Claire Parker and Bethany Black, and trans man Jason Elvis Barker, all providing fresh takes on trans living and numerous other subjects, undermining the myth that we talk about little besides our own genders.

Ultimately, the Eighties' more inventive voices – Kevin McAleer, Ted Chippington and Simon Munnery amongst them – proved the most resistant to mainstream assimilation.

In part, this was because they rose above reactionary rants about 'political correctness gone mad' that characterised some of their lazier contemporaries, who have forgotten for too long that the right to free speech works best when balanced with the responsibility to use any position of privilege fairly. Now, 30 years after the alternative revolution broke into clubs and onto screens, audiences look from *Love Thy Neighbour* to *Little Britain*, *Mind Your Language* to *Mock the Week*, and cannot always tell which is which.

New Statesman, 27 June 2011

MY TRANSSEXUAL SUMMER: THE TROUBLE WITH TELEVISION

Many of my friends are talking about *My Transsexual Summer*, which recently began on Channel Four, featuring seven people from across the gender diversity spectrum. Some are cisgender, often with little knowledge of trans living beyond what I've told them, who say the show offers accessible, sympathetic insights into the social challenges of transition. Conversely, my trans friends, some of whom had high hopes for the series, have tended to vent frustration that (besides other things) it fails to air the experiences of those who do not simply wish to move from one side of male/female to the other but find space within the gender binary.

I won't review it from a trans perspective: Sarah Lake, Dru Marland and several others have done so, better than I could. The consensus seems to be that *My Transsexual Summer* has faults – its title erases the subtleties of the participants' gender identities, and its voiceover and editing do not entirely avoid sensationalism – but that in showing trans people together, rather than disparate, isolated individuals as in previous documentaries, it demonstrates a vibrant culture on television for the first time.

This is an incremental step forward for trans media portrayal, but still raises questions about how far TV is capable of providing satisfactory minority representation. Maxwell Zachs, of *My Transsexual Summer*, has expressed some dissatisfaction with the show, whilst my own engagement with the industry has been less than encouraging.

If you didn't know (and I've had calls from media companies who'd somehow missed it), I'm transsexual, and often write about it, trying to use my experiences to open dialogue about wider trans concerns. (Apologies to my FtM friends: I've tended to focus on trans women as I don't feel as qualified on trans men.) I do this because, for years, I felt that while trans people were regularly discussed in mainstream media, used as objects of ridicule in lazy comedy shows, or attacked by certain feminists or conservatives, we were seldom allowed to frame our own stories and present counter-arguments on an even footing.

In particular, when I began apprehending myself through newspapers, films and TV, I resented the stereotypes of trans women as psychotic, criminals, or close to violent crime (*Psycho* or *Dressed to Kill*) that persisted into the Nineties (in *Silence of the Lambs*, for one). These still hadn't quite disappeared nearly twenty years later, when I decided (independently of other groups and individuals pursuing similar aims) to work within the mainstream media towards more positive representation.

After I'd written about six instalments of my Transgender Journey series for the *Guardian*, which aimed to reduce the decades-long gap between transgender theory and the broadsheet press, I got an email from someone at a company who'd produced films and programmes for the BBC and Channel 4. This person had read my blogs and proposed meeting about a possible TV drama about people in transition.

Perfect: I'd attempted something like this before writing the *Guardian* column, as I thought that a colourful, humorous narrative with engaging characters could potentially challenge preconceptions about trans people for a far wider audience. I felt that although I'd created a plausible world with interesting characters, I was average at dialogue and weak on plot. (The inevitable consequence of watching too many obscure French films where no-one speaks and nothing happens.) Now, I might be part of a well-balanced writing team with two promising young playwrights, and we could aim at a cultural landmark equivalent to *Queer As Folk* or *The L Word*.

Friends in/around the industry warned that lead-in times are always long; sure enough, we struggled to arrange the meeting. Finally, after fifteen months, resolution: the project had been shelved as 'Sky have a drama coming up about a pre-op transsexual hitwoman'. As far as the producer was concerned, this programme – which had annoyed trans bloggers even before it was cast – meant no market space for anything trans-related, no matter how different, for the foreseeable future. Perhaps, I thought, I'm best out of this.

Writers being disillusioned with the infrastructures of screen media is nothing new: think of Bertolt Brecht or Clifford Odets' disastrous inability to deliver what Hollywood producers required (the latter providing inspiration for the Coen Brothers' *Barton Fink)*, or Jean-Paul Sartre's unwillingness to compromise for director John Huston on *Freud* (1962). But the television industry's incapacity to foster formally or politically radical content is even more pronounced than its cinematic counterpart, for numerous reasons.

With so many channels broadcasting around the clock, the listings are full of unscripted programmes – sport, reality TV, panel shows – which are relatively cheap or have fixed budgets. This has the effect of making television appear a world where writers are neither needed nor wanted, but it happens because the financial and visual demands of written serials are so high. As audiences will apparently change channel unless the pace is utterly relentless, a programme like Tony Hancock's *Radio Ham,* set in one room, is no longer tenable, so screenwriters must create fast, action-packed and above all short scenes across a number of locations, keeping firmly within budget.

This is not bad in itself: these constraints offer interesting challenges to writers, and when met successfully, produce fantastic shows. (The first episode of *Shameless* is a case in point.) The key limitations are not those of form, but content: what really puts off writers with specialist knowledge are producers' prejudices about what viewers will accept or understand which, coupled with their methods of audience testing, remain the greatest barriers to any big improvements in coverage of minority subjects.

Circumventing these gatekeepers is far harder than in writing (where bloggers have successfully challenged editors' beliefs about what people will or won't read). For *My Transsexual Summer,* a number of trans people, including CN Lester, and Paris Lees of pressure group Trans Media Watch, consulted with Channel Four: the broadcaster's willingness to listen is encouraging, although all the above blogs explicate the number of compromises necessary to get this show – imperfect but still significantly better than what came before – to air. At this point, given its financial and political structures, the limited level of improvement in trans representation on TV shown by *My Transsexual Summer* is probably the best we can expect.

New Statesman, 18 November 2011

THE TURNING OF THE TIDE?

Whatever the long-term results of the Leveson inquiry, one appearance may prove a turning point for an increasingly visible and (hopefully) decreasingly vulnerable population. When Helen Belcher presented Trans Media Watch's submission last week, explaining the largely negative practices and consequences behind more than a hundred news items about transgender (but mainly transsexual) people, it felt like a turning point for a group no longer prepared to tolerate the media intruding into – and sensationalising – their personal histories.

Tabloid exploitation of transgender lives has now become so crude and so cruel that a 10-year-old is campaigning against it. Returning to her primary school in Worcester as female last September, Livvy James found her story strewn across the headlines after other children's parents took it to local newspapers and the nationals picked it up. Having been compelled to explain to the *Daily Mail* and ITV's *This Morning* why she let her child go to school as female (with the newspapers treating her decision as a countrywide concern), Livvy's mother Saffron has secured over a thousand signatures to a petition against media ridiculing of transgender individuals. Livvy felt that the abuse she took from her peers related directly to hostile print and screen portrayals.

It's interesting to note that the earliest British coverage of transsexual people was fairly even-handed: with no conventions set on the subject, the *News of the World* handled sensitively the surgical transition of athlete Mark Weston in 1936. It was not until the late Fifties, after Christine Jorgensen's fame suggested the emergence of a phenomenon that violated a fundamental social norm, that the tabloids started outing people with transsexual histories: the *Sunday Express* forced Michael Dillon into exile in 1958 and the *Sunday People* exposed April Ashley several years later.

You might imagine that after fifty years, we would have moved beyond this. The mere existence of transsexual individuals is no longer a novelty – the conservative estimate in Trans Media Watch's Leveson submission put current numbers at 7,431 – but tabloids continue to contrive stories from ordinary people's transitions.

Just because editors believe that the public are interested does not mean that this reporting is in the public interest. The detrimental effects outweigh any benefit in this systematically invasive and dishonest coverage, which at worst threatens not just the safety of individuals, but the existence of the entire transsexual population by undermining their right to gender reassignment via the NHS. In this 'age of austerity', stories attacking transsexual people for using a service to which they were entitled became frequent; the unsourced figures oscillating so wildly that Jane Fae compiled a comprehensive guide to the actual costs to the NHS. Her figures are far below the £20,000-£60,000 spread I've seen across the right-wing press.

This was another fine example of transgender people using the internet to challenge a media that has objectified and excluded them for years. On Friday, Millivres Prowler launched a stable-mate to *Gay Times* and lesbian/bisexual publication *Diva*, aimed at the transgender population. *Meta*, an online magazine catering to female-to-male and male-to-female people will likely reach a larger readership than any other trans-related journal. Its editor, Paris Lees, appeared on BBC Breakfast last week, alongside Livvy James, to expose transphobia in the media to a terrestrial television audience. Now, there's a sense that the excuses that gatekeepers of mainstream liberal and left-wing spaces have previously used to keep out transgender perspectives – that the issues are too complicated, or that transsexual people somehow undermine feminist or socialist politics – are finally becoming untenable.

Above all, there's an understanding that transgender experiences illustrate a wider point: the tabloid habit of interfering with the privacy of non-public figures when they think it will sell can potentially damage anyone. Leveson's grilling of Dominic Mohan about the *Sun*'s mean-spirited 'Tran or Woman' quiz, and Mohan's sheepish admission that "I don't think that's our greatest moment", happened before Trans Media Watch gave their evidence. This is a sign that, slowly, people in power are not only allowing transgender people to voice their concerns but also listening; and that whatever happens to our tabloid press, the situation can never be quite as hopeless again.

New Statesman, 13 February 2012

GARETH WILLIAMS AND THE PRURIENCE OF THE PRESS

"On the balance of probability," said Fiona Wilcox, the Westminster coroner working on the inquest, MI6 officer Gareth Williams was "unlawfully killed". Stating that this could not be definitively established and that the case may never be satisfactorily explained, Wilcox also lamented that the "unusual circumstances" – Williams' body was found in a padlocked holdall in the bath of his London flat – had immediately generated "endless [media] speculation" about his personal life, to the dismay of his family.

Days before Wilcox delivered her verdict, newspapers carried stories about Williams's sexual practices, suggesting that they played a part in his death without waiting for Wilcox to assert her certainty that they did not. Here is the latest example of how the press can 'monster' victims, or alleged perpetrators of crimes if they are thought to have diverged from conservative sexual or gender norms, sensationalising personal details (which they've often made considerable effort to root up) in search of saleable stories.

At its worst – during the hunt for Joanna Yeates' killer, for example – this can deny someone their reputation and right to a fair trial. In this case, as in many others, it perpetuates a victim-blaming culture, the implication that Williams' tastes caused his demise being intertwined with homophobia, biphobia and transphobia, and a curious mixture of fascination and contempt for BDSM and those who partake in it.

This prurience is as old as the mass media itself. In the Victorian era, the argument about whether or not details about sexual or gender variance should be published ostensibly concerned public morality. As Boulton and Park, two cross-dressers charged with 'conspiring and inciting others to commit unnatural offences', awaited trial in 1870-71, the Society for the Suppression of Vice urged newspapers not to document the case. The Pall Mall Gazette refused, but long before Rupert Murdoch got near it, the *Times* covered everything, including the 'medical examination' to which the Metropolitan police illegally subjected Boulton and Park in an attempt to prove that they'd had anal sex, arguing that 'its novel and extraordinary features' made it sure to be 'of interest to hundreds and thousands' (and, as such, hugely profitable).

Step forward into the 21st century and the terms have changed. It's no longer a matter of the press protecting the public from apparently unspeakable practices, but preventing the press from invading the public's privacy, especially if editors or journalists think aspects of their lives can be easily sold. This is a constant issue for Britain's transgender population: Trans Media Watch presented twice to the Leveson inquiry about how newspapers 'out' trans people for solely exploitative reasons, often accompanying their articles with 'before and after' photos, old names and anything else that will undermine their hard-fought identities, usually to their great distress.

The nastiest instance – one that parallels the coverage of Williams, rife with speculation about the women's clothing in his home – came when human rights lawyer David/ Sonia Burgess was pushed on to the track at King's Cross tube station in October 2010. The tabloids revelled in their 'man in a dress' headlines as their journalists trawled through transgender contacts sites for information on Burgess' private life, all published before an arrest was made. With so much made public about Burgess and the defendant, who was also trans, no trial could start from a neutral position, and besides dancing close to the legal line, this coverage served to intimidate anyone else trying to keep their gender variance out of the public eye, magnifying their fears that its revelation may harm their relationships or careers.

The staggeringly irresponsible behaviour of the media over recent decades, as the balance of power between parliament, the police and the press became untenably skewed, is finally being exposed, and the consequences remain to emerge. Will newspaper owners and editors realise that, with their power, comes responsibility not to prejudice investigations, or attack people of trans histories or alternative sexualities just because they can? Will they learn that just because the public may be interested in an angle, or a story, this does not mean that it is in the public interest? Will they ask themselves: whatever happened to 'innocent until proven guilty' – or respect for the dead?

The Guardian, 4 May 2012

LIZ JONES AND ME

Liz Jones and I have so much in common, chiefly that we have both documented our lives for national newspapers – her for the Mail, me for the Guardian. Our styles are quite different, though, at least gauging from reactions on social media. My sporadic blogs elicit few shares or comments, whereas it seems that every Sunday, the Twitter commentariat is livid about Jones's latest missive at Mail Online (and trying to express their outrage without linking to it and so boosting its advertising revenue). Several controversies stick in my mind, particularly those where Jones revealed particularly intimate details about her life, or when she misjudged the tone in first-person reports on individual or international tragedies.

Although Liz Jones and I came to it via different backgrounds (she wrote on fashion, editing the *Sunday Times* Style section and *Marie Claire,* whilst I covered experimental film and literature for magazines you've never read), we are both 'confessional' journalists. She has been far more successful than me, or anyone else in Britain – if you look up 'confessional journalism' online, Jones crops up repeatedly amongst the first few hits – so naturally I wanted to talk to her about the peculiar ethical dilemmas of the form.

Confessional journalists usually aim to offer insight into emblematic but individual experiences, sometimes pressured by editors to entertain or provoke (a strange contract, parodied brilliantly by Chris Morris in a *Blue Jam* sketch about a journalist who had promised to kill himself, and is writing profitably about staring death in the face). It relies on the writer being honest, and being perceived as such: the second that the reader thinks s/he is embellishing, or inventing, the edifice collapses. People defending Jones point out that few others are as open; certainly, I can't imagine another journalist who would admit to stealing a lover's sperm in an attempt to become pregnant. When I read it, convinced by its level of detail, I considered the zero-sum game of trying to shock: if Jones wanted to continue driving traffic to *Mail Online* like this, she would have to keep topping this anecdote, without stretching her (unusually elastic) boundaries of credulity past breaking point.

Combine this pressure to document unimaginable experiences, then, with the realisation that you have put yourself in a position where everything that happens to you is potential copy and things become weird, psychologically. What can or should you withhold? What can or should you do if your life just doesn't generate sufficiently interesting moments?

I agreed to write about transsexual living without knowing exactly what it would entail, and at points I found myself wishing that my gender would complicate my life more than it did. I had fleeting thoughts about putting myself in situations that might be more difficult than the safer ones I'd sought, hoping to expose more about contemporary prejudice – and generate more dramatic copy. Soon, I realised what a disgustingly privileged attitude this was, before reading about transsexual blogger Mike Penner/ Christine Daniels of the *LA Times* and seeing the tragic consequences of publicly detailing a life that became too painful to live, let alone share.

One of my favourite discussions around the ethics of contriving situations in order to write about them came in Jonathan Coe's biography of English *avant-garde* author B. S. Johnson, who asserted that a novel's content should always be drawn from its creator's own life: 'Telling stories is telling lies' was Johnson's mantra. In *Trawl,* one of his best works, the narrator's stream of consciousness describes life on a shipping trawler. Johnson worked as a teacher, but spent three weeks on the *Northern Jewel* to gather material. He was upset that its crew dubbed him "the pleasure-tripper" but it's unsurprising that he found such resentment – delving into your own neuroses is one thing, using those around you in a narrative over which only you have control is another.

Jones has attracted far more opprobrium than Johnson, or me. She has had a bullet through her letterbox, having aggrieved the people of Exmoor, was unable to sign with any High Street bank (or even a private one without a confidentiality agreement) and barred from her local pet shop. Journalism necessarily draws on the fabric of everyday lives – usually other people's – but traditionally, this means public figures, with a tacit, often problematic understanding that occupying such roles subjects them to such scrutiny, fairly or unfairly.

It's hard to say where the line between public and non-public figures sits, but wherever it is, 'confessionalism' frequently pulls people across it, without their consent. In hindsight, I was lucky not to alienate anyone important to me, particularly the NHS services facilitating my sex reassignment treatment – another structural problem that I didn't really consider when I fell into the act of first-person writing.

No wonder, then, that Jones told *The Observer*'s Rachel Cooke that "I wouldn't recommend [confessional journalism] to anyone". I often feel the same way, so I'm intrigued about where our conversation might go. Then, swiftly, the email comes: Liz has other commitments and will not be able to talk to me. Perhaps it's for the best, as we'd both be more aware than most that each may not write positively about the other.

If I've learned one thing from 'confessional' journalism, it's that sharing your issues with an audience, imagined or real, is easy, as long as you constantly consider your position on its moral challenges (or just disregard them). Forming nourishing relationships with individual people, face to face, is far harder, and as I spend yet another evening alone, looking wistfully at the lists of Twitter followers and Facebook friends who've come to me via my writing, I wonder whether I've confessed too little, or too much.

New Statesman, 25 October 2012

TRANS PEOPLE AND THE MEDIA: COMPROMISE IS NEITHER DESIRABLE NOR POSSIBLE

1. The media has a long history of humiliating and undermining trans people

The media reports on the first transsexual people were mostly reasonable, striving to understand the psychology and the science behind gender reassignment. Coverage became more sensationalistic after World War II, with the screaming headlines and "before and after" photos that came with Christine Jorgensen's transition in 1952 setting a precedent, and soon the British tabloids began outing people with transsexual histories: Michael Dillon (*Daily Express,* 1958) and April Ashley (*The Sunday People,* 1961) amongst them. This practice endures into the present.

The emergence of transsexual and then transgender people as a group since the mid-1960s changed the discourse, particularly in the liberal press. A search of the *Guardian* and *Observer* digital archives for the word "transsexual" shows – in general – a shift from medics trying to explain the processes behind transition in the 1970s, to certain radical feminists stereotyping trans people and then attacking those stereotypes for reiterating traditional gender roles (1990s-2000s), to trans people being allowed to respond, and then finally to frame the discussion (2000s-2010s). We cannot, however, draw a history of progress: the latter have not yet superseded the former, but have merely been allowed to compete.

2. Transphobia cuts across left/liberal and conservative media

Transphobia in left/liberal media tends to come, still, from this radical feminist perspective, tending to attack trans people as a category. Conservative pundits seem to focus more on isolating trans people in apparently 'public' roles, undermining their identities by exposing details about their pre-transitional lives. I won't link to individual examples, but Trans Media Watch's initial submission to the Leveson Inquiry provides plenty of evidence.

3. Most commentators (grudgingly) accept the right of individual adults to transition

The "false consciousness" arguments of Janice Raymond and other 1970s feminists are no longer fashionable: the ever-growing numbers who transition or lead gender-variant lives illustrate the scale of their failure. In the face of this, it would be not so much Quixotic as Canutian to continue attempting to deny this autonomy to trans adults *per se*, but the opponents have adapted old tactics and adopted new ones. They are usually signified by some variation on "I'm not against people having gender reassignment, but..."

4. Commentators disproportionately 'monster' trans individuals

Routinely, tabloid newspapers run stories on trans people that are not in the public interest, purely because the individual in question is trans, finding and publishing "old names" and photographs, and using demeaning language to ridicule their bodies and experiences. Frequently, the targets are linked to sex work or criminal cases, or accused of taking money from the state that could be "better" used elsewhere.

5. Editors and commissioners can no longer use the 'complexity' of transgender issues as a gatekeeping tactic

In the past, it was possible for editors to insist that "the public" would not understand issues around gender variance as they were too complicated, a position that denied writers the chance to explain them. Since the advent of the internet allowed writers to circumvent mainstream media entirely, and demonstrate that there was a large audience willing and able to understand these issues, this has become untenable. The low-cost, low-risk nature of online journalism has allowed a number of trans writers to enter the mainstream 'debate' about whether trans people should be allowed to exist and try to change its terms.

6. The refusal of trans language, culture and history is ideological

The invention of trans language, and the tropes which frame media coverage of trans people and issues, were ideological. Before the 20th century, there was no intellectual distinction between sexual diversity and gender variance, and cross-dressers were frequently arrested on suspicion of being "sodomites". As sexologists worked to understand and eventually separate the two, the medical establishment defined the terminology around gender-variant behaviour and decided who got access to treatment; as transsexual and transgender people became more visible, the media controlled the terms by which they were understood (or not).

Analysing this situation, trans people began to construct their own language to better discuss and document their experiences, and form a dialogue with medics and the media. One major problem was that there was no diametric opposite to the umbrella term 'transgender' (itself devised as an alternative to the historically loaded 'transsexual' and 'transvestite') and so "cisgender" was coined as an equal. When certain commentators claim to be oppressed by its use and question its validity, it is a political move aimed at blunting a tool that trans people have developed in a bid for equality, and against the de-normalisation of their own gender identities.

It is interesting, too, that some who are paid to provide expert commentary on contemporary social issues position themselves with "the people" when confronted with new ideas that they don't like, arguing their conceptual "people" cannot understand them. Often, they trumpet a working-class background despite not having been meaningfully proletarian for decades.

7. The focus on the cost of gender reassignment to the NHS is ideological

Public money is spent in all sorts of places for all sorts of reasons: why do the media focus on the cost to the taxpayer of gender reassignment and not (say) injuries sustained in amateur sports or on drunken nights out, or unwinnable wars launched on dubious pretexts against nations halfway across the world?

Besides ignoring the disproportionate effects of NHS cuts on people with a long-term reliance on the service, this coverage is also, frequently, more obviously dishonest: figures for the total cost of transition range from £10,000 to £80,000, often with no evidence presented for them. In an effort to combat this, Jane Fae researched and published on the topic, with the result freely available online. The regularity with which journalists who write on the costs of gender reassignment consult this resource is unknown.

8. Commentators "monster" efforts of trans community to organise

There have been efforts to organise since the 1960s, but the internet radically changed their nature, allowing trans people to engage in political action without having to out themselves to family, friends or colleagues. The internet has allowed trans people to expose the discrimination they face, and the structures that enable it, and unite against it: the media still demonises and humiliates individuals but now monsters collective dissent as well, portraying both their anger and the language used to express it as somehow unreasonable. This move is age-old, and should be familiar to anyone interested in minority activism. Given the situation, the fairest question is not "Why are they so angry?" but "Why aren't they angrier?"

9. The battleground has moved to the lives of children

In light of the grudging acceptance outlined in point four, commentators have switched their focus onto children and gender variance – the presence of trans adults around children or the actuality of schoolchildren publicly presenting as female when born male, or vice versa, even though this involves no more than a change of name and clothes, and reversible hormone blockers to delay the onset of puberty. Whenever you see the invocation of childhood innocence, consider adult malice.

10. Liberal/libertarian constructions of "freedom of speech" preserve this status quo

Defending commentators who write outright barbarous things about trans people, writers will often cite the right to freedom of speech, sometimes mistaking the refusal to give views a platform for their absolute censorship. This ignores the fact that one person's freedom of speech can, on occasion, impede the right of groups to exist without feeling persecuted, and fails to recognise that using "freedom of speech" to deny these groups a right to reply to individual aggression is in itself an attack on freedom of speech. The right to free speech is, incredibly important, obviously, but rights work best when accompanied by a sense of responsibility, and it would be nice if more commentators asked themselves: *Why am I saying this, and why am I saying it here? What power do I have, and what is the responsible way to use it?*

11. Going to the PCC is understood to be pointless

Trans Media Watch's Leveson submission stated that trans people widely regard the PCC as an "ineffective joke". The failure of the PCC's Code of Practice to protect against attacks on communities left it powerless to deal with the notorious Burchill piece referenced above; I won't insult you (or anyone else) by pointing out the problem with *Daily Mail* editor Paul Dacre being chairman of the PCC's Editors' Code of Practice Committee, and how it dissuades people from taking cases to the PCC.

12. The structures of online journalism should be considered in any analysis

Let us consider the sociopathic tendencies of online journalism, and how they affect trans people specifically. Online journalism relies on advertising revenue for its income; revenue is directly tied to hits, especially crucial when the newspaper industry is in crisis and can see no other future besides the demise of print, and so of paying customers.

Advertisers do not care whether people visiting a website support its arguments or revile them, and certain media outlets seem to have realised that orchestrating Twitterstorms through wilfully "provocative" opinion pieces will drive up the numbers. However, this has to be balanced against the understanding that gratuitous unpleasantness is bad for brands, so commentators who seek a living through this type of writing, and organisations employing them, must ask themselves: *Who can we attack? How? Will we remain brand-coherent?* These are the wrong questions, and the conclusions are frequently, if not always, misjudged.

With all this in mind, the sheer hypocrisy of a *Mail* spokesperson trying to position any connection made between Richard Littlejohn's *Mail* piece on Lucy Meadows and her death as 'an orchestrated Twitterstorm, fanned by individuals … with an agenda to pursue' should be enough to leave you burning with rage.

13. The 'outrage fatigue' generated by this model is particularly dangerous

It is widely agreed that the best response to such behaviour is to ignore it, and not to link to it. This is ultimately a zero-sum game: people who cannot afford to ignore this coverage as it impacts directly on their lives fear that if they will be demonised further if they pick every plausible battle, or simply run out of energy or hope. Consequently, the level at which these media outlets operate continually flatlines, and the only way to provoke people into making those precious hits is to noticeably drop it further.

14. This situation is self-perpetuating

Many trans people want nothing to do with the media, leaving it open to conservative and radical feminist critics, as well as lazy comedians who seek easy laughs from transphobic stereotypes. This makes it harder for trans people to enter the media, as doing so seems like an act of collaboration, creating conditions for attacks from their own community, whose support is desperately needed.

Typecasting exacerbates this: it's hard for openly trans writers to combat the stereotype that trans people are only interested in trans issues if these are all editors will commission them to discuss. It is finally becoming recognised that many trans journalists can and do write on a host of subjects, but the present circumstances are so dismal that being openly trans with any sort of media platform and not using it to critique them inescapably feels irresponsible.

15. Compromise is neither desirable nor possible

Trans Media Watch have drafted principles and offered consultation for editors and journalists for years in a bid to improve their coverage. A number of trans writers have interjected into the argument, on other people's terms, and I spent two years revealing intimate physical and psychological details about my experiences of transgender living in a bid to change those terms. None of these tactics have been completely successful as yet. This is not a situation where trans people want A, the media want to treat trans people like B and the solution lies somewhere between: it is a position that is hurtful, hateful and, at its conclusion, homicidal, and it cannot be allowed to continue.

New Statesman, 25 March 2013

AN INTERVIEW WITH JANET MOCK

Redefining Realness, the new memoir by American journalist and trans rights activist Janet Mock, opens with 'the email that changed my life'. This was a PDF of her *three-page "coming out" story in Marie Claire,* written by Kierna Mayo and published in May 2011 under the problematic headline of 'I Was Born a Boy'. Here, Mock talked about having her gender identity policed by her family and her peers, her understanding of herself as transsexual in her teenage years, and her trip to Bangkok, aged 18, for sex reassignment surgery.

The 2,300-word article immediately made Mock – a Staff Editor at *People* magazine's website – into a prominent trans woman of colour, a community under-represented in the mainstream media. Mock points this out in her 250-page book, which expands on the themes in that article: her childhood in Hawaii and Oakland; how she defined herself and found a trans community; the physical, social and legal aspects of transition; how her gender identity was policed by her family, her school and her peers; how being trans intersected with being a person of colour from a low-income family, and later, doing sex work; the challenges of finding love; and the reasons why she came out. *Redefining Realness* has already made waves in the US, not least after Mock challenged the way that Piers Morgan framed her story during his CNN programme, and has just been published in Britain by Atria Books.

Juliet: You were an established writer when you came out in 2011. What made you do it, and why did you choose to do so in *Marie Claire*?

Janet: I came out as not enough of our stories are told from our perspective. *Marie Claire* was offering the chance to be a part of a women's magazine, which often celebrates ordinary women doing extraordinary things. I thought it was very important as a young trans woman to be included in a mainstream women's magazine, countering that historical reluctance to accept trans women as women.

How has your life changed since you started talking and writing about your transition? And how have you balanced the potential problem of being typecast with the need to discuss the issues faced by trans people of colour?

My life has changed because more people know me and the personal issues I've struggled with – it's about being visible and vulnerable. I knew early on that one consequence would be having to represent all trans women, women of colour, people of colour, to some extent – it's about finding balance, remembering that I'm one person with a microphone and I'm proud to have that, but also that it's important to try to uplift the voices of other trans women. I don't feel as if I'm typecast – like any writer, the difficulty is that one facet of my identity becomes louder, obscuring the fact that I'm also a woman, a writer, a lover of pop culture and other things.

In the book, you talk about how your father thought you were "gay", and how you didn't have terms like *trans*, *transgender* or *transsexual* to define yourself. You also mention how phrases often encountered in trans narratives, such as "I always knew I was a girl", erase 'the nuances, the work, the process of self-discovery'. How difficult did you find it to render your experiences into an accessible language?

I knew what was important – the process of reading a book is very intimate, and an investment of time. Readers understand it as a complete portrait – the nuances are lost when points of our stories are reduced to media sound-bites. Writing about my personal life and contextualising my experiences, I needed to unpack and challenge certain media memes. On my road to self-discovery, only certain terms were available – I didn't use 'trans' or 'transgender' until junior high school, but I was living as trans much earlier. I wanted to bring people on that journey.

There has long been a gulf between the way the mainstream media discuss trans people – not just in the words used but also the overarching narratives – and the way we talk about our own lives. One reason you wrote *Redefining Realness* was because you weren't happy about how *Marie Claire* presented your story – but what are the advantages of telling your story through a book rather than journalism?

Marie Claire only gave me 3,000 words, which was not my entire story – but this was not my catalyst to write my book, as I was already doing it. The greatest asset of a memoir is that it's completely me, without my voice going through another journalist, editor, or TV producer. It's great to engage with the mainstream media to get messages out, but the most empowering tool is to create records of our lives, and our own images, which are not filtered through judgements, biases or misunderstandings. That's why I liked your *Transgender Journey* series – rather than a sensationalised account, you were offering an honest story of your experiences in real time.

The autobiography used to be the main way in which trans people explained their gender identities to a wider public, but hasn't been so popular with trans people in the last couple of decades. Why do you think this is, and for whom did you write *Redefining Realness?*

The reason I wrote it was because I didn't see any books by people who looked like me. I read plenty of transsexual autobiographies – Caroline Cossey, Christine Jorgensen, *The First Lady* by April Ashley, Jennifer Finney Boylan or Kate Bornstein – which were all by trans women, but didn't really cover intersections with youth, poverty, race or ethnicity. I wanted to look at being trans as one part of my identity, amongst other aspects, asking how I could tell a fuller story.

People are not always able to publish – I wanted to use privilege I had to give a voice to someone like me, who loved books. The audience is the girl I was in the library, looking for a reflection, but also cisgender women, as I wanted to build understanding, to discuss shared experiences of girlhood and womanhood, and how these concepts have evolved. If we start embracing each other as sisters, we'll take better care of each other.

The title refers not only to your ownership of your identity, but also to Jennie Livingston's film *Paris is Burning* (1990), about the African–American and Latino women in New York balls, who were judged on their "realness". The book references plenty of inspirational public figures, including Janet Jackson, Maya Angelou, bell hooks, Audre Lorde, but few trans people of colour. You found some local role models, but how important are they in popular culture?

I think for any of us, but particularly marginalised people, it's so important to be reflected in the media, and use that to suggest possibilities, encouraging people to dream bigger. Trans women of colour were never celebrated in the media – our stories were always about victimhood, violence and death. It's vital that this is discussed, but we know that these issues exist, and it's also important to see ourselves in celebratory terms, through people like Lea T, Carmen Carrera, Laverne Cox and others. People of colour have often been marginalised within the trans community, so it's especially important to suggest that more than victimhood is possible for us. One of my main objectives was to uplift trans women of colour like Sylvia Rivera and Marsha P. Johnson, who were involved with the Stonewall riots and liberation movements – I wanted readers to ask themselves "Why didn't I know about these activists and legends?" and look them up. I mentioned the Compton's cafeteria riot in 1966 as well as the more famous one in New York three years later – this probably happened so many times, when poor trans people with nothing to lose fought back against police oppression, and I wanted to mention their legacy.

Some of the British trans women were inspirational: I saw *Caroline Cossey on The Arsenio Hall Show*, which was popular when I was eight years old, and I thought "Oh my God" – here was someone from the UK, talking about being "born a boy" and transitioning. At grad school, we read books by journalists about their own lives, and I was assigned *Conundrum* by Jan Morris. She was a beautiful writer, but her experiences were very different to mine – the book resonated most when she talked about Morocco being the only place to go for surgery, and I identified with that after my trip to Thailand.

Given that LGBTQ★ lives have historically been portrayed as tragic, I think there's a lot of pressure to gloss over difficult experiences, but *Redefining Realness* is unflinching about racism, abuse and the realities of sex work as well as being trans. How hard was it to include these stories, and to publicly explore your own attitudes to them?

For me, that's the point of a memoir. I started from my most uncomfortable moments: I didn't have issues with being trans, but with how it marginalised me, and pushed me into certain traumas, such as bullying at school, sexual abuse from my stepbrother, and sex work to pay for treatment. I asked myself how I could be unflinching whilst talking about success: the media coverage I'd had suggested that everything was fine, and the book enabled me to be open and transparent about the pain, as well as the things I'm proud of.

I wasn't afraid of writing about that, as I knew that if people read the book, they would care and understand. I was more worried about the media turning parts of it into soundbites. The problem with Piers Morgan was that he hadn't read the book – *Redefining Realness* is a tool for people to understand the language that we've developed for our experiences, and there's an important difference between "assigned male at birth" and "born a boy" [the caption used when Mock appeared on Morgan's CNN show]. It's important that people read books like this in order to think about how to cover the people and issues involved in a more thoughtful and respectful way.

New Statesman, 16 April 2014

OVERCOMING TRAUMA AND INTOLERANCE AS AN INTERSEX ACTIVIST

Viloria's memoir *Born Both* tells the poignant and powerful story of h/er struggle to understand and speak out about gender identity. Calmly and with dignity, Viloria describes h/er experience and how it blossomed from the personal to the political. Today, Viloria is an activist for the intersex community. (Intersex refers to a person born with a reproductive or sexual anatomy that doesn't fit the standard definitions of female or male, such as someone who appears to be female on the outside but has a mostly male-typical anatomy inside.)

'I think we intersex folks are just one of nature's marvellous variations — like redheads in a world of blondes and brunettes,' Viloria writes. 'But each time I out myself publicly I remember that not everyone feels this way, and the fear sets in. I have to remind myself that ultimately it doesn't matter ... as much as people may view those who are different in a divisive, us-versus-them way, in actuality we are all fellow human beings who feel and want the same thing.'

Viloria's awakening emerges first out of family trauma, sexual violence and medical interrogation. H/er childhood was marked by an abusive father, anti-Hispanic racism and homophobia. Viloria, who was born in 1968 in New York, found solace and connection with androgynous cultural icons – Grace Jones, David Bowie, and Prince, and the memoirs of 19th century French hermaphrodite Herculine Barbin – who broke the silence around gender non-conformity. (After a long search for an appropriate pronoun, Viloria notes a preference for s/he and h/er.)

The book begins with an extraordinary level of violence: from Viloria's father toward the rest of the family (particularly Viloria's mother) and from racist bullies at school. Viloria finds that the advice "ignore them" not only doesn't work, but makes h/er feel powerless. Later, a nightclub rape leads to injuries to her female body parts.

This sets up the book's key political issue: the intersex community's aim to stop doctors from performing non-consensual genital surgeries on intersex infants, and allow them to decide what — if anything — to do with their bodies as adults. Having been spared such invasion as a child (despite her mother saying, in a surprisingly casual aside, that "the doctors thought you were a boy", Viloria becomes aware that h/er experiences are not like those of many people she meets through the Intersex Society of North America (ISNA).

Early on, Viloria tells a friend that both male and female "feel right," and h/er playful humour and sharp observations about gender roles derive from moments when Viloria switches between male and female, or masculine or feminine. Viloria notes the different ways people interact with h/er and the different types (and genders) of people that s/he attracts according to h/er presentation.

At one point, Viloria is arrested, as a man, for attacking police officers during a protest at the University of California, Berkeley. S/he arrives in court dressed as a woman, and the charges collapse. 'I know getting out of trouble wouldn't have been so easy if I hadn't been able to hide behind being a girl,' Viloria writes. 'I also find it interesting to consider whether any of this would have happened if the police hadn't thought I was a guy.'

As in Janet Mock's *Redefining Realness* (2014), Viloria's experiences of misogyny, homophobia, transphobia, racism and erasure of her intersex status form h/er social consciousness and draw h/er into activism. S/he tries to raise awareness through the mainstream media, making a lot of stressful decisions while earning very little.

Born Both is especially strong on the dilemmas of 'respectability politics' as Viloria details not just the challenges of deciding how to dress for high-profile television appearances (on *Oprah*, *20/20* and elsewhere), and how much of h/er self to give away in pursuit of h/er goals, but also their effects on h/er personal life. S/he splits with other activists over different approaches, for example when ISNA endorses efforts to replace 'intersex' (which denotes a physical status) with 'disorders of sex development', which Viloria fears will be used to facilitate non-consensual medical treatments.

There's a lot of sadness in this book, but no self-pity. The personal is not neglected: Viloria shares deep anguish in struggling to convey exactly what being intersex means to h/er mother, who finds various ways to avoid a full discussion; the relationship collapses in an argument about how Viloria has played down h/er father's abusive behaviour during h/er biggest television engagement.

Viloria's difficulties in reconciling h/erself with this family background tie into h/er struggles to find love, coming to a bittersweet conclusion after years of misunderstandings and violations, but the way in which s/he uses sex and sexuality to comprehend h/erself is rare in memoirs of this type. Viloria refuses to rein in h/er personality to fit some nebulous idea of a "good" intersex role model. The epilogue draws us back into a wider realm, looking at how transgender and intersex activists should support each other, with a brief reference to the Orlando massacre – a chilling reminder of this book's urgency.

Washington Post, 24 March 2017

MARX AT THE
ECOSEXUAL WORKSHOP

Paul B. Preciado's new book, *An Apartment on Uranus,* is a collection of 1500-word columns, many written for the French newspaper *Libération,* published between 2013 and 2018. As is often the case with collected journalism, the author's concerns can soon be identified, and their evolution charted over time: Preciado's key interest here is how regimes maintain borders in a time of constant movement of people, particularly across nations and between genders, and the increasingly authoritarian forms that this maintenance took throughout the 2010s. Throughout these articles, Preciado moves across Europe, from Paris as the National Front flourished under François Hollande's sclerotic centre-left rule to Barcelona during the Catalan independence referendum and the subsequent Spanish crackdown, via the Istanbul of the Gezi Park protests and the Athens of the *oxi* vote, Syriza's capitulation to the EU and the migration crisis of 2015. This may sound like a standard narrative of the left's turbulent moments of uprising and defeat in the face of rising authoritarianism over the last decade, even if it barely mentions Podemos and leaves out Corbyn's Labour entirely, but Preciado's perspective is formed as much by an interest in radical queer politics as by a commitment to wider leftist movements. These themes come together here in a way that suggests neither strand should exist without the other.

Preciado comes out against 'identity politics' here, but not in an Old Left or alt-right way: his desire, particularly for LGBT people, is to see 19th century conceptions of sexual and gender identity discarded so that we might imagine new ways of being, more appropriate to the present. (The idiosyncratic title of the collection refers to sexologist Karl Heinrich Ulrichs, who used 'Uranian' as the first term for 'homosexual' in 1867.) Preciado takes the same approach to left-wing politics, arguing against 'the gurus of old colonial Europe' who tell the 'activists of the Occupy, Indignados, crip-intersex-trans-queer, feminist' and other movements that they can't start a revolution without an ideology. Antiquated ideas need updating, and the old must listen to the young – memorably, Preciado declares that 'it is time to invite Marx into an ecosexual workshop', calling for socially and sexually liberated workers to extend their commitments to environmental movements to their personal lives.

In her introduction, writer/filmmaker Virginie Despentes explains how her ex-lover Preciado taught her the need to engage with politics with *enthusiasm*. That quality is in abundance here, in Preciado's passionate support for the #MeToo movement and for the experimental radical socialism of Rojava, and in his advocacy for a politics that unites the fights for LGBT and sex workers' rights, pro-choice and disability activism in a struggle for bodily autonomy. It is also present in Preciado's advocacy of a canon of writers who helped him to form his perspective: French writers such as Guillaume Dustan who emerged from the post-1968 sexual liberation movement; US trans activist-academics including Jack Halberstam and Dean Spade, and black activist authors like Angela Davis and Audre Lorde; and especially communist Chilean author and performance artist

Pedro Lemebel, who denounced both the Pinochet regime and an established left still unwilling to commit to LGBT rights at the height of the AIDS crisis. Preciado's approach is at its most moving in a column called 'The Bullet' that casts homosexuality and transsexuality as 'a silent sniper' that can hit any child, meaning their parents should be obliged to support them, rather using the figure of 'the child' to justify adherence to traditional family structures.

As Preciado goes on, his attention turns more to the leftist movements that emerged in response to austerity, and the migration that followed the outbreak of civil war in Syria. Once ideology could no longer maintain obedience towards finance capital, nominally democratic but increasingly authoritarian regimes took up the baton, supported by well-funded media empires. Against these, horizontalist left-wing movements had little chance – a dynamic that Preciado explores in a grimly realistic manner, without ever losing his belief that the young, and those who remain sexually and politically radical, could win this fight in the long term.

In a column about Marx, happiness and political optimism, Preciado writes that 'to be alive is to bear witness to an era'; not easy when events move so rapidly, with so many fragmentary perspectives on them available online. In theory, these types of columns allow authors to respond rapidly, receive instant feedback from readers and reconsider one's opinion as situations evolve; yet as British readers will know all too well, many columnists make a virtue of not reconsidering their positions. At its best, in these columns, the form lets writers explore a wide range of interests and develop distinctive voices within its brief word counts – and Preciado's voice, extensively articulated here, is as distinctive as one could ever hope to hear.

Tribune Issue 7, Spring 2020

SHON FAYE'S COMPREHENSIVE GUIDE TO 'THE TRANSGENDER ISSUE'

In a speech entitled 'A Humanist View', delivered at Portland State University in 1975, Toni Morrison said that 'the very serious function of racism is distraction. It keeps you from doing your work. It keeps you explaining, over and over again, your reason for being [...] None of this is necessary. There will always be one more thing.' This tactic is the foundation of the culture war, in which right-wingers use mainstream media to pin discussions of any minorities – whether of race, gender and/or sexuality – to the most unfavourable terms, forcing those minorities constantly to justify themselves rather than to advance demands for liberation. In her first book, *The Transgender Issue* (2021), trans author and activist Shon Faye sets out to make exactly such demands, opening with an epigraph from writer/performer Travis Alabanza about how the word 'trans' also means 'escape', 'choice', 'autonomy' and, above all, 'wanting more possibilities' than the ones available to us. To open up such possibilities entails addressing head-on the lies endlessly told about us, however tiresome this feels. It's a task Faye takes on with zeal: the book's title explicitly references the dehumanizing way the media reduces trans people to an 'issue'. In each chapter, she challenges a 'talking point' with a combination of facts, statistics and lived experiences, providing a comprehensive guide for anyone who wants to advocate for the community.

It's important to remember that, while plenty of trans books are being published in 2021, several by 'gender critical' feminists are also being enthusiastically plugged on social media and in ostensibly liberal newspapers and magazines. These books, including *Trans* by Helen Joyce and *Material Girls* by Kathleen Stock, aim, in part, to redefine feminism as something that can't include trans people, especially trans women. Nonetheless, in what novelist, poet and critic Roz Kaveney has referred to on Twitter as the 'Year of Trans Creativity', numerous novels, short stories, memoirs and poetry collections are striving to explore Alabanza's 'possibilities'. Pluto Press's *Transgender Marxism* anthology (2021, edited by Jules Joanne Gleeson and Elle O'Rourke), for instance, gives a scathing analysis of how poverty, precarity and austerity specifically affect the trans and non-binary community. *The Transgender Marxism* authors point towards a future that may be imaginable once Faye's demands for better healthcare, housing, social security, bodily autonomy and sexual freedom are met, but class-based analysis is central to both books.

The Transgender Issue opposes liberal approaches to trans activism that emphasise media representation and inclusion within conservative institutions, upholding prisons and the police. Faye notes how the 'Transgender Tipping Point' declared by *Time* magazine in a 2014 cover article, which suggested the US trans rights movement could no longer be stopped, was proved wrong after the ascension of former US president Donald Trump in 2016. And, while the Joe Biden administration immediately sided with trans people when elected in 2020, such progress is never smooth. In the UK, neither Trans Media Watch's submission to the Leveson Inquiry into the tabloid press' mafia-like behaviour in 2012, nor the suicide of Lucy Meadows a year later after the *Daily Mail* published an article questioning her suitability to teach primary-school children, led to better treatment. Instead, almost every major newspaper painted trans people as powerful bullies, despite there being no high-profile trans politicians or editors, and the handful of UK trans columnists present in the early 2010s being driven out of the discourse by the decade's end. Even if these writers (myself included) *had* managed to make these publications more trans-positive, this would have done little to combat the legislative assaults on trans communities in Brazil, Hungary, Poland, Turkey, the US and elsewhere, nor to alleviate the impact of the UK government's funding cuts on working-class trans people, which added years to waiting lists for NHS gender reassignment services and made it far harder for them to survive on unemployment benefits.

Faye's exploration of the difficulties facing trans children and trans sex workers is especially welcome given how little both groups have been able – or *allowed* – to air their specific needs. Her discussion of historical gender-variant people in a media climate that pretends trans is a new (and thus not valid) 'issue' is equally important. However, Faye's book is strongest when she asks how the treatment of trans people brings up 'wider, conceptual concerns about the autonomy of the individual in society': the questions of how far trans people should 'bend themselves to fit the way our society is ordered at present' and of how 'the challenges trans people present to lawmakers expose fundamental flaws in the entire system' suggest that a radical liberation movement could transform for everyone, and not just us.

Ultimately, *The Transgender Issue* is about, and *of*, public discourse. The culture war is designed to be unwinnable, but it's too damaging to ignore. I hope that, in writing this book, Faye has made it unnecessary for anyone else to do something similar – at least for a while. It's a sign of progress that publishers will now commission trans authors to tackle political arguments directly, rather than only allowing us to do so through 'confessional' genres: trans artists, writers, filmmakers and musicians can use culture to realize the possibilities that Alabanza and Faye picture, in the hope that our enemies have neither the imagination nor the talent to fight us on so many fronts.

Frieze, 16 September 2021

ARTS

I wrote on the arts before I moved into journalism about politics and the media – first, for small Arts Council-funded film magazines such as *Filmwaves* and *Vertigo,* but also literary outlets such as *The London Magazine.* I won't relitigate too much of my career here, having already done that in this collection and in *Trans: A Memoir,* but arts writing was always where my heart was, and it during a week's work experience that I wrote my first ever piece on a trans subject – the interview with performance artist Pia, for *The London Magazine'*s short-lived and more experimental *Trespess* magazine, which opens this section. Writing about the arts, and for arts publications, was often more fun, less pressured and better paid than covering trans and non-binary politics for news outlets (especially in op-eds), and far more satisfying: the essays on the video game *Alter Ego* and 'Écriture trans-féminine' were exactly what I had always wanted to write, and talking to people such as Turkish writer and performer Esmeray or 94-year-old Italian photographer Lisetta Carmi provided a beautiful correlative to some of my more frustrating encounters in political journalism.

The pieces here had a different, and more positive aim, than many of those in the previous sections – rather than calling out individuals or delving into structural problems, these aimed to help trans and non-binary people find their way to works I'd spent years discovering, and to prove to the wider world that we had a cultural canon (and to help to build that canon). This project has consistently excited me, and there is always something new to say – hence these pieces spanning almost my entire career, and being a consistent part of my work throughout, whether I was surveying a movement or going into depth on a particular artist, writer or work. The pieces cover art (installation, painting, performance and photography), film, literature and theory – I hope that, in collecting them here, they present a potted but vivid picture of trans and non-binary art and culture of the 21st century so far. I can't predict too much about how that art will develop – if I could, there would be little point in artists making it – but I do think that in literature, film, visual art, music and elsewhere, two things will happen. Firstly, the forms of representation of trans and non-binary people will become more complex, more abstract and more adventurous; secondly, more trans and non-binary artists will come through whose gender identities are not central to their work, and perhaps not even to media coverage of that work. What exactly this will produce, I cannot guess, but I'm excited to see.

TRANSGENDER ADVENTURES: AN INTERVIEW WITH PIA

JULIET: When did you realise you were gender-gifted?
PIA: From a very early age. When you go to school it becomes more apparent, because you grow up with your mother, and you see a lot more of your mother than you do of your father, so gender doesn't matter – you're just a little tiny child. But when you go to school it's clear you're intrinsically different – and not in an understandable way.

I was in a ring of children at playgroup and the teacher was asking everyone what they wanted to do when they grew up. Everyone said "train driver" or "hairdresser" until she came to a little boy called Trevor who said he wanted to be a nurse. The children rounded on him, angrily, purely because of their education about what boys can't do and girls can't do. So, I just said, "train driver".

You're allowed to dress up as children – I wanted to dress as a girl. But dressing up box stopped for me, unless I wanted to be a cowboy – I wasn't allowed anything else. Which wasn't fair: I couldn't express myself through the clearest means – clothing.

What did your transition involve?

The last 25 years of my life, getting to the point where I started transitioning. Actually doing it caused a lot of pain. It was a trial by fire. I lost money, security and many friends. Even when they know you're trans, the decision to become more female than male is often difficult for someone you meet with career and relationship goals.

Some people were fine, but initially others were hostile because I was doing something that made everything else seem a bit inane. That profound commitment to transitioning – people don't understand how gender is such a fundamental part of you, because they've never questioned it. I hate it when people refer to being a 'tranny' as a 'hobby' – you don't live and die by hobbies. You need belief that you'll survive – being into model trains isn't quite the same.

Is transition a continuous process?

It's a spiritual path – I find it's continually growing. You're learning more about yourself, having been censored for a very long time. You start to express yourself more – whereas you've been constantly tailoring your persona, you become free to let go and find your place between feminine and masculine values, which, within people's social conditioning, can be very confusing.

That's why transgender people have such a negative press. We make people question their own gender and sexuality because we intrinsically confront them about it. People ask themselves if they're gay if they fancy a transsexual – no, because gay men fancy men and lesbians fancy women. We are in the LGBT community, which is great, because we all face the same fears, which is coming out and telling everyone your darkest secret, which is "I am *this.*"

People are castrated – punished – for what they are.

Transitioning demands willingness to throw oneself off a mountain. You have to come out and say, "This is me" and if you accept me, great, but if you don't, so be it. That's what I find is upsetting when people think we are like Barbie dolls, conforming to negative feminine stereotypes – I'm like Barbie, but with a knife.

What do you think causes your gender identity?

I think you're born with it. I don't think you become transgender – I think you *are*. You can hide it. There are lots of trans people in the closet, denying themselves expression in preference of the Other – a straight, normal life. You can have a straight, normal life if you're gay, bi, trans or whatever, but stepping out of that 2.4 children construct is intimidating, and I don't know if there *is* a cause. Maybe it's a water system overloaded with oestrogen.

Throughout history there have always been trans people and they've always been revered, from the Native Americans to the Greeks and Romans, especially the Pagans, who had a lot of belief systems based on nature. In nature, there are hermaphrodites everywhere – in frogs, for example. If there are too many male frogs they'll turn into females and vice versa. I think the cause is natural – it's not a choice, and you can choose whether to hide it or be proud of it.

Who are your inspirations (trans or otherwise)?

Social mavericks: people willing to disenfranchise themselves for their beliefs. People with unshakeable beliefs with a good grounding: not in religion but in their vision of reality. If you prove one thing that isn't in the textbook, that disproves the textbook – and I think that's the essence of transgenderism.

I admire Nikola Tesla, because he, not Edison, is the father of modern electricity. Viktor Schauberger, for his theories about dynamics. Wilhelm Reich, who hypothesised that the constriction of your sexual identity and self-expression was harmful to the human spirit.

Trans people – April Ashley for her remarkable story, her strength of character and her will, as well as the *Paris is Burning* girls from New York.

How has being trans influenced you creatively?

The Seventies pioneers – Warhol superstars like Candy Darling – inspired me but as a child I didn't know them. So my creativity came from exploring gender, from within physicality. I like creativity with a message. Some art I don't see the point in. Duchamp's urinal, for example – I understand the concept, but it needs to be seen in context, and contextualising is what I'm about.

How would you describe your performances?

It's very fierce, very provocative, quite incendiary – like some bitch with tits and a cock on napalm. I'm quite humble as well, but when I'm on stage I'm on fire, and I make a formidable adversary if I'm dancing with someone. I draw on the energy of the changing seasons and the precession. My cause is for the freedom of people, particularly transgender people, to express themselves. I think it's important that people are allowed to express themselves from childhood to adulthood without being made to feel guilty. I try to have a child-like state of belief when performing – I feel like I'm becoming an adult, the adult I wanted to be when I left puberty – I draw strength from being proud of what I am, whereas before I wasn't.

I do a flag dance, which is called *Declare Independence*. I come on stage and people think I'm a girl. I have flags representing conflict facing each other – China and Tibet, America and Cuba, the gay flag opposite the Saudi flag, the cross and the arrow symbolising male and female, and on my dress, I wear 'Jesus Loves You'. As a cape I wear the Jolly Roger. I strip the flags down while dancing vigorously. I lose the flags – eventually I'm left with the Jolly Roger, which symbolises independence from everything, especially the prescribed notion of the masses, and then Jesus Loves You, which symbolises so much, including the Solstice. Then I drop that and I'm naked, and the illusion that I am a woman – and an angry woman at that – collapses, and I'm declaring independence from everything.

I do another show to *O Superman* by Laurie Anderson. I come on as a bastardised Clark Kent, and wear a rubber fuck-doll face mask, and I slowly strip in a nasty, *Friday 13th* fashion. When I shed the Clark Kent suit, you see I'm Superman, and then I take off the Superman suit and I'm a muscleman. As I remove that you see I'm a woman, but between that and my skin there's a thick layer of fake blood, as though I'm being flayed or peeling off the exterior to reveal the inner heart of Superman. As I peel the chest down, people don't see my breasts and with my mask they don't see my face – when I had my suit on, they thought I was a male stripper. Then I peel off my bottom half at the end to confuse the issue once again – first they thought I was a man, then a woman, then I'm trans. Maybe that's why Superman is so wholesome – because he's got a trans heart.

I did things at Glastonbury this year with NYC Downlow, including building a gay bar with my friend Gideon, as well as Horse Meat Disco and Jonny Woo.

In your mind, what is a man and what is a woman, and where do you fit in?
Well, men generally have a cock and women generally have a vagina. Along the spectrum of sexuality there are so many different permutations, with intersex in the middle. All of light together is white – male – and all absence of light is black – female, represented by Cybele, the Greek deification of the Earth Mother – and between there is a rainbow.

I think people would fit an explanation of gender more comfortably if society allowed wider variation. In Native American culture, if a little girl wanted to go and hunt, she could. Society is much more accepting of tomboys – if a man wants to be nurturing, it's seen as weakness. Recently we've had the New Man, Nineties Man and Noughties Man. People aren't allowed to fully express themselves yet – but that will change. Here, we're twenty years behind New York and San Francisco.

In the future, we'll start a more female age. We live on a female planet – they have more of a connection with it, because they create, they have a womb. I'm in awe of that. That doesn't make me, or men, any less. At the moment it appears the patriarchal phase is ending and the matriarchal phase is beginning, which is crucial – if it doesn't, the planet won't survive.

Trespass Issue 1, 2007

SCREAMING QUEENS (DIR. SUSAN STRYKER & VICTOR SILVERMAN, 2008)

Revolutionary movements prize history above all else. Their narratives are constructed carefully: the most powerful interests determine key battles and individuals, intending to maintain their prominence by emphasising their radical commitment from the outset into – implicitly – the future. Such movements rely upon a strong collective identity, defined both through struggle against the prevailing order and through dialogue between internal factions. Often, those factions, unified through shared oppression, come together for an epochal moment: once the dominant power is undermined, their expedient unity falters and the struggles become internal – including the struggle over history.

For the (often awkward) Lesbian, Gay, Bisexual and Transgender alliance, the definitive battle has always been Stonewall. Gay male activists – often the alliance's strongest voice – have always prized New York's Stonewall Inn riots in 1969, when gays, lesbians and transgender people rose against police brutality, as the moment when organised LGBT liberation politics began.

The relationship between transgender activists and lesbian and gay groups has often been fractious, both because transsexuality has threatened certain lesbian feminists resenting transsexual intruders upon 'women-only' spaces, but also because trans activists have very different interests. Bracketed by the dominant order as a sexual minority, due in part to the complex role of drag within gay club culture, transgender theorists have stressed that gender identity is unconnected to any specific sexual orientation. This emphasis has not always pleased campaigners for non-heterosexual relationship rights, who have often stated that same-sex desire is unrelated to gender incongruity.

Whilst the alliance has empowered the community, it has been crucial for transgender activists to construct their own history – one that overlaps with, and informs, a wider LGBT discourse but focused on 'transgender' people. This project flowered in the 1990s after Leslie Feinberg politicised the word, creating a collective 'transgender' identity, stretching from cross-dressers to transsexuals. With a definitive umbrella term, historians could write an inclusive narrative encompassing sexological research into transvestism, the possibilities of sex reassignment technology and trans-specific resistance to oppression.

Feinberg credited 'militant young gay transvestites' with leading the Stonewall fight. In 1995, historian Susan Stryker asked why the 'Lesbian and Gay History' panel at a Center for Lesbian and Gay Studies conference included no transgender speakers. One reply – that *transsexuals* were psychopaths who mutilated their bodies to conform to reactionary gender stereotypes and discredited the gay/lesbian movement – came from Jim Fouratt, Gay Liberation Front co-founder and Stonewall veteran. Stryker asserted: "I'm transsexual, and I'm not sick. And I'm not going to listen to you say that about me, or people like me, any more."

Stryker won the exchange, suggesting new interpretations of gender diversity to LGBT activists. Ten years later, Stryker presented her film *Screaming Queens*, co-directed with Victor Silverman, documenting the little-known transgender riot at Compton's Cafeteria in San Francisco in 1966, three years before Stonewall. Fouratt confronted her, decrying an Orwellian transgender hegemony erasing his experiences through historical revisionism. The audience shouted Fouratt down, and he stormed out.

The Stonewall riots were pansexual, a consequence of the authorities' ghettoising sexual and gender minorities together – and targeting trans people as the most visible members of the LGBT community. Screaming Queens' opening emphasises the conservative inability to distinguish – contemporary footage of San Francisco's impoverished Tenderloin district with ominous commentary about the city's 90,000-strong 'gay' community, warning that 'only at night do they show their true colours', as several trans women walk the streets.

Narrating the film, Stryker posits the Compton's Cafeteria riot not just as a precursor to Stonewall, but also as the transgender community's "debut on the stage of American political history". It was trans people, particularly ethnic minorities, ghettoised in Tenderloin: when frequent raids threatened Compton's sanctuary, a queen threw coffee over a policeman's face, and suddenly there was an uprising.

Hustlers kicked policemen, queens fought with their heels and handbags, a police car was destroyed and, as transsexual activist and former sex worker Amanda St. Jaymes says, people didn't care about going to jail – it needed to happen and besides, they were constantly being arrested anyway.

The riot was a crucial moment within a long history of increased trans visibility and consequent oppression and counter-oppression. Stryker and Silverman document the shifting balance between police brutality and the confidence that Harry Benjamin's exploration of 'transsexualism' gave transgender San Francisco, evoking a sense that revolution was inevitable by interviewing Tenderloin veterans from inside and outside the trans community, finding compassion from some unlikely quarters.

Sergeant Elliott Blackstone received a standing ovation at *Screaming Queens'* premiere. Asked why, as a straight man, he had fought so hard for LGBT rights after 1966, organising a church collection for hormones for transgendered people, he replied: "Because my religion teaches me to love everybody." Blackstone and the Reverend Ed Hansen, from the progressive Glide Memorial Methodist Church, offer sympathetic counterpoints to the interviews with Sixties Tenderloin's trans people (all Male-to-Female – the Female-to-Male community has its own history).

Even within Tenderloin's community, there were divides: glamorous, white queens such as Aleshia Brevard, who worked as a *Playboy* bunny, found some economic and expressive freedom in entertaining, whilst the less fortunate feared losing their insecure jobs, police harassment and a serial killer that targeted trans street workers.

The queens lacked the freedom to leave Tenderloin – not just because they were frequently arrested for "female impersonation" and interned if they refused to let the police shave their hair. Tenderloin was excluded from San Francisco's anti-poverty programmes, and its trans community denied a political voice – the hope offered by Benjamin's willingness to "give hormones to everybody" and transsexual Christine Jorgensen's high celebrity simply fuelled their resentment.

Stryker and Silverman weave in archive footage of a transsexual on television, demanding to be treated as "a normal, respectable woman", voicing the community's determination to win the right to express their inner gender with dignity. As Blackstone put it, the "unnecessary violence" used by the police at Compton's finally turned the resentment into rioting, which distilled into one of the Vietnam War era's most neglected civil rights movements.

"I knew very little about sexuality except that I enjoyed sex", confides Blackstone, who sadly died in October 2006. "I'd never heard about transsexuals before." Blackstone and Hansen helped start a welfare programme for Tenderloin's trans people through San Francisco's Center for Special Problems. Crucially, transsexuals were issued with new ID cards appropriate to their gender – the first step in their battle for the recognition of reassignment, which is still far from being won, forty years on.

"I'm so proud of those women who fought at Compton's", says Stryker. "Transgender people need to change a world that still denies us many of our basic human rights." A clearly defined history, with inspirational individuals standing against oppression, will provide a solid foundation for a trans – and LGBT – movement that will continue the global fight against subjugation. It is a history that can never again be written without Compton's *Screaming Queens.*

Vertigo Vol. 3 Issue 8, Winter 2008

RETURNING TO *THE CITY OF LOST SOULS*

City of Lost Souls does not have a strong reputation, even within the uneven oeuvre of controversial German director Rosa von Praunheim. It warrants no description even in his website's biography, eclipsed by works such as *It is Not the Homosexual Who is Perverse, But the Society in Which He Lives*, which mobilised the German gay rights movement with its portrayal of social homophobia, and *I am My Own Woman*, a semi-documentary about German transvestite Charlotte von Mahlsdorf. In *Queer German Cinema*, Alice A. Kuzniar – one of few to retrospectively address the film – dismisses it as "self-indulgent ... silliness."

Covering the film before its UK release, *Guardian* reviewer Chris Auty was even less impressed. "The latest and junkiest outing from the travelling opportunist of gay cinema, Rosa von Praunheim ... [is] as much calculated to upset a heterosexual audience as to flatter the complicity of a (male) gay one," Auty wrote on 12 April 1984. Four days earlier, *The Observer's* brief synopsis was equally scathing, but came closer to accurately describing its ensemble cast, at least realising that this was not (or at least not primarily) a gay film: "A sort of transvestite/transsexual cabaret, it looks dispiritingly like amateur night on an off-day."

A week before his colleague damned the film (when a broadsheet would offer three different takes on an underground queer musical) *Guardian* critic Derek Malcolm provided a more even-handed assessment, appreciating its spirit more intuitively than Auty or Kuzniar. "The film is a fairly comprehensive mess" wrote Malcolm, "as if it were put together by a reanimated and manic Andy Warhol" (curiously, as Warhol was still alive). "But for every exhibitionist there's a quite ordinary human screaming to get out, and von Praunheim's sympathy with this idea render the film less boring and more fun than you might think."

Story-wise, the film is a mess: Kuzniar writes it off as "little more than a vehicle for a group of transvestites [sic] to parade themselves through dance and song within a loosely concocted narrative about the employees at a Burger Queen restaurant." Kuzniar's synopsis is more accurate than her terminology, but misses the point: making scant pretence to narrative logic, *City of Lost Souls* is driven by its cast, and by theme rather than plot: its non-judgemental handling of alienation and self-realisation, and especially its anticipation of transgender identities which create space within the established 'transvestite'/'transsexual' dichotomy are what make it a (minor) cult classic.

It is no surprise that Malcolm mentions Warhol. The influence of *Chelsea Girls*, and the Paul Morrissey films *Flesh*, *Trash* and (particularly) *Women in Revolt*, to which Warhol put his name, is clearly visible. Like Warhol and Morrissey, von Praunheim allowed his actors to improvise freely, often incorporating the results into the script, lending *City of Lost Souls* a similar feel to the films of Warhol, Jack Smith, Kenneth Anger and other pioneers of queer American underground cinema.

According to *Man Enough to be a Woman*, the autobiography of *City of Lost Souls*' star, Factory actor, Stonewall riots veteran and punk singer Jayne County, von Praunheim was 'looking for eccentric Americans to be his film's Warholesque cast of outsiders. County was living in Berlin, performing her stage musical *U-Bahn to Memory Lane* – her co-star, Tron von Hollywood, introduced her to von Praunheim. After he offered County an 800 Mark advance, she agreed to feature (with Tron), giving the film its title and writing all of her own material, some of which came from *U-Bahn to Memory Lane.*

Like his New German Cinema contemporary Werner Herzog, von Praunheim liked to blur the lines between fact and fiction, saying that his output was "almost all documentary … Even the feature films are with real people – strong personalities that I build in documentary fashion into my films." Shot in six weeks, mostly in von Praunheim's basement, *City of Lost Souls* works best when he allows his cast to freely express their personalities.

The 'lost souls' orbit around Angie Stardust, who owns Burger Queen and runs the Pension Stardust boarding house. Her actual personal history is aired: after her father tried to beat her youthful femininity out of her, she became "the first black transsexual" to perform in New York, at the 82 Club (New York's biggest pre-Stonewall drag revue and later host to County and other punk pioneers), having initially been turned away because of her colour. After moving to Berlin, Angie finds that she has not escaped racism, with some who provided votes and soldiers for the Nazis surviving and passing their prejudices to their grandchildren; the generation between, she feels, were too busy enjoying West Germany's 'economic miracle' to teach their offspring to entirely reject Nazi ideology.

Rainer Werner Fassbinder's *Marriage of Maria Braun* (1979), which cynically explores the after-effects of the

American liberation of Berlin through one woman's life after her fling with a US soldier, contrasts its protagonist's lonely death with Herbert Zimmermann's famous radio commentary on West Germany's shock 1954 World Cup triumph, a famous symbol of post-war recovery. Typically, von Praunheim's depiction of everyday Fascism is more direct than that of his main rival in the New German Cinema group, juxtaposing a child singing a racist song and a white man telling the audience, in Brechtian fashion, that "I love Berlin! My grandmother used to say 'Arbeit macht frei!'" with Angie's lament that "People here don't consider the past."

City of Lost Souls is more nuanced when exploring the alienation that comes with gender or sexual minority. Tara O'Hara, who keeps bringing men back to Pension Stardust, ostensibly to "teach them English", identifies as 'transvestite' – which had a less narrow meaning in 80s Germany than in contemporary Britain.

Whilst 'transgender' had been used in several contexts by 1982, it does not appear in *City of Lost Souls*. Before this term came into common use, 'transvestite' – coined by German sexologist Magnus Hirschfeld in *The Transvestites: The Erotic Drive to Cross-Dress* (1910) – offered more scope than 'trans-sexual' for people to find space between male and female or reject the gender identity assigned at birth without pursuing medical intervention. (The modern meaning, primarily referring to those who cross-dress for sexual pleasure, is clearly signified by Hirschfeld, on whom von Praunheim later made *The Einstein of Sex*, but was only fixed after 'trans-gender' and other terms assumed this wider function.)

The tensions that developed within the 'transgender' alliance, which never quite healed the transvestite/trans-sexual division, are anticipated by Angie and Tara O'Hara – as are the passionate debates over terminology and semantics held in autonomous spaces as transgender theory evolved in the 90s. Despite his clear sympathy with Angie and Tara's difficulties in externalising their genders in a transphobic (and xenophobic) society, and his realisation that doing so has necessarily taken both Angie and Tara nearer its fringes despite supposedly being the first step towards a more settled life, aspects of von Praunheim's framing feel problematic.

A shot of Angie topless momentarily punctuates her explanation that seeing 'transvestites … with breasts' made her want to transition, giving some visual sense that she has achieved self-realisation, but whether or not this is empowering or exploitative remains open to debate, as no other context is given.

In a scene that looks improvised – County recalls that von Praunheim had a Warhol-style aloofness, preferring to '[take] a back seat and [let] people do their own thing' than provide strong direction or even script every scene – Angie has a heated discussion with Tara O'Hara about their divergent gender identities. The voiceover sets up the conflict: Tara is "a transvestite and wears women's clothes but wants to remain a man" whilst Angie "is a transsexual … her only problem is that she has a penis that she wants to have removed."

Here, von Praunheim again walks an ambiguous line between sympathy and sensationalism, but the film handles its subjects intelligently enough for this focus on Angie's physicality to convey the socio-economic stresses that come with transsexual living, rather than being simply voyeuristic. This effect is achieved when its characters speak for themselves, as Tara asks Angie: "Do you think a sex change will make you a woman?" before asserting that physical transition "is not necessary any more". Drawing on post-war antagonism between certain transvestite and transsexual activists, Tara's arguments overlap with those of the early 80s' most vocal critics of gender reassignment: a subset of 'radical' feminists who attacked transsexual people for apparently reiterating patriarchal stereotypes of femininity, an opinion that found its most aggressive and sustained expression in Janice Raymond's rabid tract *The Transsexual Empire* (1979).

Whilst transsexual responses to Raymond were published almost immediately (by writers such as Roz Kaveney and Carol Riddell), it was not until the end of the Eighties (after AIDS had seismically altered LGBT culture, and become the focus of von Praunheim's films) that gender-variant people organised politically. Written in 1987, Sandy Stone's essay *'The "Empire" Strikes Back: A Post-Transsexual Manifesto'*, became transgender theory's founding text, encouraging transsexual people to move beyond 'passing' (thus silencing themselves) and be open about their pasts, reasoning that a confident, honest assertion of a transsexual identity would undermine Raymond's critique, which relied heavily on stereotype.

The transgender alliance that arose did not always mask tensions between transsexual people who moved across the gender binary and transgender or genderqueer individuals who aimed to finds space beyond male and female. Tara O'Hara's 'transvestite' ideal instinctively anticipates the latter position, but Angie angrily tells her that it is "because of the old school that you can be what you are… We pumped the hormones, we put up with people calling us 'faggot' and 'drag queen' … Now it's easy for you, you get tits, your hair grows, you're a woman. It was harder for us, we had to act over-feminine …"

And she's right: the post-war Gender Identity Clinics administered hormones or surgery only to those who met their tough criteria on physical and mental health and in particular on gender presentation and sexuality. The transsexual women who met this obligation to dress in hyper-feminine methods and deny an attraction to other women, being unable to criticise for fear of jeopardising their treatment, all the while facing verbal and physical attacks from various quarters, often having their identities invalidated or ignored, opened space for those such as Tara O'Hara with more playful attitudes to gender.

Eventually, they reach an awkward compromise. Angie absolutely refuses Tara's suggestion to "accept yourself as a transvestite"; Tara tells her that "we're the third sex" but Angie prefers to "agree that we're the New Women". (Both of these phrases have Victorian connotations, reflecting von Praunheim's interest in *fin-de-siècle* sexology: 'the third sex' was Edward Carpenter's term for effeminate homosexuals or 'inverts', a concept that Hirschfeld and others later unpicked, while 'New Women' was a nineteenth century feminist ideal inspired by the emancipated females in Ibsen's plays.)

Later, we see Tara O'Hara with one of the men she brings home. As they kiss, she tells him that "I'm a different kind of woman … An extraordinary woman", trying to make her gender status clear before they become too intimate, knowing that revelation during sex carries the risk of a violent response (often justified by the 'panic' defence and the argument that the transgender woman has been deliberately deceptive, that often worked in transphobic courts). When he becomes suspicious, Tara says that she is "a transvestite". His response reveals that instantly, his sexual identity is thrown into crisis: "I'm not gay – you should have told me that before." Tara says, "you're not gay because you sleep with me", explaining that she is "another kind of woman" and talking him into staying: just as von Praunheim does not let Tara undermine Angie's hard-won identity, so he does not let this man reject Tara's.

Tara tells her lover that she felt "feminine" as a child, before taking steps to match her body with her feelings, suggesting some intervention (perhaps hormone therapy) despite her rejection of sex reassignment surgery. Here we see the difference between scripted films of the 1990s and 2000s that used cisgender actors to play transgender characters – *Transamerica*, *Boys Don't Cry* and *Priscilla, Queen of the Desert* for example – and the underground directors who cast transgender people as themselves, allowing them to create more honest portrayals of the experience of gender-variant life.

The presence of Jayne County, Angie, Tara and drag queen Joaquin in *City of Lost Souls* ensures nuanced representation rather than cliché – that it incorporates Angie's real-life lesbian relationship with a white woman, without comment, feels especially progressive. In this context, they are not ciphers for 'issues', members of a 'minority' or the 'freaks' that Calpernia Addams complained that trans actors often end up playing, but simply people, with some of their challenges being gender-specific and others not.

Man Enough to be a Woman was one of few transsexual autobiographies not to be centred around surgery – which County ultimately declines – breaking with the genre's convention by showing her gender identity's evolution within a queer context rather than as a struggle to hide it in order to maintain a 'respectable' heterosexual life. (This, of course, was an honest representation of her personal history.)

In *City of Lost Souls*, she plays cisgender woman Lila, who goes from supporting Reagan – to the extent of singing '(I Want to Be the One to) Push the Button' – to becoming pregnant by a Communist who promises to make her a People's Artist of the German Democratic Republic. Which happens: Lila ends up on East German television singing 'I Fell in Love with a Russian Soldier' and declaring her love of Karl Marx – warmly appreciated by the American outsiders feeling oppressed in their anti-Communist homeland and West Berlin (and not entirely aware of the realities of life in the East).

Then, dancer Gary, due to be deported the next day, sets fire to his room: he and Tron are killed and, as angels, look down on the other characters, who obliviously continue dancing as the fire brigade arrive: there is a threat to their hard-won liberation as real, and fatal, as the HIV virus that began to ravage gay and transsexual communities as the film was conceived.

Tron von Hollywood fell to AIDS a few years before County's book was published in 1995, but he was not the first cast member to die. Tara O'Hara's 'freedom' proved chimerical: she too contracted HIV, according to *Man Enough to be a Woman*, but was not killed by it. In 1983, she was found severely beaten in a ladies' room in Tiergarten and taken to hospital, lying in a coma for weeks until the doctors pulled the plug. (Charlotte Cooper's tribute is particularly moving.)

I feel that *City of Lost Souls* has aged better than Kuzniar or Auty would have guessed: with gender-variant people slowly gaining mainstream media respect and representation, it's fascinating to see the debates in which they worked out their gender identities staged before online communities, transgender-specific fanzines or Queer/Transgender Studies courses – all crucial to the development of organised transgender politics.

Lagging behind gay and lesbian history, a transgender cultural canon is still being defined. Rosa von Praunheim emerged at a time when 'gay' retained a function as shorthand for a range of gender identities and sexualities fighting shared oppression, and so became known as a 'gay' director. Which he was, but his output often explored gender as well as sexuality, better fitting more recent ideas of 'queer' filmmaking, and several would slot well into a historiography of transgender film, even after considering the problems in retrospectively transposing the concept onto people who preceded its contemporary usage.

Rather than being 'self-indulgent', its characters are trying to understand their identities in the face of prejudice – not just transphobia but also homophobia, xenophobia and racism – and far from trying to 'upset a heterosexual audience', or even 'flatter the complicity' of gay male viewers, its transsexual and transvestite characters were fighting for the freedom to be themselves. Consequently, they provide an inspiration to a culture that has had to prize this struggle above all others, and still has relatively few role models: in doing so, they raise *City of Lost Souls* far above the limitations of its plot.

3:AM Magazine, 4 January 2012

PARODYING EVA PERÓN: ON COPI

Sixty years since her death, dramatisations of Evita's life and early death abound. The most famous remains Tim Rice and Andrew Lloyd Webber's musical; the most notorious is still *Eva Perón* by Copi, whose premiere in Paris in 1969 was disrupted by Perónists who hurled stink bombs, tore down the set, attacked the cast and threatened to burn down the Théâtre de l'Epée de Bois before the police intervened.

Born Raúl Damonte Botana in Buenos Aires in 1939, the son of an anti-Perónist politician and periodical editor, Copi (from *copito de nieve*, Spanish for "little snowflake") spent years in Uruguay and New York before settling in France in 1962. He set up as a costume designer before joining the Panic Movement, founded by Fernando Arrabal, Alejandro Jodorowsky and Roland Topor in response to a sanitised version of Surrealism becoming co-opted into mainstream culture.

The Panic group fused ideas from the most sexually and politically radical Surrealists – *Un Chien Andalou* co-director Luis Buñuel, authors Antonin Artaud and Benjamin Péret – and American and Viennese performance art to create confrontational, chaotic happenings. Copi took this aesthetic into theatrical scripts, influenced by Jean Cocteau, Jean Genet and Tennessee Williams, and the transvestite and transsexual performers of Parisian cabarets. Copi and his works outraged French critics: reviewing *Eva Perón*, conservative newspaper *Le Figaro* called him 'sinister, inept, indecent, odious, nauseating and dishonest'.

Calder Publications released *Plays: Volume 1* in 1976, Copi's only publication in English (*Drag Ball,* from his novel *Le Bal des folles*, was planned but never appeared). Now reissued by Alma Classics as *Four Plays*, Anni Lee Taylor's versions provide some idea of why his dramas caused such controversy – and why *Eva Perón* remains best known and most staged.

The use of drag queens heightened the furore around *Eva Perón*. Originally, La Grande Eugène, one of Paris's best known artistes, was intended for Evita, but attended rehearsals drunk and, used to lip-synching, couldn't learn the lines: Copi tried starring himself, but director Alfredo Arias cast Argentine-born Facundo Bo in a golden gown. *Figaro* objected to a 'grimacing transvestite' representing Evita, but who portrayed her didn't matter. Queer interpretations of femininity were embedded into all of Copi's texts, working to strongest effect in his savaging of the Peróns' private and public politics.

Set during her final hour, Evita's first words set the tone: "Shit! Where's my presidential robe?" Besides referencing the *"Merdre!"* that initiated Alfred Jarry's proto-Absurdist *Ubu Roi* about a grotesque power-hungry King, starting a near-riot on its 1896 debut, Copi launches a play about Evita's image: her obsession with it, and the gulf between her family's treatment of her and their planned manipulation of her posthumous cultural meaning.

Former actress Evita's apparently apolitical connection with Argentina's working classes, particularly women, was crucial in securing popular support for her husband's regime, but fearing her growing influence, the army crushed her plans to run for vice-presidency. Copi frames this conflict within her home, casting Juan Perón as an unprincipled opportunist and her mother and brother as calculating gravediggers, impatient for cancer to kill her – vested interests which Evita sees full well.

Giving her little substance, Copi portrays Evita as a foul-mouthed, morphine-addicted hedonist whose primary interest is how her body will be embalmed and displayed. ("You told me it's the same man who did Stalin. But he's Spanish. Don't you think we should have got an American?") However, the audience are still invited to sympathise with her. Copi's Evita is a tragic heroine, not exempt from her family's culture of cruelty – she hits her mother before telling her that "In a month's time you'll be back in Monte Carlo getting yourself screwed by French gigolos" – but mistreated by the men around her and desperate to escape.

The atmosphere is paranoid: Evita accuses her husband of poisoning her, blaming him for her cancer. All four plays operate on the fringes of reality and delirium, however, and having rejected radio bulletins on her health, Copi's Evita fakes her own death, murdering her nurse and absconding without disclosing the numbers for her Swiss bank accounts, undermining not just Juan Perón's sanctifying epitaph ("Eva Perón is not dead, she is more alive than ever") but his patriarchal, militaristic style of governance.

Copi's refusal of logical narrative or character development works best in *Eva Perón*, his hallucinatory humour failing to carry his plots when his satire is less pronounced. Each play is less comprehensible than the last, and his attempts to shock haven't always aged well. *The Homosexual (or the Difficulty of Sexpressing Oneself)* is amusing, but the twist that several characters (including Greta Garbo) have visited Casablanca for sex reassignment surgery offers less sensation than in Coccinelle's day, and there is little else to hold the interest – that Taylor offers no information on its first performance is telling.

The Four Twins is equally farcical, with two sets of sisters fighting over ill-gotten money, incessantly killing each other, reviving themselves and killing each other again. Passing too far beyond the edge of possibility, Copi cannot create tension, but by over-playing the fundamentals – sex, crime and death – renders theatrical drama as ridiculous as Perón's depthless politicking.

In *Loretta Strong,* an astronaut travelling to Betelgeuse murders her co-pilot and launches into a surreal, scatological monologue. As in Cocteau's *La Voix humaine,* we hear one end of a telephone conversation, but the scenario is too baffling for an audience to fill the gaps. Perhaps Loretta could *only* be played by Copi – who did so in Paris and Washington as part of the American bicentennial celebrations, wearing just high heels and green make-up.

One critic described Copi, who died of AIDS in 1987, as "more than an eccentric, less than a genius", and this feels a fair assessment. Three of the *Four Plays* strike as bizarre period pieces, but *Eva Perón* periodically revived on the stage across the world, remains a minor classic of queer theatre. Its return to print in English reminds us of its distinctive place within the plethora of works on Evita – and of its sustained power to surprise.

New Statesman, 17 April 2012

ON *THE QUEER ART OF FAILURE* BY JACK HALBERSTAM

Every year – at least until this year – the discourse around GCSE results has been the same. Are they too easy? Are they getting easier, and (by implication) are barriers to "success" thus opened to the "unworthy"? This debate was raging when I got mine, fourteen years ago, but I didn't care. My aims at secondary school weren't to get the best grades (as long as I got into sixth form, as I enjoyed learning for its own sake) but to express my queer gender and sexuality as much as possible without being beaten up, and to resist pressure to pursue heteronormative "achievements": I had no interest in marriage, children, home ownership or the conventional career structures suggested by our school advisors.

I never believed the rhetoric that anyone could be successful in this way as long as they put their minds to it, already aware that there were too many economic, educational and social bars for this to be true. The questions I wanted answered, but never heard raised, was: *Who decides what constitutes "success" and why should I want it on their terms?* So I looked for other options, gradually discovering the alternative cultures and relationship models created by queer people who had previously been excluded, trying to create my own space rather than campaigning for access to the most conservative institutions.

Various writers have questioned the desirability of such tactics, most recently American academic and theorist Jack Halberstam in *The Queer Art of Failure,* published by Duke University Press last year. Like Mattilda Bernstein-Sycamore's *That's Revolting! Queer Strategies for Resisting Assimilation,* a volume of essays by those marginalised within American LGBT politics, Halberstam explores queer history for forms of activism that avoid working with the established order, but also mines popular culture for ways of moving from childhood to adulthood that place collectivism over individualism.

Non-heterosexual parenting may slowly erode the practice of guiding children into normative 'desires, orientations and modes of being', but disavowal of the competitive selfishness encouraged by educational and political authority figures looks ever more necessary after the collapse of the neoliberal economy. Halberstam finds this in Pixar's animations, arguing that in *Finding Nemo* and *Chicken Run,* the most important lesson for their protagonists is not the trite "be yourself" or "follow your dreams" but how to work together for a fairer society. This is because Pixar remember that 'children are not coupled, they are not romantic, they do not have a religious mentality, they are not afraid of death or failure, they are collective creatures [and] they are in a constant state of rebellion against their parents' – their films are 'successful' precisely because they subtly react against the very concept.

Halberstam asks if queer culture should reject negativity about its place in contemporary society as much as it has, given that this stance is never apolitical. This may be a response to the historical association between same-sex love and loss, but Halberstam cites Laura Kipnis' assertion in *Against Love* that 'we tend to blame each other or ourselves for the failures of the social structures we inhabit, rather than critiquing the structures (like marriage) themselves'. The fact that societies that prohibited sexual or gender variance, or cast them as inauthentic, control the terms on which it is eventually accepted is forgotten, which leads activists to disregard intersectionality as they pursue goals specific to their minority.

This leads Halberstam to explore divergent strands in queer politics: resistance to oppression, especially that which does not appear 'active' (such as the very existence of the butch lesbians documented by Brassaï in Thirties Paris); and collaboration with it, particularly that of a minority (mostly men, and some masculine women) with the far Right from their presence in the *Männerbunde* in Nazi Germany or the British Union of Fascists to the Islamophobic Jörg Haider and Pim Fortuyn in 21st century Europe. Understandably, queer historians have emphasised Fascist attacks on feminine men, particularly those around Magnus Hirschfeld's Institute for Sexual Science, finding it harder to address questions about the ethics of collaboration. Explicitly disowning any suggestion that such collusion represented an ideal for masculine homosexuality, Halberstam implies that here many than anywhere, we identity with the losers, and ensure that we do not ignore the complexities around their defeat.

Freely jumping from subject to subject, sometimes too quickly, not all of Halberstam's arguments work: an attempt to form a theory about forgetting leading to new kinds of knowing in a reading of *Dude Where's My Car* doesn't quite come off (although Halberstam anticipates this). Halberstam is most convincing in contrasting liberal narratives of queer progress, in which freedoms gradually unfold, with wider radical histories in which struggles often end in defeat, from the Paris Commune of 1871 to the insurrection of May 1968 and beyond, and from which lessons *have* to be drawn. What becomes clear is that the victory of equality in a conservative world may be pyrrhic, and that making failure into a style (as it was for Quentin Crisp) or even a way of life (as for Foucault) may bring far more positive results than the unquestioning pursuit of "success".

New Statesman, 24 August 2012

RETURNING TO *ALTER EGO*

I knew at the time that I was wasting my teens. Not drinking, smoking, doing drugs and having sex. (This would not have been wasteful.) I spent most of mine, as a deeply depressed boy in a small Surrey town, in my bedroom, watching football, writing lyrics for terrible punk bands, furtively cross-dressing whilst suppressing my wish that I'd been born female, and playing computer games, mainly on my Commodore 64.

The ones I preferred, besides shoot-'em-ups, football and platform games, were those with an unusual concept. I was intrigued by, but too young to understand space trading epic *Elite* or the surreal 3D world of *The Sentinel,* but engaged with some interesting ideas elsewhere. I tried to get into the mysterious world of *Hacker,* in which you had to break into a mainframe computer: it came without instructions and opened with a stark 'Logon Please', crashing if you failed to guess the password before letting you in via another route. Then, I discovered *Frankie Goes to Hollywood,* the magnificently bizarre collaboration between Futurist record label ZTT and coders Denton Designs, where you had to help 'Frankie' develop a personality by solving puzzles and mastering various sub-games before he could escape Mundanesville and enter the Pleasuredome.

It wasn't just *Frankie* that invited me to live an 8-bit life. I explored *Deus Ex Machina,* which came with an audio tape to be played alongside it, narrated by Ian Dury, actor Donna Bailey, E P Thompson and others. Here, you controlled the progress of an 'accident' born inside the 'machine', trying to keep it away from the Defect Police (voiced by Frankie Howerd) who want to terminate it. Although *Deus Ex Machina* was a fascinating experiment, I much preferred *Alter Ego,* published by Activision in 1986.

Alter Ego was a text-based 'fantasy role-playing game', frequently cited as one of the best C64 games ever made. The 'role' was that of a person: specifically, a cisgender, heterosexual Westerner, as an only child born into a two-parent family with a married mother and father. I first read about *Alter Ego* in an old issue of *Zzap! 64 magazine.* I was immediately attracted by the tagline – 'What if you could live your life over again?' – and desperate to play it after *Zzap!* awarded it 98 per cent, stating that 'the writer. . . displays a great sense of humour and a surprisingly perceptive view of all the problems both the young and old face in their lives', calling it 'original, unusual, compelling [and] varied'. There were male and female versions: the male one was released first, and it was this that I managed to find, ten years after its release – by which time the male version was a rarity, the female one virtually untraceable.

Both editions were created by Dr Peter J. Favaro, a clinical psychologist who interviewed hundreds of men and women about their most memorable experiences, putting those that 'many people shared' into the game, along with others that he devised. (Favaro also discussed an infant version called *Child's Play* with Activision, but this collapsed due to financial difficulties.) He understood that *Alter Ego* could only ever be a small quotation of life: the instruction manual asserted that '*Alter Ego* is first and foremost a game. It was designed to be entertaining, not clinical. There are certain insights that can be gained from playing the game, but life improvement or self-analysis should never be the goal.'

The manual also said that 'Because of the authenticity of the life experiences explored in the program, *Alter Ego* contains explicit material which may not be suitable for computer users under the age of 16', and in the US, the game was not to be sold to them. There were no such restrictions in Britain, and in any case, they would have been impossible to enforce by 1996, so with all this in mind, I clicked on the game's first experience icon and threw myself into its alternative reality.

Immediately, it became clear that *Alter Ego* posited life as a selection of choices above all else. 'You are in a warm, dark, comfortable place,' said the narrator. 'This has been your place since you became aware that you are alive. It's almost time to enter a different world now.' There followed the invitation to 'Select an action': 'Come out fighting', 'Come out peacefully' or 'Stay in a little longer'. If I chose to 'come out', the game offered another chance to reconsider; if I kept opting to stay in, eventually my alter ego would be born by Caesarean section, and my mother might subconsciously resent me.

'Happy birthday and welcome to the world,' continued the narration screen. 'From now on, life will begin to change rapidly. You will have to learn to accept responsibility, build up resources, and manage yourself physically and emotionally', it said, implying that progress is a matter of individual choices of mood and action, with no suggestion that your development could be shaped by socio-economic factors, dumb luck, or much else beyond your control. Interactions with your parents would affect your character, but you did not directly inherit any traits, perhaps because this would have required the game to generate personalities and circumstances for them, and for a potentially limitless number of people (family, friends, lovers, teachers and colleagues for starters) whose actions and behaviour influenced yours, and the technology that allowed something close to this, in *The Sims* and later *Second Life,* simply was not available in the mid-1980s.

Next, however, *Alter Ego* offered not a life experience but a questionnaire, designed to generate opening percentage scores in personality 12 categories: Familial, Intellectual, Physical, Social, Vocational, Calmness, Confidence, Expressiveness, Gentleness, Happiness, Thoughtfulness and Trustworthiness. (You could let the computer determine these, but the instructions recommended doing it yourself, and I always did.) There were 26 to be answered True or False, but if you answered True to number 6, 'I think that questions like this are stupid and meaningless', it terminated early, and you began with lower Intellectual, Social and Thoughtfulness ratings.

These rose or fell as you negotiated *Alter Ego* 's Emotional, Familial, Physical, Intellectual, Social and Vocational scenarios, presented as icons on a flow chart, with seven stages: Infancy, Childhood, Adolescence, Young Adulthood, Adulthood, Middle Adulthood and Old Age. You could start anywhere, playing sections more than once or skipping them entirely, with the narrator commenting on your progress at their end. As you got older, more icons appeared: Risks, Relationships, High School and Work in Adolescence; Family, College and Major Purchases in Young Adulthood. At these points, you could find education, jobs or partners were denied because poor decisions meant that your status scores were too low – you couldn't play certain vignettes without a job, or a steady partner, or a child.

Alter Ego expected you in play in character, with its other 'voice', your Conscience, pointing out uncharacteristic choices, or when your status suggested that you were incapable of achieving the desired outcome. For instance, in the male version, you could, as a married man, offer to drive a shop assistant home and have sex with her, but if this was inconsistent with your previous behaviour then your conscience would tell you that 'You have been a very trustworthy person so far. This trustworthiness causes you to feel terribly guilty about having sex with this young man. As a result, you are thrown into a deep depression. You leave feeling resentful and foolish.'

★

Two things got me addicted to *Alter Ego*, both in the mid-Nineties on floppy disk and a decade later, when I found it at playalterego.com. The first was the sheer wealth of options it presented, which often lead to unexpected outcomes. In one of the earliest episodes, I chose to cry when my mother went to answer the door. I thought that the game would tell me that this was an inappropriate way to get attention – several Infancy vignettes focus on this – but it turned out that she was grateful that I helped her to get rid of a salesman.

The second thing I loved was its tone. The narrator could occasionally be a touch sanctimonious, but *Alter Ego* was mostly funny and friendly: subversively complicit in harmless youthful misbehaviour; gently scolding of choices in which you denied yourself the full richness of life, particularly in Old Age; stern when you did something reckless or callous; and rewarding when you demonstrated kindness, open-mindedness or selflessness. The mood could shift in an instant: in Childhood, for example, you could go from being caught by your parents playing 'doctor' with a friend of the opposite sex to being abducted by a child murderer outside your home, and the first time I encountered this, offering to help a stranger find his 'nephew' before being told that 'This man is very sick. You are tortured, killed and buried in a landfill. Your body is never recovered. This game is over,' I felt genuinely numb. (The next time, I chose different responses and got him arrested.)

From the start, your experiences were emotionally complex, weighing against playing as the nastiest, most self-destructive or irresponsible person possible – for example, in Childhood, if you opted to keep playing with a box of matches, ignoring your conscience's repeated exhortations for you to stop, you could burn down your house. You would not be killed here (although one approach was to find all the choices that could lead to your death – I died in a car crash, took an overdose, committed suicide, ignored an ultimately fatal illness and collapsed during a senior citizens' softball game), but you could cause considerable damage and traumatise your parents; one of the most striking moments in *Alter Ego* came with the ice-cold conclusion that 'You are never punished, which somehow makes you feel worse.'

My favourite episode, then and now, came in Childhood, with an elderly woman known as 'the witch' because she kept calling the cops on kids, screaming at them, keeping her light on at night and staring out of the window. Her light goes out for a few days, and your friends gather outside, singing 'Ding Dong, the Witch is Dead'. If you select 'Happy' as your mood and 'Sing with everyone else' as your action, the narrator explains that: 'Sometimes children don't realise how mean they can be. The woman can hear you taunting her outside, and spends her days crying, wishing for her life to come to a peaceful end. Then she could be with the people whom she loved and who loved her. Three weeks later she really does pass away. Almost no one in the neighbourhood notices.'

If you select 'Sad' and 'Try to see if anything is wrong', however, and persist in reaching out to her, she eventually says that the bulb is broken. If you offer to fix it, she tells you that she once had a husband and a child, about your age, who were both killed by a freight train after the child got his (or her, in the female version) foot stuck on a railway line and the husband tried in vain to free him/her. At this point, you can choose to do more odd jobs for her, whereupon you are told that: 'You have done a much kinder thing than you can probably imagine at your age. You've given this woman a reason to live.'

★

By my final years at secondary school, I'd realised that the experiences glamorised by TV shows and valorised by my peers weren't for me, and *Alter Ego* helped me to accept that I wasn't really bothered about getting drunk, taking drugs or having sex – not straight sex, anyway. The Risks option in Adolescence just amused me, offering the (potentially fatal) chance to see how fast a car could go, amongst other things: I was so introverted that I was most likely to die listening to my Walkman, deep in thought, and not looking before I crossed the road. Sometimes I wished I was wilder, or more sociable, but as *Alter Ego* told me when I tried to ingratiate myself with free-spirited arty types at a party, as I was starting to do in real life: 'You aren't capable of making such a radical change in your personality.'

The more I played, the more I struggled with the heteronormative future that it offered. I liked having the chance to act this out, graduating from college before starting a career, going steady with a woman and then getting married and having children, but I knew this path to be off limits for me. I appreciated that the game's practical and technological limits (the C64 had 64 Kilobytes of Random Access Memory, not all of which could be used) meant that not every life experience could be featured, and tolerated its American setting and ethnocentrism, but by my mid-teens, I was sick of people assuming that I'd want this particular life, telling me that I would soon even if I didn't now – and I got sick of people assuming that I was content to be male, and that I would want to behave and be perceived as such. The kind of person I wanted to be seemed no more visible in *Alter Ego* than s/he was anywhere else.

In *Alter Ego*, I could never be gay, bisexual, queer or transgender. Its set up meant these things would have to be presented as choices, which would have been deeply problematic, and making a character turn out to any of these things would doubtless have angered certain players, and possibly required an explanation. However, there were passing references to gender variance and sexual diversity. In one Adolescent scene, I could accept a manicure from a young woman: my friends would mock me, but I scored with her, so the (mild) gender play was placed strictly within a straight setting. In another, a usually happy-go-lucky friend called, sounding upset, and told me that he was 'homosexual'. I opted to be 'Accepting' and referred him to a specialist – the best set of choices, the narrator said. Soon after, a classmate told me that he was bisexual, and *Alter Ego* had prepared me to be 'Accepting' despite not yet feeling comfortable with my own identity.

Still, the game provided more positive information about sexual diversity than I got at school. In Section

28-era Britain, all we had was a 1970s video about two boys who "go camping", before our Religious Education teacher told us that their orientations were "probably just a phase". That came a few weeks before our final exams, by which time Morrissey, Oscar Wilde and others had shown me queer alternatives to the futures suggested by our Personal and Social Education classes. There, we were shown a PC program called Kudos, a career test that aimed to show us which jobs would suit our personalities. This gave us a series of simple Yes or No questions – whether or not I wanted to work with children, travel, or look after the elderly, for example. After repeatedly being told that 'There are no suitable careers for you', I decided to see which other outcomes were possible; once it concluded, to my amusement, that I should become a TV presenter. *Alter Ego* was similar, but more evolved: I could join the Peace Corps, sell a recipe or write a book, but these were incidents rather than vocations, and it put careers, comprised as jobs, at the core of adult life.

I had no career plans at all, and found the very concept absurd – all I knew was that I wanted to write. But deep down, I thought that the adult world would reward my interest in ideas and people, as *Alter Ego* usually did, and that my depression would lift as I got older, as my Happiness and Calmness scores tended to rise throughout the game. Certainly, I thought, the future would be far removed from the Mundanesville of secondary school, and that somehow I'd escape the monotony of jobs, but I did not realise that my lack of interest in financial matters, and my disdain for the principle of accumulating wealth, would not prove as practically or psychologically inconsequential in real life as it did in *Alter Ego*.

Nor did I fully appreciate how choices made in my teens would affect my opportunities later on, despite *Alter*

Ego relying on this premise to keep me hooked. By the time I realised that I wanted to be an architect, it was too late – partly because I didn't take Art as a GCSE 'Option' and because I dossed around in my Communications and Graphics classes, but also because my parents had no interest in it, and their newspaper of choice, the *Daily Mail,* railed against anything built after 1387, so I did not encounter the *avant-garde* visions of Mies van der Rohe, Le Corbusier, Antonio Sant'Elia and others until I was a second-year undergraduate, and could not qualify to take a degree in Architecture.

★

In 2009, aged 27, I finally decided to begin the process of gender reassignment. At the same time, I found *Alter Ego* online, and became addicted again – not least because now, the first choice you made was whether to be born male or female. Would I have been happier, or better adjusted, if my body and mind had been aligned from the start? Here was a chance, however limited, to live out the girlhood I felt I'd been denied.

As it turned out, the Female version was not all that different. Many vignettes were only superficially different: for example, in Male Adolescence, you would be embarrassed when buying condoms from the local chemist, especially as an attractive girl from school worked there; here, you had to get 'feminine products' from the cutest guy in the year. Some differences bothered me more than others: in the Male version, you could form a band with friends; here, this became the chance to meet my favourite DJ. Why couldn't I join a group like The Slits?

That said, feminism did occasionally feature in the Female version. As a student, I was confronted by a sexist Professor who told me that 'the new generation of young women is going after material possessions more than any other before it'. I decided to contest this, but was told that he 'outmaneuvers you with logic' but respects me more and gives me an A grade for the course. In Young Adulthood, there was an encounter with 'Mary Lou Stoker', who called herself a 'staunch feminist', but 'The truth is that she is not a feminist in the true sense of the word; she simply despises and resents men, misapplying the feminist philosophy to suit her needs.' That episode ended with my closest friend and me agreeing not to take Mary Lou seriously, but mostly, *Alter Ego* invited you to make instinctively feminist choices rather than engage with its ideas – indeed, active politics played little part in either version.

There was a sense, though, of the social difficulties for women in a male-dominated world – in school, relationships and work – but the biggest differences were physical ones, with the two often converging around sex. In one game, I lost my virginity at a party, opting to 'Give Him What He Wants', before being told that I 'feel like crying afterwards'. I couldn't tell if this was because of my status sheet, or if this choice, and the power relations that its phrasing implied, would always draw this conclusion.

Before that, near the end of Childhood, I had to negotiate learning to masturbate, buying my first bra and having my first period. 'For a time, you may feel a curious mixture of sadness and joy at being grown-up,' the narrator told me. 'Some people say that this is the beginning of "womanhood" and that is scary, too. Getting used to all of the changes in your body makes this time of life difficult. It's like walking into a house that you've known for years and finding all of the comfortable furniture has been replaced by new pieces.'

Later, I became pregnant unexpectedly and had an abortion. My partner was supportive, but I had to deal with anti-choice campaigners at the clinic, and got no help from my family, with the game informing me that 'Many women undergo severe depression after an abortion' and that 'You are one of the unlucky ones. You can't stop thinking about what your son or daughter might have been like. Eventually, however, life goes on.' Planned pregnancies, however, were difficult: in several games, I tried repeatedly for a baby without success, and was particularly aggrieved to discover that I could only have children if I was married.

The Female version, it seemed, had the same strengths as the Male one, and similar weaknesses – it was just as witty, sensitive and intelligent, and equally heteronormative. The queer and feminist challenges to the ideas that upheld male dominance of various areas of society were still being formulated in the mid-1980s, and made little impact on *Alter Ego*: the female youth it showed me was no more desirable than the male one, really, and the future that it offered – one of balancing a family with a career – was no more appealing. Could I "have it all"? Did I want *any* of it?

★

When *Alter Ego* went online, the game's hosts put up a Wish List of features that 21st century players wanted added to it. They said that they got more requests to include homosexuality than anything else, acknowledging the problem of choice, as well as some new episodes that would be needed – such as encounters with your parents, coming out, and dealing with prejudiced employers.

These would form an interesting starting point for a newer, queerer *Alter Ego*. Perhaps in late Childhood, the game might offer the chance to cross-dress, and a situation where a same-sex friend gets intimate with you, before asking you how you feel, and what action to take next. If you then played as lesbian, gay, bisexual and/or transgender, or polyamorous, many of the existing episodes (from going to the Junior Prom to health problems in Old Age) would become complicated by your gender and/or sexuality, and there would be a range of new ones specifically related to them.

Sexually diverse scenarios would include coming out to family, friends and colleagues, deciding how to disclose, and who to. Misfortunes in *Alter Ego* tended to follow successive poor choices, but life is often arbitrarily cruel, and the game might explore the consequences of being outed. Hopefully, such a vignette might teach people just how nasty an action this is in a still homophobic society. You might have to think differently about your sexual health, and how you check it, or get involved in different types of activism, either campaigning for LGBT access to social institutions or setting up autonomous queer communities.

A range of experiences might follow your discovery of gender-variant people in the media or your area, or the first time that you cross-dress. As well as coming out, and finding the right language to your gender with those around you, the game could address the resulting difficulties in social navigation, asking whether you want to 'pass' in your acquired gender, how you might handle transphobic abuse or violence, or how you might cope with hostility within radical circles that you had hoped might accommodate you.

Maybe there would be a Transition icon that you could click at any time, with episodes about the Gender Identity

Clinic, and how you present yourself to the psychiatrists who decide whether or not to refer you for hormones or surgery, whether or not you want them, and how you cope with their effects. Do you want to ensure that you can have children before hormones or sex reassignment surgery leave you sterile? Do you want any other operations to change your body? How do you deal with intrusive questions, or being treated differently at home, school or work due to your gender? A new version of *Alter Ego* could invite players, whatever their gender or sexuality, to consider such problems, and might generate a far better level of self-understanding or empathy.

Of course, the existing versions are of their time, as everyone involved with them knows. Besides, I was no more capable of imagining my future than was the game. These days, to my quiet astonishment, I travel the country, delivering talks about my transgender youth, how I came to understand and accept myself, how I saw gender identity presented in the media, and how and why I came to write about this issue. Afterwards, the beautiful people in the crowds, a decade younger than me or more, ask that if I could live my life over again, would I prefer to be born female, and I'm never sure which option I'd choose.

New Statesman, 9 August 2013

TYPES OF AMBIGUITY: ON QUEER ART AND CULTURE

Alice Austen's photograph of herself and two other women dressed as men was taken in New York in 1891, anticipating the female masculinity of Radclyffe Hall and others. It's one of the more than 200 images in Phaidon's *Art and Queer Culture,* edited by Catherine Lord and Richard Meyer, which charts the shift from the 'homosexual' identities formulated by 19th century sexologists and lawmakers to the fluid conceptions of gender and sexuality that characterise contemporary queer culture.

The first section, covering the years from 1885, when the law against 'gross indecency' was passed in Britain, to 1909, when Magnus Hirschfeld distinguished between homosexuality and transvestism, is full of portraits, like Austen's, which can be read as queer, but were ambiguous enough to make it past the censor. The ambiguity, and the censorship, haven't gone away. The Alice Austen House, Meyer says, has made it clear that researchers linking Austen to lesbian history are not welcome.

The precariousness of queer archives and the defiance of queer people in the face of denial or violence is a recurring theme in Lord and Meyer's book, from the Nazi sacking of Hirschfeld's Institute for Sexual Science in 1933 to the vandalising of LGBT, AIDS and women's health books in the San Francisco Public Library in 2001. Amy Conger made *Queer Reader Mandorla* by dyeing the slashed pages of *A Queer Reader* in high-contrast shades and pasting them into a collage around the cover image of a sailor in lipstick.

In the earlier parts of *Art and Queer Culture*, queer people are often subjects for investigation by straight photographers and writers. Lord and Meyer include one of Brassaï's famous shots of sexual dissidents at Le Monocle, and a conversation between André Breton, Benjamin Péret, Jacques Prévert, Raymond Queneau and others in January 1927, which reflects the Surrealists' anthropological view of homosexuality. Queneau and Prévert expressed their disdain for the 'extraordinary prejudice against homosexuality' within the movement; Breton was vehemently homophobic but awkwardly tolerated Claude Cahun, one of whose *Cancelled Confessions* closes the second section, 'Stepping Out 1910-29'.

In his introductory essay, 'Inverted Histories: 1885-1979', Meyer quotes Nayland Blake's assertion that 'the discourse of the postmodern is the queer experience rewritten to describe the experience of the whole world,' as Susan Sontag's *Notes On Camp* questioned the categories of 'man' and 'woman' and associated behaviours, as well as the boundaries between 'high' art and the 'low' culture in which queer people often had to express their desires.

In 1965, hand-drawn symbols started to appear beside the photographs in *Physique Pictorial*, published by the Athletic Model Guild. Subscribers who wanted to know what the symbols meant could send off for a copy of the so-called Subjective Character Analysis chart; experienced readers would know what 'late riser' and 'very affable' really meant.

The increasing confidence after the Stonewall riots in 1969 created tension between gay, lesbian and bisexual activists, as gay power and the Gay Liberation Front led the fight for 'homosexual rights'. (Their difficult relationships with gender-variant activists receive less attention in Art and Queer Culture, perhaps because they were played out in theoretical texts more than art.) But it also gave rise to a sense of a strong cultural heritage, and of the underlying queerness of modernism, evident in Ulrike Ottinger's film *Freak Orlando*.

One of the last images in *Art and Queer Culture* is a portrait by Nan Goldin of the actress and writer Cookie Mueller. Taken in 1983, it was one of the 15 photographs that Goldin collected in *The Cookie Portfolio 1976-89* after Mueller's death from AIDS six years later. Lord and Meyer's caption describes Goldin's regret that 'photographing couldn't keep people alive'. No image in the book captures the long, constantly shifting balance between defiance and sadness that characterises queer history quite as much as this one.

London Review of Books blog, 13 September 2013

MARINA ABRAMOVIĆ: 512

It was night now in my mind, I was alone in the semi-darkness of the booth and I was thinking, protected from outer torments. The most favourable conditions for thinking, the moments when thought can let itself naturally follow its course, are precisely moments when, having temporarily given up fighting a seemingly inexhaustible reality, the tension beginning to loosen little by little, all the tension accumulated in protecting yourself against the threat of injury — and I had my share of minor injuries — and that, alone in an enclosed space, alone and following the course of your thoughts in a state of growing belief, you move progressively from the struggle of living to the despair of being. (From *Camera* by Jean-Philippe Toussaint, 1989)

*

Wednesday 6th August 2014, 8.30am. I'm getting dressed, as if for work, worrying about what might be appropriate. I'm going to see Marina Abramović in *512 Hours*, her durational performance at the Serpentine Gallery. She is there every day, 10am-6pm, her only materials being herself, the audience, and a selection of props which she may or may not use. In this respect *512 Hours* has parallels with her *Rhythm 0* performance, where she stood by a table covered with objects and told the crowd to do as they pleased: one event famously ended with a loaded gun held to her head. Wishing that Abramović had specified a uniform, I decide upon a plain white T-shirt, black trousers and pumps, with no make-up —if I do interact with Marina then I want *my* appearance to provide as little stimulation as possible.

512 Hours aims to induce a state of mindfulness —total immersion in the present time and space. I'm ambivalent: I dream of this, but I think it's impossible, agreeing with Jenny Diski that its current popularity is understandable in a society dominated by smartphones and social media, but that it serves as a mechanism of control, discouraging individuals from learning from the past or planning for the future.

Seemingly forever, I've been trapped in a Western malaise of depression and anxiety, with my mind always wandering away from details in friends' conversations or plot twists in films. It came to a head when I was 25, watching a friend's band, only to find my head couldn't leave my dismal data entry job, and I decided to see a therapist. Every week I would pry deeper into childhood alienation and detachment, agonised each time she said my fifty minutes were up. I recall the second session best, when I left with my mind clear for what felt like the first time. Within minutes, however, the clamouring voices returned, screaming about money, love, fitness, work, clothes, diet, sex, family, health, dragging me away from what I cared about most, writing, leaving me terrified that I wouldn't leave some worthwhile work before I died, and I wanted to die soon.

These concerns infused themselves throughout my body, making me desperate to break out of it until I resolved to shift from male to female. It started building as soon as I realised my gender dysphoria, aged ten, and became paranoid about who would find out, my shoulders always hunched. Twenty years later, in Charing Cross Hospital after my sex reassignment surgery, a fellow patient abandoned her attempts to massage them because my brain wouldn't allow it. I thought back to the first transsexual woman I really knew, a performance artist called Pia who did a striptease to Laurie Anderson's *O Superman*. She told me that once I became comfortable in my body, the familiar and unbearable imperative to do everything *now* would dissipate.

My mind bore so many marks of transition – the fear of harassment, mockery, violence, rejection – and my body language changed to fend off intrusive questions and abusive comments. My frame itself had become scarred by the operation, though all have faded, two years after my week on the ward. Now, I leave Lancaster Gate tube, trying not to get impatient as the pedestrian light stays red for ages, becoming annoyed with the tourists who block me from jabbing the WAIT button, even though I know I'll have to queue outside the Serpentine.

I have soundtracks for when I want to calm or slow myself. During my second night in hospital, after I came off the morphine and couldn't sleep, wracked with pain yet happier to stay alive, I put on the final track of *Königsforst* by Gas, a ten-minute loop of a single melody, soft scratching and two bass notes, one rising, one falling, providing respite if not rest. Now I listen to *Anglepoised* by Fridge, built around a pulsating bassline that varies just slightly, the drum line subtly shifting as synthesized sounds shimmer over the top, inviting me to fall into its groove rather than ordering me to march to its rhythm.

The track suits the otherworldly feel to Hyde Park, with the beautiful fountains and marble basins in the Italian gardens. I love the view from the bridge over the river, every branch hanging in the right place, the swans and geese so carelessly at ease. Recently, I worked nearby at St. Mary's Hospital: Marina Abramović arrived just before my contract expired, which already feels like an eternity ago. In the same seat in the same room, three days a week, with nothing to do and nowhere to go, I had so little motivation that one lunchtime I came here and wondered who would notice if I spent the whole afternoon in the gallery. I would pretend I'd been at a meeting if anyone asked, but I never quite dared.

In the line at the Serpentine, I find my friend Alexandra Lazar, a Serbian artist. I tell her I'm trying to freelance, speaking about a piece on transgender people and radical feminism, absurdly long at 8500 words that I sent to my editor at 1am, for which I'm expecting ambivalence from trans people, anger from journalists and death threats from extremists. Alexandra talks about how Serbia is trying to adopt the neoliberal economics which the European Union imposes on new members, and how this manifests in the hideous 'Belgrade on the Water' cultural scheme with a blue Chinese bridge dumped over the river, ruining the sulphur yellow house style of the city.

We reach the entrance. A woman, dressed in black, tells us to put our possessions in a locker, and advises going to the toilet now as once we leave, we won't be allowed back without queuing. In the bathroom, I get an email: my article is online. I put the link on Twitter and Facebook, take a deep breath and step inside.

Alexandra has entered already, and I'm worried that I've lost her. I lock up my phone, purse and keys, trying to let go of the dread I feel whenever I'm without them. I think about how I never dare do anything spontaneously, and then, tentatively, start to ask myself if I'll be able to give up fighting this seemingly inexhaustible reality, even temporarily, and follow the course of my thoughts.

I thought there was no talking, but Marina Abramović sits, whispering to an invigilator. I read the text outlining the concept and put on headphones, wondering if she's dictating a soundtrack, but there is no sound. I try another pair, realising then that they cancel noise. It reminds me that I've always had music on, whenever I'm alone in public, using it during the year-long Real Life Experience of "living as a woman", before hormone treatment to drown out the abuse from strangers, but well before that to silence the constant chattering inside myself.

I enter the gallery, its walls are blank and people are sat on chairs around a podium, some staring ahead, others down. The invigilator leads me silently to a seat, gesturing at me to close my eyes. I do so for some time, then I decide to join a few other people on the planks of wood in the centre, exposing myself to the gaze of the audience, and the potential humiliation this brings. *Are my flies done up? What if I slip? Or if I start sneezing or coughing?*

I remember all the times I've relinquished control of my body: in fetish clubs, or in private with a master or mistress, no longer protecting myself from the threat of injury but wilfully submitting to it. They tell me what to wear, making demands of my dress and deportment like the Gender Identity Clinics used to before people challenged the cruelty of this. We then enter some otherworldly environment where my punishment for some unspecified transgression will be enacted, and they take me on a chain, tying and blindfolding me before smashing the tension out of me, little by little. I have no way of knowing when the attacks will start or stop, or even who is delivering them, let alone halting them; briefly savouring those moments when they flit from brutality to tenderness before the beatings resume, and it's incredibly liberating.

Growing up in a small town, with nothing to do and nowhere to go, I could always discern the hour and minute with an uncanny degree of accuracy, but under their supervision, this ability leaves me. Time, so oppressive when I was waiting for the Clinic to prescribe hormones or set a date for surgery, becomes erotic duration: being left so helpless is one of my favourite feelings, perhaps the only time that the voices realise there's no point in harassing me, and when I'm finally unbound, they never tell me how long it's been, and I never want to ask.

I step into one of two rooms filled with camp beds and sheets. The invigilator invites me to lie down, providing the public space to nap that I've always craved: the tyranny of the nine-to-five has never let me rest, reminding me that humans are the only animals to sleep in one block. I welcome her offer. Horizontal, I wish that I could transcribe every thought directly from my brain, but accept that some will remain as others vanish, trying to trust myself to keep the most important. In an age where everything is recorded and broadcast, there's something freeing about this, especially as writers are now practically obliged to be on Twitter, worrying about how to shape every brainwave into a brand that stands out from the incessant noise. Then I realise that the very process of writing trammels my thoughts, and that a piece like this can only ever be an approximation. I've read translations of Surrealist 'automatic writing' where they tried to record a stream of consciousness with as little mediation as possible, but the results were always dull and aimless, being far better when they structured things, especially when they talked about sex.

I get up and sit back down. Marina Abramović sits next to me, taking her time to breathe. When I think about transition, or my life as a transsexual journalist, I see that film of her, inhaling and then hurling herself into a wall. She closes her eyes, and I want to take her hand, knowing that talking is forbidden but certain that we can still communicate. I want her to know that the pain that makes her throw herself into a wall, or put herself in a position where people hold loaded guns to her head, that's my pain too, I've known it all my life, and her sharpness in expressing it makes me feel braver.

Somehow, it feels more beautiful to leave her alone, and I go to the foyer to chart my reflections. Alexandra has left at more or less the same time, and the moment is broken: we cannot return. Outside, normal life rushes towards us: I have an email about temporary public sector jobs, but just as I think about how I never want to go back to that, I bump into Lizzie, my old manager at NHS London, who let me go home when I got my date for surgery and was going crazy about how soon it suddenly seemed. Then, having tried so hard to suspend any consideration of it, I remember my article: I check Twitter on my phone. It's gone viral. *How can so many people possibly have read so many words while we were in the gallery?* Amazed, I tell Alexandra that my whole life has been building up to this moment – when I challenge forty years of 'radical' transphobia head-on and people finally listen. She hugs me, buys me a cup of camomile tea in the café, and tells me to relax.

Written for an unpublished Penny-Ante Editions anthology in 2014, published by *ARC* in July 2020

TRANSLATING THE SELF

To the outsider – and particularly to one interested in contemporary art and Western popular culture – it may seem like there has been an explosion in transgender visibility during the last few years. In the US, former Olympic athlete and reality tv personality Caitlyn Jenner has appeared on the cover of *Vanity Fair*, and *Orange is the New Black* star Laverne Cox on that of *Time*, with online shows such as *Transparent* and *Sense 8* (co-directed by Lana Wachowski, who announced her transition in 2012) attracting international audiences. In Britain, publications across the ideological spectrum are focusing on trans people and politics more than ever before, often featuring openly trans writers, and broadcasters are making trans people the centre of comedies, dramas and documentaries in an unprecedented way.

Numerous contemporary artists have either expressed their own transgender identities, worked with gender-variant subjects, or both. EVA & ADELE, Boychild, Micha Cárdenas, Yishay Garbasz, Juliana Huxtable, Evan Ifekoya, Shigeyuki Kihara, Amos Mac, Raju Rage, P. Staff and others have brought their gender positions into photographic, performance or digital works; Heather Cassils, Zanele Muholi, Marc Quinn, Ryan Trecartin and Wu Tsang have made sculptures or films documenting the bodies and lives of trans people.

This phenomenon may seem fairly recent, with subjectivities that move beyond 'male' and 'female' entering the mainstream, but there are precedents buried within what is often termed 'queer culture'. A number of earlier examples exist of artists using photography or film to create a direct record of people who transgressed established gender boundaries through clothing and cosmetics or medical interventions. Mostly, they did so before concepts of sexuality and gender identity were separated and codified into identity positions, with a strict focus on *practices*: the most notable artist to explicitly state discomfort with the binary was Claude Cahun, who, as early as 1930, said that 'neuter is the only gender that always suits me', but who has often been claimed as part of a lesbian canon.

Gender-variant people in the 1960s US underground, including Candy Darling and Mario Montez, appeared in the films of Andy Warhol and Jack Smith, as well as Peter Hujar's photography, with this visual representation meaning that they had no obligation to define their genders within written language. Over the following decade, gender identity clinics categorised what made 'the transsexual' eligible for reassignment, discouraging service users from being open about their histories. The gay and lesbian politics that followed the Stonewall riots (led, to some extent, by trans women of colour) often characterised trans people both as conformists to gender norms and as deviants likely to discredit 'respectable' activism, before the AIDS crisis put the focus on sexual activity and institutional prejudice rather than physical embodiment or identity formation.

Besides the artist Greer Lankton, who started off modelling for Nan Goldin, gender-variant people were rarely visible in the post-AIDS queer art scenes of the 1990s, and play with gender worked mostly at the level of performance. People who had transitioned became involved with

transgender theory, which reacted against the medical establishment, feminist and conservative transphobia, sensationalist mass-media coverage and tropes in transsexual autobiographies. Authors such as Kate Bornstein, Leslie Feinberg
and Sandy Stone urged readers to move beyond 'passing'
and be open about their experiences – significantly, Stone's
manifestos circulated in early online communities and
Bornstein, writing in 1994, explored possibilities for playing
with identity offered by the internet's mixture of connec-
tivity and anonymity. The result has been more confidence
in delineated gender identities and the constant generation
of new ones, as well as a stronger sense of community: this
has made it harder for old-style gay rights movements,
especially those with the type of assimilationist politics that
have led as far as the UK Independence Party marching at
London Pride, to co-opt or subsume trans people, or to
marginalise or silence them.

With these tensions in mind, P. Staff's *The Foundation*
(2015), a video and installation, is particularly interesting.
Staff's half-hour film was made at the Tom of Finland
Foundation in Los Angeles, which serves both to collect
Tom's documentations of a hyper-masculine sexuality
that was changed irrevocably by the onset of AIDS, and
as somewhere for gay men interested in what his work
recorded to meet, bringing together generations from both
sides of the epidemic. Staff provides a sense of new identities
emerging, in a more oblique way than (for example) Mac's
photographs of trans people or Garbasz's flick-book showing
how her body changed during transition, by hinting at how
new possibilities can emerge from established subcultures.
Through interviews with people at the foundation – one
of whom assures the ambivalent Staff that 'you'll grow into
[…] being a man' – and in a choreographed segment shot at
Spike Island in Bristol, there is a sense of the artist achieving

self-definition both with *and* against an older companion: Staff's presentation occupies a 'queer' space, its ambiguity offering room for a gay male identification to shift into a trans-feminine position.

At face value, Juliana Huxtable embodies a stronger sense of futurism, although her work, too, is also rooted in a historical counter-culture – the underground clubs that have been relatively welcoming of queer and trans people since the house scene and vogue balls of 1980s New York. Like many of this wave of trans and genderqueer artists, Huxtable did not emerge from a fine art background, instead developing a following on Instagram and Vimeo, working with the House of Ladosha art collective and DJ-ing at Shock Value, the 'nightlife gender project' that she co-founded.

She featured prominently in the New Museum's Triennial this year, as the creator of four inkjet prints – two poems and two self-portraits. These photographs suggest radical possibilities for self-creation and self-expression. *Untitled in the Rage (Nibiru Cataclysm)* (2015) shows Huxtable naked (besides an ankle bracelet), facing away from the viewer, her body tinted sea-green and her hair yellow: through this colouring and the ethereal surroundings, Huxtable references the Nuwabian religious group inspired by Islam, Ancient Egyptian culture and cosmological ideas. She also modelled for Frank Benson's life-sized 3D sculpture *Juliana* (2015), shown alongside her own work. It's a stunning piece, its metallic sheen recalling the cyborg theories of Donna Haraway that rejected the boundaries dividing 'human' from 'machine', which were a strong influence on Sandy Stone in particular.

But is such a direct use of an artist's identity problematic – either when representation is handed over to a third party, or when it is enacted by the self? Perhaps it runs counter to queer theory which suggests that there is *no* fundamental 'self', creating considerable tension for artists reacting against essentialist concepts of gender, but there are deeper psychological problems too. Benson told *The New York Times* that he sent an 'intense email full of historical references' to persuade Huxtable to pose nude: for an artist (or writer, as I found when documenting my own gender reassignment), such exposure can be nerve-wracking and draining, coming with concerns about how much it shatters stereotypes and how far it indulges the 'curiosity' of outsiders about transgender bodies, not to mention how it can lead to artists being typecast.

It can be argued, too, that personal 'stories' – relatively easily co-opted by large institutions and mainstream media – take the focus away from wider political issues for a minority that still faces many legal and social challenges worldwide. The radicalism of *Juliana* lies not just in the technological potential that it signifies, but also in the very act of bringing a trans woman of colour into a prominent New York gallery. Not only does this confront the audience with a body that defies conventional categories, but it also suggests possibilities to people who may not have seen someone like themselves in such a space before. Individual and collective concerns can have a symbiotic relationship: the self-realisation enabled by encountering works such as *Juliana* or *The Foundation* leads people into communities, and into exchanges that will not just generate new identities but also engage meaningfully with their wider contexts. The durability of this interest, and of the engagements it produces, remains to be seen.

Frieze Issue 174, October 2015

ON JT LEROY

Back at the turn of the millennium, LeRoy's debut novel
Sarah (2000) marked the arrival of a phenomenal new voice
into American literature. It was praised not just by writers
as influential as Dennis Cooper and Chuck Palahniuk,
but also musicians who had moved from underground
scenes to international fame without compromising their
integrity – PJ Harvey, Lou Reed and Tom Waits amongst
them. Quoted in Corsair Books' recent reissue, Cooper
said: '*Sarah* is a revelation … [It] has a passion, economy,
emotional depth, and lyric beauty so authentic that it seems
to bypass every shopworn standard we've learned to expect
of contemporary fiction'.

Many others were effusive about LeRoy's prose, but
Sarah's impact was heightened by the author's life story,
which apparently informed its narrative about a teenage
hustler in a small-town America of interstates and motels,
born male but living mostly as a woman with a group
of transgender sex workers. This sounds like a publisher's
dream and, as a friend put it, "catnip for counter-culture",
especially as the book also took in S/M sex and the 1990s
zeitgeist of the "fucked-up" teen, but there was a problem.
LeRoy, apparently the 19-year-old son of a sex worker from
small-town West Virginia, dealing with gender dysphoria

and HIV, was too shy to appear in public. No matter: others performed readings from *Sarah* in his place, and fans took to wearing raccoon penis bones around their necks, like the 'lizards' who turn tricks in the book.

Despite his absence, the LeRoy legend grew. Admirers soon included Debbie Harry, Courtney Love and Michael Stipe, Gus Van Sant and John Waters, Carrie Fisher, Matthew Modine and Winona Ryder. Then it spun out of control. Jeff Feuerzeig's documentary *Author: The J. T. LeRoy Story* (2016) explains how Laura Albert – the New York mother and thirtysomething punk musician who had actually written *Sarah* – saw sister-in-law Savannah Knoop in sunglasses and a blonde wig and decided that Knoop looked close enough to 'LeRoy' to play him in public. Now, things were very different to Amandine Dupin writing as George Sand, or Mary Ann Evans as George Eliot, to get ahead in a sexist world; it went beyond the many heteronyms that Fernando Pessoa created to write in different voices, and it took 'LeRoy' into a strato-spheric level of fame, with Cooper's endorsement repeatedly endlessly by magazines and newspapers who would never have dreamt of profiling Cooper himself.

As Albert/Speedie and Knoop/LeRoy became ever-present at parties and premieres, they began to lose sight of how they got there. A friend told 'LeRoy' that 'writing is all you have,' bearing in mind that fame is always fleeting if one does not periodically back it up. (This was just before the explosion of reality television, and social media that means that people's fifteen minutes never quite end like they did in Warhol's time.) So, in 2001, a new LeRoy volume appeared: a set of interconnected stories entitled *The Heart is Deceitful above All Things*. Its main character was seemingly a younger version of *Sarah*'s, who recounted physical and psycho-logical abuse inflicted by a truck-stop prostitute mother and various lowlifes.

The Heart is Deceitful cemented the author's popularity, and 'LeRoy' became involved with film, writing the original (eventually unused) script for Gus Van Sant's *Elephant* (2003) and getting close to director Asia Argento, who had optioned the book for adaptation. However, cracks were appearing in the public persona, even as numerous US publications were running features on LeRoy. Knoop ran out of a Q&A session immediately after a reading – although this was interpreted as an example of LeRoy's shyness rather than fear of exposure. One British journalist told me how he was commissioned to cover LeRoy, but knew something was up when he saw 'Speedie' conferring with Knoop and told his editor that he could not file his piece – although he maintains that *Sarah* was 'a brilliant novel'.

It was not until January 2006, after Argento's film had been released, that the *New York Times* ran an 'unmasking' of LeRoy by Warren St John. St John correctly identified Knoop as the public face, stating that this added to a 'mounting circumstantial case that Laura Albert is the person who writes as JT Leroy' – as suggested by the *New York Metro* the previous autumn. Amid the anger from many who had 'believed they were supporting not only a good and innovative and adventurous voice, but [also] a person', as LeRoy's literary agent Ira Silverberg put it, St John asked: *'It is unclear what effect* [this] *will have on JT Leroy's readers, who are now faced with the question of whether they have been responding to the books published under that name, or the story behind them.'*

The response was unlike that which met Claudio Gatti's recent 'investigation' into Elena Ferrante, with Gatti cast as intrusive, undermining Ferrante's valid reasons for writing pseudonymously. Albert and Knoop fell out of their celebrity circles overnight; many former friends stayed silent (and declined to be interviewed for Feuerzeig's film), although the fact that 'LeRoy' had claimed to be HIV positive in early phone calls to various celebrities and literary figures caused disquiet. A decade later, Argento told *The Guardian* that "I should have seen it at the time – how are you [Knoop] so joyful when your life is so miserable?" and that she had felt so embarrassed that she had not directed again for ten years.

People wanted to punish Albert: but for what? Eventually, a fraud case was brought, for signing a contract with Antidote Films for an adaptation of *Sarah* as 'J.T. LeRoy'. The *New York Times* reported on 23 June 2007 that the trial hinged on LeRoy's 'purpose in the world', as an 'avatar' or 'respirator' for Albert's inner life, or to enhance the value of the work. (Any critique of the publishing industry and its vested interests in 'marketable' authors was either not reported, or not made.) Albert was found guilty, and ordered to pay $116,500 to the company, but even their lawyers 'admitted a grudging admiration' for Albert's talent, and performance.

There was also sympathy, as the eight-day trial covered Albert's history of institutionalisation and sexual abuse, a poor self-image and thirteen years of telephone therapy, during which 'LeRoy' emerged as a character. Albert has since expressed the wish, in Feuerzeig's film and elsewhere, that "I had been born a boy", and to be addressed by gender neutral pronouns, 'they' and 'their'. After that, the voices that discussed LeRoy were not Albert's – Savannah Knoop published *Girl Boy Girl: How I Became JT LeRoy* in 2008, and the novels faded from view.

Revisiting the footage of Knoop at packed literary events, sweating under the wig, barely able to utter a word, it is barely credible that this was not where things unravelled, but when LeRoy – accompanied by 'Speedie' – made a similar transition into superstardom to his celebrity fans, and befriended many of them. (Perhaps strange, but it's worth recalling that this world, built on the intersections of US literary, film and music culture, has accommodated believers in far larger, and more damaging 'cults'.) Perhaps, as one of Feuerzeig's interviewees suggests, editors wanted to believe in LeRoy as exciting discoveries in fiction were rare – one reason why 1990s publishers looked towards 'misery memoirs' for new voices – and they transmitted this desire to believe onto readers.

Sarah's appeal sprang from how it put 'misery memoir' tropes (childhood abuse, rape and sexual trauma, desperation to escape) into a narrative register closer to *Alice in Wonderland* than *Angela's Ashes,* with humour that would have felt inappropriate were it not for its deftness of prose. This 'coming of age' story, where the nameless protagonist tries to become the best 'lot lizard' to outshine a neglectful mother, was captured well by critic Stephen Burt, who described it as a fantasy about the thrills of playing with identity, and the pitfalls of worshipping 'authenticity'. Indeed, one reason that it stood out was its lack of self-pity, and its refusal to delve into the psychological trauma of being in the 'wrong' body. Instead, the central character (nicknamed 'Cherry Vanilla' but often self-identifying as 'Sarah') constantly flips between male and female, sometimes at will, sometimes under order.

Sarah's main strength is its voice, which recalls Genet or Burroughs, as well as Salinger's youthful rage. Establishing a convincing teenage idiom as an adult is not easy, and perhaps this explains why so many believed it *was* by a 19-year-old. That said, it's not realistic: it's hard to imagine someone like the protagonist writing: 'I feel a conspicuous ache of pleasure combined with shame that I am not sharing her probable rightful place as a religious icon, on account of her having lost her innards probably thousands of times and giving birth to me without knowing it'. (The dialogue is much sparser.) Crucially, it's funny: make readers laugh, as *Sarah* often does, and they will forgive almost anything.

It seems to work like song lyrics do, more than like a conventional novel does – for me, *Sarah* felt more like Modest Mouse's 1997 album *The Lonesome Crowded West,* with its evocations of isolation, frustration, and alienation in pastoral America, than anything else I've *read.* The only book that springs to mind as a comparison is *Cobra* by Severo Sarduy, a gay Cuban author writing in French. This was a postmodern fairy tale about a transvestite obsessed with physical transformation, achieving it through Tantric Buddhist rituals and initiation into a motorcycle gang, with the author constantly breaking the fourth wall to remind readers that Cobra was an avatar, not a character. Certainly, *Sarah* shares with *Cobra* a sense of ascent that is missing from *The Heart is Deceitful,* which keeps readers in a relentless cycle of abuse with its fragmentary structure, and only occasionally brings in the funnier, fanciful elements that offset its predecessor's more visceral aspects.

When *Sarah* first appeared, barely any fiction by trans women about trans women was in print, and there was a cultural need for trans-identified authors that LeRoy briefly filled. One of the few antecedents (in a way) is Roz Kaveney's semi-autobiographical *Tiny Pieces of Skull,* following trans sex workers in Chicago in 1979-80. It was written in 1988 but not published until 2015, as enthusiastic editors could not persuade Eighties directors to take it. (One said his house had published 'too many quasi-experimental novels by sexual deviants'.) Like Leslie Feinberg's *Stone Butch Blues* (1993), Kaveney's characters pragmatically navigate a transphobic world, without *Sarah*'s magical elements. Imogen Binnie's *Nevada* (2013) and Casey Plett's *A Safe Girl to Love* (2014) – two prominent works from New York-based Topside Press, set up in 2011 to publish openly trans authors – do something similar, taking trans characters out of their (relatively) safe urban environments and into rural ones. They share *Sarah*'s stylistic lightness, but not its combination of abuse and alt-religious fantasy.

★

Somehow, I'd missed LeRoy's celebrity and its subsequent collapse at the time, despite being a queer, transgender teenager who loved punk and post-punk, the Velvet Underground and REM, reading Burroughs and Salinger when *Sarah* came out. Verso Books, who had recently published my gender reassignment memoir *Trans,* asked me to introduce a screening of Feuerzeig's film, at the London Review Bookshop in July last year, because they knew the issues it raised – about the line between autobiographical writing and fiction, the nature of authorship and how it intersects with the publishing industry, whether or not Albert's use of transgender characters constituted cultural appropriation, and whether this was a hoax, an Andy Kaufman-style piece of sustained performance art, or something harder to define – would intrigue me.

I was stood backstage, waiting for the event to start, when a stranger passed me a phone. "Hello, is that Juliet?" I said yes. The accent instantly switched from a naturalistic New York to a turbo-Cockney of a type that probably never existed but if it did, I explained, would now be more likely found in Essex than East London, where visitors will mostly hear the charmless Home Counties tones of gentrifiers like me. Immediately, I recognised Speedie, who fulminated: "This film's about me! Not Laura! Me!" I laughed, weakly, wondering if I'm being recorded. Then, Laura Albert broke character, insisting that the affair was "like *The Great Rock 'n' Roll Swindle*", the film that Temple made after the Sex Pistols imploded, telling things from Malcolm McLaren's point of view.

I'm still not sure what to think about LeRoy. The affair has shaken my notion that if you publish anything, you must be prepared for whatever reaction it generates, and accept that it often won't be what you anticipated, or desired. After all, texts don't go into the world alone: they come with a backstory, marketing strategies and champions, and the decision to publish comes with decisions about how often to appear in public, how to present oneself, how much to acquiesce to a publisher's idea of what is marketable and how much to argue. My thinking on this has changed since the person who handed me the telephone before the screening – a friend of Albert's – told me that she had known from the start that Albert was LeRoy, and that the author had taken *Sarah* to publishers as Laura Albert and repeatedly been turned down.

Albert lost her grip on the 'avatar', and the revelation left people embarrassed, wondering how they failed to see through LeRoy/Knoop's ridiculous get-up. However, there wasn't a sense that while lines had been crossed, there was a political point consciously being made. Albert, it seemed, never had a grand plan – Feuerzeig's film gives an impression of LeRoy emerging first on the phone to a therapist, then in conversations with publishers (who forgot their due diligence) and finally in response to an unexpected wave of support. In that sense, the comparison to *The Great Rock 'n' Roll Swindle* is apt: that film, too, tries to convince viewers that the Sex Pistols' meteoric rise and fatal (for Sid and Nancy) fall was rigorously choreographed, and falls short.

All this, though, doesn't make me think of Johnny Rotten asking, "Ever feel like you've been cheated?" as the Pistols disintegrated on stage, but of his decision to use his birth name, John Lydon, and form a new group, Public Image Limited. Supported by Keith Levene and Jah Wobble, Lydon escaped the myths that McLaren had built around him, and recorded music far more inventive than the Pistols' ultimately conventional, three-chord rock. The person who once wrote as Jeremiah Terminator LeRoy is now working on a memoir, as Laura Albert – maybe hoping for rehabilitation, or maybe because it feels important to counter all the negative assumptions and judgements that were made after the 'reveal' of 2006. If it's anywhere near as good as *Metal Box* – the second PiL album, and one of the finest of the punk/post-punk movement – then it will be a fascinating coda to a very strange story.

Canal Issue 1, 2017

THE CRYING GAME

On its British release in 1992, *The Crying Game* was marketed as a film in which politics and love became inseparable, with 'Desire is a Dangerous Game' as its tagline. Using *When a Man Loves a Woman* as its soundtrack, the trailer focused on the romantic affair at its centre, and particularly on Dil – 'a woman with a secret' and the centre of attraction for Fergus (Stephen Rea), a Provisional Irish Republican Army soldier played by Stephen Rea. This ambiguity is reinforced by the stock used for the trailer, a grainy material with the feel of 16mm or VHS that contrasts with director Neil Jordan's crisp 35mm cinematography.

Dil's 'secret' was as crucial to the film's success in North America as its sympathetic portrayal of an IRA member was to its muted reception in Britain, especially as an IRA bomb campaign was in full swing across London in autumn 1992. Jordan later reflected that because the Anglo-Irish issues were less well understood in the US, its distributors (Miramax) could play up the sexual politics – creating a frenzy by begging audiences not to reveal the 'twist'.

The Crying Game was written in the mid-1980s and filmed in the early 1990s, just before the World Wide Web became part of everyday life. In the internet age, such protection of a crucial plot device is no longer tenable, despite the 'spoiler warnings' that accompany so many online discussions of film and television. Unlike reviewers of the time, who stated that giving it away was uncharitable, I am going to reveal the 'secret' – so if you've somehow managed to last 25 years without finding out, look away now:

Dil is transgender.

You *did* know, didn't you?

★

I use 'transgender' anachronistically. The word existed in 1992 but hadn't moved far beyond publications written by and aimed at people more often termed 'transsexual' or 'transvestite', and doesn't feature in *The Crying Game*. This was amongst the first of an international wave of 1990s films, from *Ma vie en rose* (Belgium, 1997) and *All about My Mother* (Spain, 1999) to *Priscilla, Queen of the Desert* (Australia, 1994), via *Orlando* (UK, 1992) and *Different for Girls* (UK, 1996), as well as *Tales of the City* (US, 1993) and *Boys Don't Cry* (US, 1999) to feature gender-variant protagonists. But while it shows certain challenges of cross-gender living, it doesn't dwell on struggles to assert identity or navigate the reassignment process, or handle relations with family or friends. We see Dil only through a male gaze – be it her lover Jody, who is taken hostage by the IRA, or Fergus, who inadvertently kills him – without any 'self-discovery' backstory or discussion of whether her body is as she wishes.

It's not so much that *The Crying Game* leaves these questions unanswered: more that it focuses on Dil's present, with other characters' pasts and futures anchored on her.

This is really a film about male sexuality, that sometimes casts the feminine as deceptive, from the moment that Jude (played with unimpeachable cool by Miranda Richardson) lures Jody into the IRA's trap to the point where Fergus reacts to the now-infamous 'reveal' by vomiting (a response parodied in the 'gross-out' comedy *Ace Ventura: Pet Detective,* released in 1994). It takes in Fergus' discomfort at having to handle Jody's penis so that his hostage can piss, and the sense of Jody passing Dil onto Fergus, as 'property' for which Fergus becomes responsible.

The middle of the film examines the way in which trans women (again, not a term available to its characters) complicate male sexuality. Dil presents as high-femme: she is first seen working as a hairdresser, wearing tights and heels, with frizzy hair and manicured red nails. Her life pivots around three locations – her home, her workplace and the Metro, a queer pub in East London, frequented by people of various colours, genders and sexualities, but enough straight white men to make Fergus feel comfortable.

The viewer sees the world through Fergus' eyes: when he returns to the Metro after the 'reveal', it is far more obvious that it is a queer venue. The pub crowd serve as Dil's family and friends, and the most likely source of potential suitors. She still seems isolated, and we witness no deep relationships with anyone besides Fergus – or Jimmy, as he calls himself, as he keeps secrets from Dil, far graver than what she hides from him. There is transphobia in the background, even though this isn't explored as a reason why Dil might not be upfront about her body and presentation, or for Fergus' 'revulsion', described by Kate Bornstein in *Gender Outlaw* (1995) as 'an admission of attraction' that does not endorse his reaction, but shows how common it is.

Judith/Jack Halberstam, in *In a Queer Time and Place* (2005) was more critical. Halberstam praises the 'relatively unknown' Jaye Davidson's 'feat of credibly performing a gender at odds with the sexed body even after the body has been brutally exposed', and while Jordan's script has Dil accept 'blame' for Fergus 'not knowing', it also allows her to gently rebuff Fergus' "Should've stayed a girl" with "Don't be cruel" and a swift affirmation of their love. The film others Dil on grounds of colour as well as gender, and castigates Northern Ireland for its racism whilst not examining it in England (notorious for its post-war 'No Blacks, No Irish' attitudes to community-building) and subscribes to the trope of presenting happiness and satisfaction as impossible for trans people.

In this sense, *The Crying Game* is of its time, but despite its faults, it presents Dil as someone with genuine agency and strength, a generous spirit who nonetheless has the freedom not just to be imperfect, but outright *bad,* whether she has to be, or just wants to. However much the film defaults to the 'straight' white man's gaze, it allows a trans woman to love and be loved, by both the male protagonist and the audience – something rarely shown on screen before.

Commissioned by the BFI for the liner notes for their
DVD release, 2017

A FANTASTIC LEAP: TRANS CINEMA'S BREAKTHROUGH MOMENT

A Fantastic Woman, Chilean director Sebastián Lelio's best foreign language Oscar nominee, is not the first film about a trans woman to be in contention for an Academy Award. Some argue that playing a trans character is a sure-fire way to contend for a statuette – look at the nominations for John Lithgow for *The World According to Garp* (1982); Jaye Davidson for *The Crying Game* (1992); Hilary Swank in *Boys Don't Cry* (1999); Felicity Huffman for *Transamerica* (2005); Jared Leto for *Dallas Buyers Club* (2013) and Eddie Redmayne for The Danish Girl (2015). What is new is that Lelio's lead actor, Chilean actor/singer Daniela Vega, is herself trans, and was briefly in the running to become the first trans person to be nominated for best actor. Vega missed out, but her performance as trans woman Marina, whose older lover Orlando dies in her arms, leading to her being ostracised by his family and suspected of murder, was integral to the film's Oscars recognition.

Those interested in trans representation did have something to celebrate with Yance Ford's nomination for *Strong Island*, which made Ford the first trans director to be considered for an Academy Award – for best documentary. That Ford's film does not directly deal with LGBT issues, but with his brother's murder by a white man who was never brought to trial is significant for a community so often typecast. However, Vega's prominence has raised another question, which has become more prominent as advocates have broken into mainstream media in the last decade: should trans characters in feature films be played by trans actors?

Historically, there has been a divide: underground films in which trans people play themselves, often with improvised dialogue that uses their own experiences; and mainstream films in which A-list, cisgender actors portray a trans character. The latter doesn't have to be worse than the former, or bad in itself – a talented actor can produce an interesting and intelligent performance, given a well-researched and sensitively written script. As a trans teenager, I found films such as *Priscilla, Queen of the Desert* (1994) or *I Shot Andy Warhol* (1996) helpful, as they showed the difficulties of cross-gender existence with nuance and wit, never degenerating into cliché or melodrama.

Leto's Rayon in Dallas Buyers Club met with hostility not just because it embodied so many stereotypes ("a sad-sack, clothes-obsessed, constantly flirting … drug-addict prostitute" as Steve Friess wrote in *Time*) but also because no trans consultants were enlisted, and because Leto used his speech on winning the Golden Globe for best supporting actor to talk about how that "tiny little Brazilian bubble butt was all mine" rather than anything he had learned about the realities of trans living.

The Crying Game was notable for not using a big-name actor, unlike *Priscilla* with Terence Stamp or *Myra Breckinridge* (1970) with Raquel Welch. The film's twist, zealously protected by its US marketers (just before the internet made this impossible) relied on Jaye Davidson, who played Dil, the main romantic interest, being unknown. This meant the viewer realised Dil was trans at the same time as protagonist Fergus – played by the more established Stephen Rea. *The Danish Girl* is a strange case. Adapted from David Ebershoff's novel, it is loosely based on the life of Lili Elbe, who died in 1933 after one of the first sex-reassignment surgeries. The film took 10 years to get from a script to the screen. It was long delayed by financiers pulling out, worried that the story was not commercially viable, and the inability to secure a big name to play Elbe. Originally, Nicole Kidman was lined up to star and produce, but the film went through three false starts and six directors before its eventual release with Eddie Redmayne as its lead.

During the 15-year lag between Ebershoff's novel being optioned and Redmayne receiving his best actor nomination in 2016, much had changed. Telling the story through a cisgender woman (Alicia Vikander, who won in 2016 for best supporting actor) struggling to accept her lover's trans identity, felt old-fashioned, the reverse-mirror shots of Elbe modelling for her painting utterly clichéd. The scene where Elbe gets beaten up by people who ask: "Are you a girl or a boy" felt heavy-handed, plastering a familiar transphobic trope over a situation that was far more nuanced. Again, though, the problem was not so much Redmayne's interpretation of the role as the hackneyed script and ponderous direction, and for me, the film's worst crime was being boring.

During that interregnum, there had been one other significant Hollywood portrayal of a trans woman: *Transamerica*. When I saw it in 2005, *Transamerica* felt like an exercise in compromise, written in the awareness that studios would not cast a trans actor as a lead, but trying to make space by using trans people in supporting roles.

The first person on screen was trans woman Andrea James, teaching Bree (Felicity Huffman) how to feminise her voice. Despite this, and a scene where Bree attends a party for trans women, played by trans women, Huffman could not escape the need to establish her character's transsexuality through a series of clichés: putting inserts in her bra; applying make-up in the mirror (while dressed all in pink); seeing a psychiatrist who praises her "authenticity". Even this timidity, though, outdid *The Danish Girl*.

For now, trans actors still aren't cast in those roles, partly because producers feel there aren't any qualified to play them. But trans people are seldom given other parts (and if they are, don't get nominated for awards for their "brave" portrayals of cisgender characters) so the problem persists. Technological advances have offered ways around this: Netflix made space not just for Ford's *Strong Island*, but also Laverne Cox's rise to prominence as trans inmate Sophia Burset in *Orange is the New Black*, which led to her cover appearance on *Time*'s Transgender Tipping Point issue in May 2014.

Cox's success showed the film industry that it wasn't just a handful of activists who wanted to see trans actors playing trans characters. The following year, a surprise, low-budget hit confirmed this: Sean Baker's *Tangerine*, which also relied on digital advances to get around traditional barriers. It was shot in Hollywood on an iPhone 5, a process that, unlike traditional films, did not require a permit. Baker used two trans actors, Kitana Kiki Rodriguez and Mya Taylor, from a Los Angeles LGBT centre, who brought their own experiences of sex work, poverty and transphobia into the script.

This way of working has a long underground tradition. Several of the New American Cinema filmmakers, including Jack Smith, Ken Jacobs and Ron Rice, assembled groups of outsiders, including gender-variant individuals such as

Mario Montez and Francis Francine, pointed a camera at them and turned the results into a film. Plot wasn't usually their main concern – the films were more about celebrating their own survival, and creating spaces away from straight society where they could express themselves without restraint. This movement arose in the early 1960s: Jacobs's *Little Stabs at Happiness*, Rice's *Chumlum* and Smith's *Flaming Creatures* were all made between 1959-63, with Smith's film confiscated by police and censored by the Supreme Court.

Paul Morrissey and Andy Warhol took a slightly more structured approach, in their films with the Factory's trio of transgender superstars, Jackie Curtis, Candy Darling and Holly Woodlawn. The point wasn't so much that they were trans, but that being so placed them on the margins, where *Trash* (1970), featuring Joe Dallesandro as a heroin-addicted hustler and Woodlawn as "Holly" was set.

In Europe, two notable directors followed this lead. The first was German film-maker Rosa von Praunheim, whose films are more intelligent and interesting than (heterosexual or cisgender) critics realised. *City of Lost Souls* (1983) was badly received on its release for its minimal plot; certainly, its scripted parts are its weakest. Like Warhol, Von Praunheim brought misfits – specifically, queer Americans in West Berlin – together, and let them improvise dialogue. The film's best scene, has transsexual performer Angie Stardust and transvestite Tara O'Hara, playing themselves, arguing about whether surgery is necessary to be a woman. Angie's passionate explanation that "it's because of the old school that you can be what you are" wins the debate. Maybe someone with no direct experience could have performed their heated but humane conversation with similar clarity and conviction – but it's unlikely.

It's not impossible, though. The greatest film about trans living is Pedro Almodóvar's *All About My Mother*, which won the foreign language Oscar in 2000. Antonia San Juan's performance as Agrado, peaking in a brilliantly observed monologue on being an "authentic" transsexual woman, was so good that speculation about her gender was intense: she later said "I'm not a transvestite or transsexual, and that's all there is to say about that", but the rumours did not go away.

Whatever San Juan's history, those who maintain that the only criteria for trans casting should be good acting should consider Stanislavsky's "system", which made "emotional memory" of a real-life situation central to its realistic depiction. Given this, it is far more likely that a trans person would be best placed to portray trans life, and the performance of non-professional trans actor Stéphanie Michelini in Sébastien Lifshitz's *Wild Side* (2004), where she plays a transsexual woman trying to reconcile with her dying mother, is more subtle and less predictable than the ones recognised by the Academy.

Likewise, I found Daniela Vega's stoic responses to endless micro-aggressions far more convincing than they might have been if played by an outsider. It helped that Lelio wrote *A Fantastic Woman* after extensive consultation with Vega, letting her draw on her experiences without crossing the line between feature and documentary, and letting him take his storyline beyond the basics of transgender living. The result is a vibrant combination of romance, fantasy and detective story, unlike any of its predecessors. Whether or not it tears down the barriers for trans actors is yet be seen – but it's certainly a huge step forward.

The Guardian, 2 February 2018

MAKING *REVIVIFICATION:* *ART, ACTIVISM AND POLITICS* *IN UKRAINE*

I arranged my residency at the Izolyatsia Platform for Cultural Initiatives in a back-to-front (and arguably *wrong*) way. Rather than coming up with an idea and then addressing the practicalities, I met someone from Izolyatsia in London, liked the idea of spending a summer in Ukraine and only then came up with a project to justify it. Lots of my travels to post-Soviet or post-Yugoslav countries in the last four years put me in touch with similar scenes: queer and/or feminist artist-activists, inclusive of trans/non-binary people and sex workers, most likely to call themselves anarchist if they adopted an ideological label, but often interested in finding queer or feminist histories within their male-dominated Communist or Socialist pasts, and how their perspectives could influence leftist movements in future. I guessed that Kyiv, where the Orange Revolution in 2004-05 and the Revolution of Dignity nearly a decade later began, would have as vibrant a queer/feminist scene as Zagreb or Bishkek. Having long been frustrated by how badly Western (liberal) journalists understood LGBTQI+ issues in post-Soviet contexts, and especially Russia, I decided to look for this subculture and make a documentary on it, aiming to improve understanding of LGBTQI+ culture in Ukraine and provoke further thought about among outsiders (myself included).

I had a few predecessors – all within the last four years, after the Russian invasion of Crimea – itself after the Pussy Riot case and the emergence of Femen – made Western filmmakers take an interest in Ukraine never previously expressed. The one that caused the most discord was an episode of a series called *Gaycation,* made by Elliot Page and Ian Daniel for *Viceland* – *Vice* magazine's online TV network – in 2016. I'd not heard of this – I've never paid much attention to *Vice,* nor (for the last few years, anyway) the kind of Anglo-American activism premised on the assumption that neoliberalism is essentially fine but just needs a little more 'diversity' and 'tolerance', which looked like the show's starting point. Formally, it bored me. I particularly hated the constant cuts to Page and Daniel looking sad whenever they heard how hard it was to be LGBT in Ukraine, centring but not questioning their position as Western visitors, putting themselves above, or at least *outside* the concerns of their Ukrainian interviewees.

I imagined Page and Daniel as the kind of people who put a poster of Hillary Clinton up in their bedrooms in early 2016, and still haven't taken it down. Soon they reproduced the cardinal sin of recent Anglo-American liberal media, giving over half the show to far-right nationalists in the hope of 'understanding' their ideology and thus allowing them to promote it, protecting them by blurring their faces, not giving any time to anti-Fascist activists, or anyone pursuing LGBTQI rights within a movement addressing the rampant individualism and inequality of a post-Soviet Ukraine that prioritised 'de-Communisation' above all other cultural change.

So, I looked at what *Vice* did and planned to do the opposite. I decided to keep myself out of the film, or at least the frame, as much as possible: I thought about problematising my position but soon thought this as self-indulgent as *Gaycation*'s constant close-ups. Far better to make an issue of this only if my interviewees did.

Finding those interviewees wasn't too difficult. I felt unprepared but, my interviewees said, I'd done more homework than *Vice,* having the advantage of working with Izolyatsia. Lina, the residency co-ordinator, gave me a list of interesting contacts and helped me find a Director of Photography, Oksana Kazmina who had made films with several of the people Lina mentioned, and knew most of the others. I won't talk too much here about the specific artists – you'll have to wait until my film is screened – but my expectation that the scene would be intelligent and interesting, fortunately, proved correct. I met a clothing co-operative called ReSew, who work on a fair trade, horizontal basis, who hold workshops on art and activism in Ukraine, reusable sanitary products, and to teach people how to make the clothes they dream of, or simply *need.* Tetiana Korneieva is a performance artist whose work deals with the uses and limits of *visibility,* such a prized concept for LGBTQI+ activists (including myself in my *Guardian* series). Both were involved with Pride events, delivering presentations and performances that feature in my documentary.

I also met Anatoly Belov, a graphic artist and musician who sings with a group called Lyudska Podoba, who have large following in Kyiv, and not just in the queer and feminist communities. AntiGonna, an artist and performer whose video works look at the brutality and beauty of sex, with a gorgeous film called *gporn* that reminded me of Carolee Schneemann and Maria Beatty, talked about how her work explores sexuality and death, and how difficult she has found it to get her works sown in Ukraine. Alina Kleytman, from Kharkiv, told me about her videos, and *perestroika*-era Russian pirate TV star, performance artist and drag queen Vladislav Mamyshev Monroe – one of the period's few visible queer people, and an inspiration for a new generation of artist-activists trying to find space outside the dispiriting battle between neoliberalism (that appropriated the Marxist concept of 'the end of history') and the backwards-looking far-right, instead hoping to use queer and feminist perspectives to revivify left-wing movements, and I took this idea of *Revivification* as my half-hour documentary's title.

I spent a fascinating hour with US Fulbright scholar Jessica Zychowicz, who talked about how Ukrainian art between the revolutions of 2004-2005 and 2013-2014 was often an archaeology of the Soviet period, with artists forming collectives (such as REP) and working in public squares. In this, they were inspired by the *avant-garde* Constructivists and Suprematists – many of whom worked in Kyiv and Kharkiv in the decade after 1917, and remained highly influential over Ukraine's visual culture (and the most interesting works in the National Art Museum's collection) despite efforts to marginalise it with the rest of the area's Soviet history. (Indeed, Yulia Tymoshenko – a crucial figure in the Orange Revolution, and the country's first female Prime Minister – had a personal aesthetic that deliberately harked back to the 19th century, with her hair in braids like the national poet, Lesya Ukrainka.)

Valentina Petrova was a joy to talk to, opening her interview with a manifesto on her feelings about public speaking, asking for people to be more self-conscious in their statements. Then she told me about her conceptual practice, investigating labour and poverty from a feminist standpoint, with a strong interest in protecting workers' rights and the position of women within trade unions in the post-Soviet context. I mentioned another interviewee, Maria Kulikovska, in my last letter. We talked further about how the paramilitaries who occupied Crimea drove her from her home and destroyed her soap sculptures of female bodies – "their own performance", she said, "to show what would happen to *real* bodies who opposed them".

Maria also discussed this year's Pride march, where we took our camera (unlike *Vice,* who showed very little of it when they visited). But that's a story for next time ...

Tinyletter, 3 July 2018

KYIV PRIDE 2018

The last time I went to Pride was in Brighton in 2011. I hadn't done that with great enthusiasm – the organisers had solved the problem of the event's increasingly unmanageable popularity by charging £15 for tickets to the party, which had always been held in Preston Park at the end of the parade, and which had always been free, which seemed to me like the completion of its corporate takeover. I was happy to march with my employers at the time, the NHS Primary Care Trust – at that point, being subjected to its own corporate takeover after the Conservative and Liberal Democrat coalition announced the white paper on health and social care reforms – and equally happy to leave as soon as I could. I moved to London that autumn: I've never been to Pride there, taking Huw Lemmey's word for it that if anything, it's even worse, with occasional flashpoints over efforts to intimidate and exclude trans people making me feel even less inclined to bother with it.

Kyiv Pride wasn't a regular occasion the last time I attended a march. Given my long-standing interests in queer culture and post-Communist politics, I was aware of some of the attempts to hold Pride events in Serbia and Croatia during the first decade of the 21st century, almost all of which ended in the state, and especially the police, failing to protect the marchers from neo-Nazis. (I learned more about that in a fascinating conversation between Ukrainian filmmaker Mykola Ridnyi and Croatian video artist Igor Grubić, whose *East Side Story* (2006) documents attacks in 2001 and 2002.)

There was a small Pride march here in 2003, but in 2008, the city authorities told organisers to cancel their IDAHO event due to the likelihood of friction. Four years later, the organisers of Kyiv Pride themselves cancelled their parade, fearing for their safety – at that time, Viktor Yanukovych's government had introduced a draft bill against 'gay propaganda' into the Ukrainian parliament. They moved the march to a secret location in Obolon, on the banks of the Dnipro river. Someone in the police leaked it to a Fascist group, who attacked the marchers – two of the organisers were beaten up and gassed.

With LGBTQI+ groups and far-right nationalists becoming more visible after the Euromaidan revolution, the police refused to provide protection in 2014, after the local government had banned it the previous year. Kyiv's mayor, former boxer Vitali Klitschko, declared that it would be frivolous to hold Pride when 'battle actions' (in the Donbas) were going on, satisfying the Love Against Homosexuality group's demands to have it stopped. Later that year, Fascists set fire to the Zhovten Cinema during a screening of *Les Nuits d'été* in the LGBT strand of a film festival. The revolution may have led to the new government's decision to drop the propaganda bill, but there was – and remains – far more to do. The following year, Yanukovych's successor as President, Peter Poroshenko, over-ruled Klitscho's attempt to cancel Pride again, but stated that he was only allowing it to meet the European Union's demands on equality, and that as a practising Christian, he was personally opposed to it.

The 2015 event set the tone for the next few years: a brief march in a restricted area with far more police than participants. The secret location was again leaked, resulting in further attacks; marchers were told to leave in small groups and avoid the Metro, where neo-Nazis might corner them. Since then, police have protected events in Kyiv, which remain the biggest in Ukraine: marches in Lviv (2015) and Kharkiv (2017) were also targeted, and at Pride events in the days before this year's Equality march, I met several people who had travelled from other cities.

★

This year's march began at 9am, reminding me of how the police in England ask for football matches between bitter rivals to kick off at midday so troublemakers are less likely to turn up drunk. The city centre had to be closed at 7pm the previous (Saturday) evening: the authorities told anyone who complained that it was the LGBTQIA+ community's fault for demanding a march, rather than supporting it, or blaming the far-right for necessitating so much security.

I dressed down, not wanting to attract attention, and arrived alone to see dozens of cops on the steps of the National Opera. I saw a man holding a placard over his face: I couldn't read the text but when I saw 18:22 at the end, I guessed it was a Bible passage. Then I noticed a man in a 'Make America Great Again' T-shirt and wondered if these Christian fundamentalists were funded by US organisations, as LGBTQIA+ groups in Kyrgyzstan told me happened there. When I saw a group of men chanting and holding up a banner with a silhouette of a man and a woman holding a child's hand, surrounded not just by police but also the fire service, I realised I was on the wrong side of the cordon. I briefly wondered how many of those men had been in the stadium with me when I'd seen Dynamo

Kyiv on my first visit, back in March, and went through the airport-style security to join my cinematographer, Oksana, to film the parade.

There were just as many riot police inside the cordon as outside. Oksana and I took a few shots of them, and then filmed some of the people. We saw Amnesty International, and other groups with a more homonationalist approach, perhaps adopted to persuade those outside the fence screaming 'Homosexuality is not Ukrainian!' that this was not the case. We spoke to a trans group and the Ukrainian Bears. Then, suddenly, a huge scrum of photographers rushed over to the front of the parade, which was yet to begin. A far-right group had smuggled in a rainbow flag with an anti-gay message on the front, and briefly chanted against the march before the police removed them. Oksana and I wondered if this was the best approach – given that they weren't armed, and seriously outnumbered by a record Pride attendance, it might have been worthwhile at least try talking to them, but equally, nobody was sorry to see them removed.

The appearance of a float full of drag queens dancing to loud music brightened the mood, and Oksana and I spent most of the short parade following them. (We were amused that they played *Sound of da Police* by KRS-One, given the complex relationship between Pride and the cops.) Reaching the end by 10.30am, we asked to be let out of the compound, and found a café on Kreschatyk Street to hide in while the crowds dispersed. It certainly had a very different set of problems to Brighton Pride or Pride in London, and was an important reminder to me of why such events are necessary. I won't be back next year, but I won't forget about it, either.

Tinyletter, 9 July 2018

AN INTERVIEW WITH ESMERAY

Since Occupy Gezi launched popular protests against the rule of Turkish leader Recep Tayyip Erdoğan in 2013, Turkey witnessed a crackdown on dissent that has alarmed international freedom of speech activists. After his government resisted a military coup in July 2016, Erdoğan has become increasingly autocratic, ruling Turkey in an ongoing state of emergency. Last year, he declared himself President after a constitutional referendum with 1.5 million unstamped votes. During that time, academics, authors, and journalists were imprisoned or exiled.

In consolidating his power, Erdoğan has relied on fundamental Islamic support, and nostalgia for the Ottoman Empire. No laws have yet been passed against lesbian, gay, bisexual, trans, queer or intersex citizens, but cultural expression has been curtailed, with Pride bans in Ankara and Istanbul. In 2016, LGBTQI activist and sex worker Hande Kader was raped, tortured and killed by a gang.

This suppression has intensified since the socialist, pro-Kurdish Halkların Demokratik Partisi (HDP) [People's Democratic Party] passed the 10% threshold to enter government in the General Election of 2015. Trans activist Diren Coşkun, imprisoned in Tekirdağ prison on the charge of 'membership to terror organisation', recently ended her hunger strike, held to demand access for trans-specific healthcare in Tekirdağ prison.

I recently visited Istanbul to co-judge the 'Love and Change' political documentary strand of the !F Film Festival (which hosts an annual Rainbow party in support of the LGBT community) and met Esmeray, a transsexual journalist, feminist and LGBT activist.

Juliet: How would you describe the situation for trans people in Turkey at present? I understand that the situation has worsened in the last five years.
Esmeray: It has always been tough for LGBTQI individuals. In the 1990s, I was a sex worker – there were no regulations. Now, before any interrogation, the police must ask for an ID; back then, they would just drag sex workers around by their hair. Thanks to the solidarity of LGBTQI organisations, there was greater public visibility before the Gezi protests of 2013. After that, we've had approximately 100,000 people marching on İstiklal Street *[the main street]* for Pride, several times. Since the coup attempt in July 2016 *[when a faction within the Turkish armed forced attempted to seize control of key locations in Ankara, Istanbul and elsewhere, but were defeated]*, there has been repression of the LGBTQI movement. They didn't directly target organisations, but in Ankara, the mayor has outlawed Pride and all activities with an LGBTQI theme.

What resistance do you think is possible?
When the Pride march in Istanbul was banned, the committee decided to disperse across all the streets, rather than proceeding through İstiklal, so people walked everywhere in the Beyoğlu district. The city authorities only

banned the march: all other events, like seminars and film screenings, went ahead. The official reason for the Pride ban was that it overlapped with Ramadan. All active LGBTQI organisations are still trying to resist.

What are those organisations doing?
There are emergency phone lines for LGBTQI individuals, and there is still a support network and therapy for trans people in transition. I am not involved in any organisations, but they are still organising panels and seminars with academics and the public. Personally, I work to increase the visibility of LGBTQI people in art.

Do you feel that art and culture are a useful way to mindshare LGBTQI experiences and educate people about the issues?
My play, *Cadının Bohçası (The Rag Bag of the Witch)* deals with the experience of a trans woman, not just as a one-person story, but with how wider social factors shape it. I reached out to people who might form an audience – not just the usual targets. Now, it feels like a social responsibility to perform it. It's often hard for people to put on one-person plays, they often burn out after one or two years, but I've been going for 11 now.

Are there any other artists or performers working on LGBTQI issues in Turkey who interest you?
The most remarkable is Huysuz Virjin ('Grumpy Virgin'), a transvestite or drag queen who prefers 'he'. He has been active in showbusiness for the last fifty years, but there is a crucial difference between this and art, because he is

not critical of the situation for LGBTQI people, capital-ising instead on the public representation of a specific gay culture. In some ways, the drag acts damage the cause by misrepresenting trans people, by giving the impression that our identities are performances rather than lived experiences – this allows them to opt out of the politics around those experiences. Bülent Ersoy *[the popular actor and singer who began her career as a male singer before finishing gender reassignment in 1981]* identifies as a woman rather than a trans woman and isn't advancing any cause either. She might be friends with Erdoğan, but that doesn't do anything for the wider community.

Most feminist and LGBTQI movements have had little choice but to support the left. We have been oppressed because of our visibility, but left-wing groups have been stigmatised because of their support for us. The main opposition party, Cumhuriyet Halk Partisi *[the social democrat Republican People's Party],* have supported some activities like the International Women's Day marches in Beşiktaş, and other LGBTQI events, but haven't changed their constitution much. When asked, the CHP said they had no LGBTQI agenda – they were more interested in the war in Syria *[in which Erdoğan launched a major offensive in Afrin in January 2018].*

There is another party that is an offshoot of the far-right *Milliyetçi Hareket Partisi* (MHP) *[Nationalist Action Party]* group in parliament. They were looking for delegates near where I live, and invited me to join, even though they know I am a trans woman and support the HDP. They said they wanted me *because* I supported labour and human rights! The guy who offered me a place lives in a rich district in Anatolia – I didn't understand why he claimed to be on the side of the workers. I challenged the war and said I couldn't exist within his organisation.

The AKP has an LGBTQI organisation, albeit a terrible one. It's for apolitical LGBTQI people, of which there are many – I'd guess that 70% of the population votes for the AKP. If you check the Facebook profile pictures of many trans sex workers, you'll find a picture of Erdoğan, or the leaders of the July 2016 coup attempt.

Those with pictures of Erdoğan – is that because they support him, or to keep themselves safe?
They are not conscious about politics, and on the side of power and money. Our conservative movement, unlike Britain's, does not permit gay marriage.

The British press gives the impression that it's now impossible for the LGBTQI community to organise in Turkey, and that it's being destroyed.
Because of the Orientalism in Europe, they like to see countries like ours as the most improbable places for LGBTQI people to exist. When I took my play to the West, people thought it was impossible for me to be Kurdish, Turkish, trans and involved in art.

What can people from the West do to help?
It's not as if Western Europe has been completely free from homophobia. I think we should eliminate artificial borders, form solidarity between organisations in Turkey and elsewhere, and then look at how we can work together. We will never be free for as long as the heterosexual men from the United States rule the world.

How can we form an international solidarity that transcends elitist, racist and classist power structures?
I don't have an easy answer. Many LGBTQI organisations here have 'Turkey' in front of them, and vocally support Turkish military operations in Syria, so we have a similar problem – there are huge numbers of trans sex workers being murdered here but they're not focusing on that. We should fight transphobia, homophobia, racism and imperialism together.

What support (if any) are trans sex workers getting?
LGBTQI organisations provide support for those in transition (as mentioned) and provide legal help for people who are being harassed, but their main focus is visibility. They want the parliament to recognise that sex workers are *workers* and provide rights accordingly.

Do you have any cause for optimism? What do you think might change?
Of course, things could be much better, but we have succeeded in making LGBTQI communities visible in public, and this is a huge accomplishment. Families are becoming more supportive of LGBTQI people and that's important too.

PEN International Blog, 3 August 2018

ÉCRITURE TRANS-FÉMININE?

The notion of women engaging with and documenting the physical and sexual realities of their own bodies as a distinct style of writing was first articulated by French theorist Hélène Cixous in 1975. In her essay 'The Laugh of the Medusa' ('La Rire de la Méduse'), she argued that this kind of 'women's writing' – what she termed *écriture féminine* – would enable women to enter public discourse in new ways and liberate themselves from a patriarchal stranglehold over art and culture. An intoxicating blend of poetic prose, postmodern theory and feminist activism that combined the Surrealists' interest in political (Marxist) and libidinal (Freudian) challenges to traditional power structures with the opposition to conventional literary styles adopted by French *nouveau roman* authors, Cixous's essay called for women to engage with their designated 'otherness' in the established patriarchal order.

Underpinning 'The Laugh of the Medusa' was a strong focus on the cisgender (non-trans) female body: it advocated the discussion of menstruation, lactation, pregnancy and clitoral pleasure. This was, in part, a reaction against linear texts that reproduced the structure of phallo-centric climax, countered with a celebration of women's sexual and intellectual power. Cixous told readers not to be put off by the idea that writing was for 'great men', nor to be held back by 'the imbecilic capitalist machinery' of the publishing industry. She was aware that her essay was initiating, not concluding a process: 'Since these reflections are taking shape in an area just on the point of being discovered,' Cixous wrote, 'they necessarily bear the mark of our time'. (That time being the mid-1970s: the height of the US second wave feminist movement, left-wing insurrections in Italy and West Germany, and the unleashing of radical energies in France that followed May 1968.)

Certainly, Cixous opened doors for writers to reconsider ideas of femaleness, femininity and womanhood, offering them a readily adaptable set of tactics. Without 'The Laugh of the Medusa', it is hard to imagine the foundational texts of transgender studies, especially '*The "Empire" Strikes Back: A Post-Transsexual Manifesto*'. First published by trans artist, media theorist and activist Sandy Stone in 1987, the manifesto had a similar power and poetry to Cixous' essay, and made a similar call for people to explore their bodies as part of a literary and political project. However, it was not a direct response to Cixous, but to radical feminist Janice G. Raymond, whose anti-trans diatribe *The Transsexual Empire: The Making of the Modern She-Male* (1979) cast male-to-female transsexuality as a plot to infiltrate the second-wave feminist movement. Arguing that transsexual women appropriated female bodies to exercise male dominance, Raymond qualified it as an act tantamount to rape. Stone's response began, however, not with dismantling Raymond's trans-exclusionary arguments but with the conventions of the transsexual memoir. Having established itself as a distinct genre in the fifty years since Lili Elbe wrote the first specimen, *Man into Woman* (1933), the memoir form defined the first wave of trans writing. Focusing on Elbe and Jan Morris' *Conundrum* (1974) – for years the most read book of its kind in the United Kingdom – Stone challenged these writers' conflation of received gender roles with physical sex, noting that: 'Each of these adventurers passes directly from one pole of sexual experience to the other. If there is any intervening space in the continuum of sexuality, it is invisible.' Stone concluded: 'No wonder feminist theorists have been suspicious. Hell, *I'm* suspicious!'

One reason for these authors' elision of this transitional sexual space, suggested Stone, was the binary imperative propagated by the Gender Identity Clinics, which handled transsexual patients in the United States and the United Kingdom. They insisted that service users do their best to 'pass' in their chosen genders and live in 'stealth', not disclosing their transsexual histories on either side of transition. This made it impossible for them to publicly discuss terrain beyond the male/female binary, or the ways in which the Clinic forced them to adhere to traditional ideas of masculine or feminine behaviour as a condition of treatment – a protocol designed, perhaps, to protect cisgender people from exposure to transitioners. This also formed the basis of radical feminist claims that transsexual people (especially transsexual women) were dupes of the patriarchy who willingly conformed to outdated stereotypes.

Stone called for a 'post-transsexual' breaking of this silence by 'constituting transsexuals not as a class or problematic 'third gender,' but rather as a *genre* – a set of embodied texts whose potential for *productive* disruption of structured sexualities and spectra of desire has yet to be explored.' This demand inspired a generation of trans artists, activists and academics throughout the 1990s and 2000s – such as novelist and activist Leslie Feinberg, playwright and performance artist Kate Bornstein, and genderqueer artist Greer Lankton – who in turn influenced the trans voices who broke into the mainstream media during the 2010s.

Originally published in 1994, Kate Bornstein's *Gender Outlaw: On Men, Women and the Rest of Us* followed Stone's imperative to 'mix genres', both in its author's refusal to identify as male or female and in the book's hybrid structure. Combining personal reflections and political commentary, including some of her plays and transcripts from chat room interactions, Bornstein hoped to pin down 'a transgendered writing style' that would consequently 'produce an identification with a transgendered experience.' She listed antecedents and contemporaries whose work could offer ideas as to how this might look: essayist Jamison Green, who discussed the visibility of trans men in a culture more interested in male-to-female people; activist Riki Ann Wilchins, who said trans people needed to reclaim the definitions placed upon by sexologists and medics, and define their own terminology; and photographer Loren Cameron, whose use of portraiture to familiarise (or even confront) the viewer with bodies that did not fit into conventional models of 'male' or 'female' became a familiar tactic, subsequently borrowed by Amos Mac, Zachary Drucker, Rhys Ernst and numerous other artists – not all of whom called themselves trans or non-binary.

I should add here that given the infinitude of gender expressions, and the extent to which they have sometimes conflicted with each other, we cannot speak of a homogenous 'trans' group. These positions grew, in part, out of what has become known as a second wave of *écriture trans*: writers discussing their gender dysphoria – the sense of their identity not matching the one assigned at birth – and how it could be conveyed. The leading lights of this second wave, which began with Stone's manifesto, wrote theory (Bornstein and Judith/Jack Halberstam, noted for their books on *Female Masculinity* and *The Queer Art of Failure*), political manifestos, novels and histories (Leslie Feinberg, who called for a trans liberation movement that was part of a wider revolutionary programme), or assessments of the limitations of this line of writing (Viviane K. Namaste, whose *Invisible Lives* aimed to shift the conversation away from artistic or academic circles towards the discrimination and violence that trans people faced in the 'real world'). The main thing they had in common was that they all rejected the linear memoir *form*, which led a generation of trans people who turned to their writing to share Stone's suspicions about that genre.

This second wave turned into a third, which had a strong focus on media representation, and on bridging a gap that had developed between trans activism and the wider world sometime during the late 2000s. It also included more British and European voices, in contrast to the overwhelmingly North American second wave. Three key texts were Julia Serano's *Whipping Girl* (2007), with its influential critique of mainstream media portrayals of trans people, and how they lagged behind academic and activist discourses; Susan Stryker's *Transgender History* (2008), which placed the second wave into a far wider context, showing how it evolved out of a long process of legal discrimination, the emergence of sexology and sex reassignment surgeries, and sensationalist media coverage of transsexual people, who then wrote autobiographies to counter it; and *Testo Junkie* by Paul B. Preciado (2008), which combined ecstatic recollections of using testosterone with reflections on how society, industry and pharmaceutical technology manipulates human bodies. This led to the emergence of 'non-binary' as a prominent gender identity, defining a presence as important to this third wave as 'transgender' had been to the second, and 'transsexual' to the first.

There was a recognition that trans theory – now as recognisable a genre as transsexual memoir – incorporated plenty of autobiographical material to reinforce its arguments. Earlier writers had used their life stories to undermine transphobic stereotyping in activist and academic circles, a tactic outlined by sociologist Carol Riddell in her essay *Divided Sisterhood* (1980), which also responded to Janice Raymond. During the 2000s, their successors saw these stereotypes perpetuated by radical feminist journalists in liberal media outlets and took a similar approach to that advocated by Riddell. They infused their autobiographical writings with lessons from trans theory, but with a crucial difference in their target audience.

While second wave trans writing had aimed largely to build a community, with trans people talking to each other in an unprecedented way, and in reaction to a first wave of trans authors who had spent most of their energy justifying their existences to outsiders, the third wave sought to bridge these two approaches. Having formed their identities not just by reading the second wave authors but also through extensive online interaction, they entered the mainstream media, where they went into established literary, artistic and political discourses and tried to change them, armed with and emboldened by ideas developed in preceding theoretical and political works. Consequently, they became more prominent in fiction (with trans-only publisher Topside Press issuing novels and short stories by Imogen Binnie, Casey Platt and others, which presented transition and other trans-specific experiences as part of the tapestry of their narratives, rather than narrowly focusing on them), poetry (varying from neo-Classical poet Roz Kaveney to left-wing *avant-gardists* such as Nat Raha or Verity Spott), pop music (ranging from Laura Jane Grace of punk band Against Me! to electro-pop artist Sophie) and other cultural areas, expressing themselves across an unprecedented variety of genres and forms.

It was in this context that I published *Trans: A Memoir* in 2015, a book that built on my *Guardian* blog *A Transgender Journey* (2010-12). I wanted to place that series' narrow focus on the gender reassignment process within the wider context of my pre- and post-transitional relationship with my gender identity. It encompassed my discovery of the trans theory published during the 1990s, unknown to me at the time, and how I saw trans people represented in mainstream media, and the successes and failures of my attempts to work within that media to improve this representation.

In the five years between my first *Guardian* post and my book, much had changed. In May 2014, *Time* magazine put *Orange is the New Black* actor Laverne Cox – one of the first openly trans women to play a leading role in a popular film or series – on its cover, announcing a 'Transgender Tipping Point' for cultural visibility and civil rights. In the US, this was followed by a Vanity Fair special edition on *Trans America* in August 2015 (its title nodding back to the flawed but culturally significant film *Transamerica*, released a decade earlier with cisgender actor Felicity Huffmann playing a transsexual woman) and, in Britain, a landmark piece in the *London Review of Books* in May 2016 by Jacqueline Rose, a prominent writer known for her interests in psychoanalysis, feminism and literature.

This new visibility proved to be a double-edged sword. Sweeping through several important legal decisions (from the decision to annul transsexual model/actor April Ashley's marriage to Lord Arthur Corbett in 1970 to the passage of the Gender Recognition Act in 2004), numerous transition memoirs and theoretical texts, as well as government reports on transgender equality, Rose concluded that while trans people are 'brilliant at telling their stories', their visibility was not sufficient to secure legal reforms or wider acceptance. Indeed, being more visible brought a different set of problems, as transphobes learned more about the people they hated, and how to hurt us.

For all the trans community's lucid, frank self-narration, Rose identified one key elision: sex. Not the discussion of physical sex, or the exploration of the space between 'one pole of sexual experience [and] the other,' but sexual desire and intercourse. (I have many frustrations with how badly the English language copes with trans experiences but having just one word to cover those two things, with all the resultant confusion, is one of my largest.) One notable exception to this, argued Rose, was Kate Bornstein, both in *Gender Outlaw* and in her more recent memoir, *A Queer and Pleasant Danger: The True Story of a Nice Jewish Boy Who Joins the Church of Scientology and Leaves Twelve Years Later to Become the Lovely Lady She is Today* (2013). This felt like a transitional text between the second and third waves: written by one of the most prominent and provocative of the 1990s trans authors, it brought Bornstein's personal exploration of gender issues into a wider narrative rather than making them the narrow focus of either a memoir or a theoretical work. Even more than her previous books, *A Queer and Pleasant Danger* also featured plenty of discussions of sex, including a long BDSM interlude that Bornstein invites readers to skip if it might prove too much for them, it cut against the consistent pressure on trans people not to talk about sex.

I have written, in *Trans* and elsewhere, about a particular double-bind for trans women who want to express, let alone explore, their sexual desires. Those who 'pass' for cisgender women can become fetish objects for heterosexual men, turned on by the idea of a woman who has, or used to have, a penis. Rose's *LRB* piece opens with an anecdote about a man who 'took pleasure in regaling us with stories of the male-to-female transsexual prostitutes' he met in Berlin, 'and how difficult it was to 'complete' the transaction since the transsexual body interprets the surgically created vagina as a wound which it tries to close.' (Post-operative transsexual women must dilate, three times a day for the first months after their lower surgery and thereafter with decreasing frequency; it was after ten weeks of this that I realised I had a working clitoris, feeling stimulated by contact with the Perspex dilator.)

Those who don't 'pass' are frequently ridiculed – often, as I found, on the street – with the idea that they could never be sexually attractive to *anyone* being a central plank of that derision. The most dangerous thing, in my experience, was an encounter during which I ceased to 'pass'. One time, a man accosted me when I'd ill-advisedly walked down a dimly lit alley at night, grabbed my face and kissed me, and then asked: "Are you a boy or a girl?" I walked off, intensely relieved that all he did was yell, 'Can I stick my dick inside you?' It was only when I got home that I realised that, at that point, all bets about how he might react were off.

I want to say that we should refuse to be cowed by this prejudice, but I know how difficult it is to write openly about sex and sexuality, in a climate where, at least until very recently, any individual's words or actions become burdened with the representation of the entire community. While I feel like this burden has now been shared across the sheer number of trans people who have broken into mainstream culture, this difficulty has long been intensified by the second wave feminist movement's aspects not just of transphobia but also of opposition to BDSM, which casts people who want to transition, or otherwise move beyond the categories of 'male' and 'female', and people who want to engage in sadomasochistic practices as dupes of the patri-archy, reproducing internalised misogyny.

In my memoir, I wrote of several occasions when I was sexually assaulted to show the level of transmisogyny (as Serano named it in *Whipping Girl*) that I faced, but I barely mentioned any consensual, pleasurable sex. I used an anecdote in my first draft about a trip to a fetish club in Brighton in 2006, where I switched from bottom to top, playing with cis and trans women, experimenting with flagellation and bondage, drawn almost verbatim from my diary. *Trans* had few scenes about sex and fewer about long-term relationships; inspired by Bornstein, I wanted to bring in my sexual desires, which had been marginalised and stigmatised as much as my gender identity, often by the same people. Immediately, my fears about publishing doubled, and I was relieved when my editor cut it as it didn't fit my overarching narrative about retaining jobs, friendships and family ties after I came out as transsexual. The evenings of sexual experimentation did not lead to deeper relationships and so were deemed irrelevant. The taboo I broke instead was to talk about my lifelong depression. Avoiding the pressure to present myself as a happy, perfectly adjusted person in the face of stereotypes that cast us as miserable and broken, I opted for placing my mental health issues, and my difficulty in sustaining a conventional relationship, within the context of late capitalist society.

The most loving sex scene in *Trans: A Memoir* is in the first half of the book, dealing with my pre-transitional life of presenting as a man. (I felt that transsexual life stories did not always make enough of how their authors managed their assigned genders, physically or psychologically, and I'd had no space for this in my *Guardian* series.) Aged 22, I was seeing a man in Brighton, who I'd met through an amateur theatre production. He noticed my chipped nail varnish and offered to fix it; then he put me in a black dress, false eyelashes and blonde wig, did my make-up, took some photos and then fucked me. I had not experienced such a visceral rush of energy – such a sensation of a fundamental part of me being unlocked, that I would never adequately be able to capture in language – since I first wore women's clothes, aged ten. Then, I was floored by a huge rush of energy, undeniably sexual but, as I instinctively knew, significant of something beyond erotic desire and beyond language.

Excited, I would wear make-up and women's underwear when I wanted to feel attractive – but soon found this was not attractive to *him*. We stopped seeing each other, and then I had a brief romance with another guy who dumped me *during* sex because he found my feminine self-presentation unappealing. At this point, I had to admit to myself that I was *not* a gay man – a label I'd adopted during my teens, hoping that for my family and friends, it would account for *any* behaviour that wasn't 'straight' – and that I needed to think more seriously about my gender identity before I could be clear about my sexual orientation. This led me onto the 'journey' at the core of *Trans: A Memoir*, into publicly presenting as a woman, following the NHS gender reassignment pathway to hormones and surgery, and identifying as queer – someone who is sexually attracted to men, women and anything between or beyond those categories.

Thirty years after Stone's manifesto was first published, and with nearly a century of writing by trans-identified authors behind us, I feel like the possibilities for écriture trans (and, from my perspective, *écriture trans-féminine*) are more open than ever before. It feels now like it is equally valid to aim our texts either at trans people, or at outsiders, or to search for some place in-between. (In interviews, I always said *Trans: A Memoir* was aimed at people who were just starting to work out their trans identities, and sympathetic outsiders who wanted to understand more about our lives, than for people who were already immersed in trans discourses.) The rise of so many trans and/or non-binary people working in so many forms surely means that we can build on the works not just of Bornstein, Califia or Feinberg, but also emerging authors such as Andrea Long Chu or Paris Lees, who have talked extensively about how sex and sexuality intersect with trans bodies and identities – and we now have our own publishers and journals to further conversations that cannot (or should not) yet be taken out of our community.

As the content and form of trans writing evolves, so the need to write in the theory/memoir dichotomy, or to have a 'debate' set by hostile outsiders should diminish. The current strategy has been to appeal to medical or media gatekeepers to prioritise trans/non-binary voices rather than keep us in an endless argument with people who feel we should not be allowed to exist. Instead, I think we can hope to see more of us writing poetry, plays and fiction, making music and radio or television programmes, art and films, or even creating new genres as readily as we have created new genders. To examine the ways in which being trans or non-binary complicates or changes a whole range of experiences means no longer excluding the reality of sex and sexuality from the picture; incorporating it into an expanded *écriture trans* may help us to overcome any fear of transphobic detractors, and take the creativity unleashed by Cixous, Stone and others into unprecedented places. Through this, we might even realise the French equivalent of the English 'transgender' and become truly *trans-genre*.

Mal Issue 1, Autumn 2018

A SENSE OF COMMUNITY: ON LISETTA CARMI

On New Year's Eve 1964, Lisetta Carmi was invited to a party in Genoa. A former concert pianist who was four years into a new career, Carmi was not yet well known as a photographer, although she had a reputation in her home city for her recent series, 'Genova Porto' (Genoa Port, 1964), for which she had pretended to be a local docker's cousin to gain site access and then documented the harsh conditions under which they worked. The party was for Genoa's clandestine community of male-to-female cross-dressers and transsexual women, who mostly lived in the former Jewish ghetto of the Via del Campo neighbourhood in the city centre. Some of them worked at the docks by day and cross-dressed by night; one provided Carmi with this exclusive invitation, trusting her to depict them sensitively.

Carmi spent the next few years taking photographs of the group, moving to the city centre to be closer to them. She did not ask them to pose for her images, preferring to show them going about their daily lives – dressing and putting on make-up, cooking and dining together or (in some cases) earning a living through sex work. Rather than exhibit them, Carmi chose to collect her inquisitive photographs into a book, *I Travestiti* (The Transvestites), which was published in November 1972. Accompanying the images were texts by the renowned psychoanalyst Elvio Fachinelli, who helped her find a publisher (Essedi Editrice) for a project that not many people wanted to touch. Fachinelli's interviews focused on the participants' educations and family backgrounds, including how much their families knew about their gender identities, but the process was far from easy: he even had to ask Carmi to sit in on the conversations after the interviewees started kissing him and pulling his trousers down.

The earliest stirrings of the Italian LGBT movement were occurring as Carmi was documenting Genoa's gender-variant community, yet she found that booksellers were as reticent as publishers about her work. Asking around, Carmi discovered that the few shops who had agreed to stock the book kept it under the counter. Writer and journalist Barbara Alberti rescued *I Travestiti*: she bought every copy, quietly distributing them to 'intelligent people' who would not baulk at the subject matter. Carmi never attempted to reprint *I Travestiti*, but now, almost 50 years later – at a time when trans and non-binary people are far more visible, if not accepted, across the Western world – and 35 years after she gave up photography, these images are finally being exhibited, most recently at Galerie Antoine Levi in Paris, the Centro Pecci in Prato and the Museo di Roma in Rome.

Carmi's portraits are intimate and empathetic, giving the subjects a rare chance to reveal themselves: sometimes literally, as in the photograph of an unnamed transvestite hitching up her skirt to expose the top of her stockings, or another pulling down a part of her dress to reveal her breast, the lighting and angle (most likely deliberately) making it impossible to tell if she is a cross-dresser or transsexual. The important thing, which Carmi manages to convey, is her subjects' mixed feelings: not about their gender identities, but about the joy of finding a time to express it, and about capturing it in a photograph that will record a moment that cannot be permanently lived, at least not without painful social consequences. Such bittersweet emotions frequently spring from loneliness, but Carmi was careful to portray something often absent from early representations of trans women: a sense of community. Her subjects are seen helping each other with their dress and make-up, smiling and hugging one another, tenderly expressing their love for each other in their bedrooms, or enjoying the embrace of a man.

In one especially striking image, the transvestite who adorned the original cover of Carmi's book holds up a framed photograph of herself as a man; only her distinctive nose reveals that she is the same person. Several pictures subtly bring in another contrast: between religious conservatism and self-expression. They may not directly reference the Biblical passages that forbid a man to wear women's clothing, but the images of Christ and other holy figures above some of the transvestites allude to a powerful system of oppression. If such contrasts feel like tropes or clichés now, they did not at the time – very few people had thought to collect images of cross-dressers or transsexual women, except to illustrate sexological texts that were barely known beyond their professional circles. The conditions for such individuals were similar everywhere, with many people feeling the schism between their male and female identities in isolation or being ostracised for coming out. Carmi, to her credit, did not employ the before-and-after canard used in so many transsexual narratives, and certainly did not give in to voyeurism or sensationalism, which helps explain why her work has aged so well.

One new revelation that has emerged from the recent exhibitions of Carmi's work is her use of two cameras: a black and white one, with which she took the photographs in *I Travestiti*; and one that captured colour images, rediscovered by the manager of Carmi's archive, Gianni Martini. The shadowy monochrome pictures emphasize her subjects' night-time existences, hinting at a sense of marginality, but the colour ones feel less melancholic and far more playful. The influence of post-war Hollywood glamour on Carmi's subjects – many of whom named themselves after actors and singers – also becomes more obvious, notably in the photographs of Cristina, a transsexual woman with an astonishing blonde beehive, thick black eyeliner and mascara, sat on her bed in stockings and a mauve nightdress that matches her lips. In the fullness of their colour and divorced from Fachinelli's accompanying texts, I found it easier to connect emotionally with these women, placing them amongst my trans foremothers and wishing I could have spoken to them about their lives and identities. In an interview, Martini told me that only one was still alive and able to visit the recent exhibition, but many of Carmi's subjects had maintained a friendship with her beyond the end of the project and were grateful that their existences had been marked in a way that – we can only speculate – those of so many other trans people were not.

I was unable to talk to Carmi about her photographs – she is now 95 years old, quite deaf and does not leave the small village in Puglia where she lives – but, in a previous interview, she stated how she wanted to be a boy, like her two older brothers, when she was growing up, and that she did not wish to fulfil the social convention for young women by getting married. Her guiding principle for *I Travestiti* was very simple: she felt that everyone should have the right to express themselves as they wished. Having been expelled from high school when Benito Mussolini passed the racial laws against Italian Jews in 1938, forcing her family into exile in Switzerland until the end of World War II, Carmi knew the huge personal cost of discrimination and had developed a strong sense of empathy: like many in Italy after the collapse of fascism, she supported the Communist Party for a time. She got into photography when she brought a camera on a trip to record the ancient songs of Puglia's Jewish community and found that people were impressed by her images.

Carmi's practice was incredibly varied: she took pictures of Provo – a group of left-wing artists and activists from the Netherlands who staged non-violent insurrections against the Dutch authorities in 1967 – and reported from the Troubles in Northern Ireland in 1975. As well as chronicling the *travestiti*, Carmi took many portraits of noted figures, such as the artist Lucio Fontana, the filmmaker Joris Ivens and the poet Ezra Pound – notorious for his vocal support of fascism after he moved to Italy in 1924. Despite having begun her photographic career in reaction to an exhibition of fascist-era art in 1960, Carmi felt appalled by the US military's decision to keep Pound in a steel cage for three weeks after he was arrested for treason when American troops found him in Pisa in 1945. Twenty years later, she sought to depict the humanity that lay beneath Pound's poetry (which she held in great esteem) rather than the inhumanity behind his politics, but Pound, by then in his early 80s, was no longer speaking. Carmi did not need words: she knocked on his door, spent four minutes taking 20 photographs of the writer in his dressing gown, then left. The images show Pound looking startled, haunted, regretful and yet calm; they end with him turning away. Other journalists only saw a doddering old man and felt they had wasted their time; Carmi's series won the prestigious Prix Niépce for Italian photography.

After meeting a guru in Jaipur in 1976, Carmi founded an ashram in Cisternino three years later and retired from photography altogether in 1984. Her images of Pound may have remained famous, but her portraits of the previously voiceless trans women of Genoa deserve to be far better known – slowly, the world is starting to see the same humanity in them, and people like them, as did Carmi.

Frieze Masters Issue 8, 2019

GENDER GENRES: ON THE EMERGENCE OF TRANSGENDER LITERATURE

Two novels issued this year by large publishers – *Paul Takes the Form of a Mortal Girl* by Andrea Lawlor (Picador) and *Confessions of the Fox* by Jordy Rosenberg (Penguin Random House) – suggest the emergence of a transgender literature that is ready to make an impact on mainstream culture. Or, more accurately, the emergence of a literature that puts trans and non-binary characters at its heart, written by openly trans authors who draw from lived experience.

We can trace trans representation in literature back to the post-war period, with gender-variant characters appearing throughout the 20th century, and especially after US transsexual woman Christine Jorgensen shot to global fame in December 1952. Gay male authors often featured cross-dressers, transvestites or transsexual people in their narratives – Jean Genet's *Our Lady of the Flowers* (1943), Gore Vidal's *Myra Breckinridge* (1968) and Severo Sarduy's *Cobra* (1972), for instance. Yet, these characters usually served to show the diversity of queer subculture or to make a point about the rules of gender, rather than to illustrate the realities of trans living. That task was left to the transsexual memoir, with *Christine Jorgensen: A Personal Autobiography* (1967) and *Conundrum* (1974) by British travel writer Jan Morris its most famous examples. In 1987, trans artist Sandy Stone published her influential essay 'The "Empire" Strikes Back: A Post-Transsexual Manifesto', in which she argued that previous memoirs had not properly addressed the space – physical, psychological or social – between 'male' and 'female'. Stone concluded that trans people should publicly explore such terrain through writing, creating not just new gender identities but also new genres to convey them.

This prompted a 1990s wave of North American trans writers documenting their experiences in texts that combined memoir, theory, activism and cultural criticism – all published on small presses or in underground zines, such as *Gender Trash from Hell* (1993-95). However, there are few examples of noteworthy fiction. One exception is Leslie Feinberg's *Stone Butch Blues* (1993): barely fictionalised, the book's protagonist shared many of Feinberg's experiences but its classification as a novel freed the author to write a work of social realism. Many of Feinberg's contemporaries also rejected the conventional memoir format, but most stuck to non-fiction: their texts aimed to help a traditionally disparate community organise against transphobia. Questions were asked about who represented trans people in fiction and how but, *Stone Butch Blues* aside, the task of answering them through creative practice remained secondary.

Throughout the 2010s, trans people – in the West, at least – have won more rights and representation, although the scale of reaction from both the conservative right and trans-exclusionary feminists means that these victories remain far from secure. Nonetheless, authors inspired by Stone, Feinberg and others have increasingly begun to explore what a literature by, about and for trans people (though not exclusively) might look like. Small publishers have played a key role in this – notably New York's Topside Press, established in 2011 exclusively for trans authors. Works such as Imogen Binnie's *Nevada* (2013) and Casey Plett's *A Safe Girl to Love* (2014) helped demonstrate that fiction could convey trans experiences to a broader audience than theoretical texts. In the UK, trans authors have also found creative expression in forms other than fiction, including the poetry of Jay Bernard, Nat Raha and Verity Spott, among others. Roz Kaveney crossed between the two with *Tiny Pieces of Skull*: a semi-autobiographical novel written in 1988 and rejected by publishers before finally being issued by a small press, Team Angelica, in 2015.

As well as using writing to help shape the future of the community, trans academics and activists have explored its past, looking not just at the development of hormonal and surgical treatments for transsexual people but also at how legal, medical and social discourses have constituted their identities. When postmodern approaches to history assert that we should not retrospectively ascribe identities to people, how should we depict cross-dressing individuals who lived before German sexologist Magnus Hirschfeld initiated a gender-identity language in *The Transvestites* (1910)?

Fiction can be a useful tool in such cases, allowing the writer to speculate about a character's motivations in times when gender dysphoria could not be openly expressed. Rosenberg's *Confessions of the Fox* (2018) re-imagines the 18th-century British criminal and jailbreaker Jack Sheppard as a trans man: there is no historical evidence that Sheppard was trans, so Rosenberg invents it. Meanwhile, US author E. J. Levy's forthcoming novel, *The Cape Doctor*, about

Irish surgeon James Barry, has already caused controversy. Assigned female at birth, Barry lived as a man until he died in 1865. Levy, however, has used female pronouns when describing Barry despite clear evidence he used male ones and asked not to be undressed before death to avoid his identity being discredited.

My own historical fiction – including 'The Woman in the Portrait' (2014) and my forthcoming volume of short stories about British trans people from the Victorian era to the present – has avoided speculation about real-life characters whose gender identity might be contested. The fact that such issues can come to the fore, however, suggests that the trans and non-binary community is gaining confidence in its creative expression and is able to fight on more fronts than against legal or social injustices alone. These debates will feed into a literature that is politically dynamic and aesthetically daring, with Lawlor's and Rosenberg's works heralding its arrival into a wider critical consciousness.

Frieze Issue 203, May 2019

PAUL TAKES THE FORM OF A MORTAL GIRL BY ANDREA LAWLOR

Paul Takes the Form of a Mortal Girl is a cross-over novel. Not only in the sense that its protagonist, Paul, shifts continually between sexes and genders depending on what he considers the most exciting, or expedient. But also in that Lawlor originally published the book in 2017 via an independent outlet, Rescue Press. Its popularity with critics and readers alike has led a larger publisher, Vintage, to reissue it in Lawlor's native United States, and Picador to publish it in the United Kingdom. Together with *Confessions of the Fox*, which – written by Lawlor's friend Jordy Rosenberg – reimagines the eighteenth-century English thief, jailbreaker and folk hero Jack Sheppard as a trans man – it has become one of the first novels by a trans or non-binary author to move outside smaller presses. Does this mark the point when fiction by and *about* (if not exclusively *for*) trans and non-binary people – a genre that has not existed for very long, but which draws on a long line of autobiographical and theoretical writing – breaks into the literary mainstream? Might bringing such trans and non-binary perspectives and discourses to an audience help to change the way in which authors more widely think about gender?

Like *Confessions of the Fox, Paul Takes the Form of a Mortal Girl* is set in the past. Lawlor's is a recent past, though, and one in which trans authors were still finding their voices: the early 1990s. In an influential text first published in 1987, The "Empire" Strikes Back: A Post-Transsexual Manifesto, trans theorist and artist Sandy Stone argued that since Lili Elbe's *Man into Woman* was published in 1933, transition memoirs had failed to adequately explore the physical, psychological or social space in between 'male' and 'female'. In this void, Stone argued, transphobic feminists have been able to dominate the narrative about transsexual people's conceptions of gender expression and motives for transitioning, and the medical and social structures through which trans identities were constituted. In response, Stone asked trans and non-binary authors to write not just more honestly but also more inventively about their experiences. Seeing themselves as inscribed bodies, whose very existence disrupted established notions of sex and gender would, in turn, help them to create new textual genres to narrate their lives.

Stone did not mention fiction; at that point, there had been little published by trans or non-binary authors. Most of those who took up Stone's demand over the following decade mixed genres in their quest for what American author, performance artist and playwright Kate Bornstein called, in her influential text *Gender Outlaw: On Men, Women and the Rest of Us* (1994), 'a transgendered writing style'. Sticking mainly to non-fiction, these authors combined autobiographical material with reflections on gay and lesbian activism, second and third-wave feminist theory, as well as the representation of trans people in the media. They did so to directly challenge widespread transphobia, publishing works that talked about how discrimination manifested itself in media and culture, employment and (the lack of) public safety, interpersonal relationships and other parts of everyday life. One notable exception was Leslie Feinberg's *Stone Butch Blues* (1993) – subtitled 'A Novel' to state that the book complicated this category. Feinberg said in an interview that loosely fictionalising hir life story (and deliberately choosing a 'bad' pseudonym, 'Jess Goldberg', for the central character) allowed hir to 'be more brutally honest' about the challenges faced by gender non-conforming people in the United States around the time of the Stonewall riots in 1969 – when *Stone Butch Blues* is set – than 'if I were telling my own story.' Beyond this, this wave of authors used their writing to challenge transphobia and to build community, dealing directly with social and political issues. This left a gap that has only recently begun to be filled: Topside Press was established in New York in 2013 with the aim of publishing works by trans authors, having early successes with Imogen Binnie's road-trip novel *Nevada* (2013) and Casey Plett's volume of short stories, *A Safe Girl to Love* (2014). Meanwhile, British author Roz Kaveney's semi-autobiographical *Tiny Pieces of Skull*, rejected by publishers in 1988, finally reached print in 2015 through Team Angelica, a London-based independent press dedicated to LGBT-themed works.

Written over a fifteen-year period, *Paul Takes the Form of a Mortal Girl* gestures towards this Nineties gap. Adopting a similarly conversational tone to Bornstein, Feinberg and others, it uses a clearly fictional form to answer Stone's call for writing that creates new genders, if not genres. Its protagonist, Paul Polydoris, is a young bartender at the only gay club in Iowa City in 1993, who studies queer theory and film (where he reads Derrida and Foucault but not Bornstein or Feinberg, although Judith Butler almost inevitably pops up), makes zines, and has a 'dyke best friend'. His world is, in many ways, a Nineties update of Goldberg's in *Stone Butch Blues*. Lawlor sets it up with a similar vivacity, introducing bars with 'five or six dykes with chains on their plaid pants, tattoos on every surface, fucked-up hair', grunge bands playing whose lyrics reference Maya Deren, the mostly female gig-goers staying up all night and having sex in dingy toilets.

Paul spends a lot of his time dating and fucking, practices that are both complicated by his secret ability to transform his body, instantaneously, through sheer force of will. (How this power works is not something that is documented in any detail, though it is something that Paul appears to use relatively casually.) Over time, Paul's brief relationships and sexual encounters as a gay man and a lesbian aggregate into a complex history. Notably, Lawlor resists assimilating Paul – who is often called Polly by his friends and lovers – into a 'normal' (that is, *straight*) context. Rather, Paul only feels comfortable around people who *like* being queer. That subculture *is* the novel's world – a world that consists of gay and lesbian bars, BDSM clubs, women-only festivals, Riot Grrl bands and zines, and Film Studies classes that focus on underground queer filmmakers like Kenneth Anger. All this differentiates *Paul Takes the Form of a Mortal Girl* from the transition memoirs Stone critiqued, which often followed a male-to-female person through a process of coming out as transsexual, and then the struggle of trying to retain a stake in bourgeois society. Such conventions appear to only flicker on the edges of Paul's consciousness, as he *detourns* ACT UP's slogan about silence into 'Heterosexuality = marriage = death'.

Paul Takes the Form of a Mortal Girl is fun, and frequently hilarious. Those familiar with academic cultures will appreciate Paul's ranking of his professors' stylishness by discipline and area of historical interest, where he concludes (correctly, I would say) that 'Marxists and queers in any period always shot to the top'. The brief gag about Paul reading Michel Foucault's *Discipline and Punish* in a BDSM club feels a touch predictable; the line about him wanting to be a classy submissive 'like Genet or Violette Leduc', meanwhile, comes as an amusing surprise. At the same time, Lawlor's prose is full of subtle asides about how gender is performed, such as Paul's self-assured observation that 'pretty girls were always doing stuff to look less pretty', and his eventual failure to become a convincing drag queen when trying to find a way to earn money provides an intelligent plot twist. For all his lengthy analysis of songs that 'fuck with gender', fucking with gender in a more typically queer way – that fans of, let's say, Ru Paul's Drag Race might recognise – proves beyond him, because his constant shape-shifting means that he has not learned the high-camp stylings of drag performance, but instead has found a more restrained gender expression that will allow him to 'pass' as a woman.

Though Lawlor's novel is not overt in its formal experimentation (besides the incorporation of a few fairy tale asides into its chapters), it is written in a way that short-circuits not just the established transition narrative, but also the need that many trans and non-binary people feel to clarify their identities, and have them understood by others. Although the narrator uses male pronouns for Paul throughout, rather than gender-neutral ones, his gender identity is never fully clarified. His feeling that he 'belong[s] in all the genders' is crucial to the plot from its outset; the narrator casts him 'with all the other girls' even when he presents as male. His ability to change his body on a whim, rather than through the lengthy Gender Identity Clinic process, frees Lawlor from the linear conventions of transition narratives; it also moves Paul beyond the question of 'passing' as a woman in order to avoid transphobic violence. Instead, choosing clothing becomes something more positive, and more enjoyable: a matter of 'the story he was telling' on a night out – that is, who he hopes to attract. 'Passing' becomes something *playful* rather than repressive, as Paul watches the women he finds desirable and enjoys the process of becoming more like them, shifting between gay male subcultures and lesbian ones with relative ease.

As the novel progresses however, it becomes clear that while these transformations are socially complex, requiring that Paul keep two sets of gender norms afloat in his mind, the physical mutations aren't so simple either. Maintaining his 'girl body' for long periods of time proves to be exhausting, and still incurs anxiety over 'passing'. When he attends the notoriously trans-exclusionary Michigan Womyn's Festival – in infatuated pursuit of animal rights activist and committed lesbian Diane – he spends much of his time worrying about being exposed, even at the same time as he feels himself to have been 'victorious over his erstwhile penis'. When they do finally get together, Diane worries that Paul/Polly will eventually tire of being a girl and change back. Their relationship falters as a result: the very power that removes the issue of Paul's body being read differently to his gender presentation, it turns out, creates just as many problems as it solves.

Lawlor's is a queer novel as much as it is a trans one, and Paul's experiences are shaped by his experience of homophobia as much as they are by prejudice against gender non-conformity. Paul is aware, though, that such distinctions hold little meaning for their oppressors or, as he bluntly puts it: 'They don't worry about alienating us when they're beating the crap out of some baby drag queen.' Why be polite to straight society, Paul suggests, when it will never be reciprocated – a point Lawlor reinforces with a subtle reference to a headline about a 'Woman Who Posed as a Man … Found Slain With 2 Others', whom readers may recognise as Brandon Teena, raped and murdered in Nebraska in December 1993 after being outed as a trans man. In addition to the ongoing violence perpetrated by those Bornstein terms 'gender defenders', the spectre of HIV/AIDS haunts the novel. Lawlor quietly hints towards it when an important person from Paul's past dies, and deals with the way people at the time often felt unable to speak honestly about this cause of death by presenting a list of Paul's memories about his deceased ex. Meanwhile Paul reflects on how his youth offers some 'protection from what the older guys, those memorial-weary men in their twenties, thirties, forties, what they were losing'.

One of Paul's most intelligent conclusions is about how becoming cool requires work, and is 'relational and conceptual', making it a more meritocratic aspiration than being attractive. Paul's preference for people who make the effort to be cool (especially if they do not always flaunt it) over the 'aristocracy of genetics' is expressed near the end of a novel that is full of sex, in a way that most trans memoirs are not. (An obvious exception is Kate Bornstein's *Queer and Pleasant Danger*, published in 2012, which is full of graphic descriptions of sadomasochistic encounters, and which also subverts the conventions of such memoirs, which had become quite unfashionable amongst trans writers, by focusing on Bornstein's life before and after her time with the Church of Scientology rather than before and after transition.) By telling a story about how unconventionally gendered bodies have sex through a shape-shifting protagonist, Lawlor avoids any prurience or sensationalism about trans or non-binary bodies, while also threading the difficulties of learning and re-learning codes of sexual attraction throughout the plot. In this, the novel feels as much like a worthy, contemporary response to Virginia Woolf's *Orlando* (1928) as it does to Sandy Stone's manifesto: Lawlor manages to find an intriguing middle-ground between Woolf's playful modernism and the perhaps more realistic, observational approaches of Binnie, Plett and Kaveney. How much space the novel opens up for trans and non-binary writers remains to be seen, let alone how far such writers might, in the future, come to influence the ways in which cisgender authors write about gender identity and sexuality. But it feels like it could herald a new wave of trans and non-binary writing – one which engages with the transition memoir and transgender theory but also thinks about how the use of characters who move beyond the old categories of 'male' and 'female' might reshape established literary genres.

The White Review, 5 July 2019

POETIC POLITICS

The Argentine-Brazilian anthropologist, sociologist, and poet Néstor Perlongher was one of the most important figures in Latin American literature, and among the most influential cultural theorists to emerge from Argentina's gay liberation movement of the 1970s, which was just as febrile as its French, Italian, British and American counterparts. He is little-known in the Anglophone world; however Frances Riddle's translation of *Plebeian Prose*, a volume of essays, poems, interviews, and stories selected by Osvaldo Baigorria and Christian Ferrer originally published in 1997, has brought Perlongher's forensic, furious, and often humorous writing into English for the first time. Published by Polity, it includes an introduction by Cecilia Palmeiro that promises that despite Perlongher's AIDS-related death in 1992, his work 'provides the tools to formulate a radical critique of the new Alt-Right's focus on identity and nationalism'.

Born in Buenos Aires in 1949, Perlongher joined the Trotskyist *Partido Obrero* (Workers' Party) as a student but soon left, disappointed over its failure to support 'the gay cause', and specifically the *Frente de Liberación Homosexual* (FLH). He agitated for the FLH to take an 'ultra-leftist' line, working to combine their struggles despite the Argentine left – echoing a line taken elsewhere – seeing homosexuality as an imperialist perversion. Seeing patriarchy as a construction that led to (and certainly pre-dated) capitalism, and disillusioned that the Cuban and Russian revolutions did not dismantle that patriarchy or even homophobic oppression, Perlongher wrote about how opposition to the machismo that ran through Latin American society might be expressed through writing, political movements and the human body.

After a set of sixty-nine questions and answers that gently introduce his thought, *Plebeian Prose* opens with its strongest section, compiling Perlongher's articles on Desire and Politics. Deft editing means readers are thrown straight into Perlongher's assessment of Argentina's homosexual archetypes, and his defence of the effeminate, openly gay *locas* and *maricas*, who suffered from homophobia, misogyny and policing of self-expression far more than the more traditionally masculine *chongos* who only occasionally had sex with other men, and were eventually disowned by gay movements that sought greater 'respectability'. Perlongher, who referred to himself in the feminine and sympathised with women, drag queens and transsexual people, especially the sex workers who were frequently murdered in a style he denounced as paramilitary, had a simple demand of politicians, the police, and wider society: 'All we want is to be left to our own desires.' (This also applied to drug use: Perlongher endured a stretch in prison for his recreational consumption.)

The entries that trace the history of Argentina's FLH, and chart the country's regulation of sexuality back to the 1930s (considering its relationship to the military and the church) are fascinating, but it is Perlongher's documentation of a subculture vanishing before him that are most provocative. His analysis of how the 'normalisation' of homosexuality stripped it of its mystery, perpetuated divisions within queer groups and enabled those who crafted a socially acceptable 'gay' model of behaviour to move 'to the centre', marginalising others in the process, is acute – and will be familiar to those who have followed a similar process in the global north. Writing about how AIDS brought bodily fluids and sex back into a rights-based discussion that had tried to forget them, Perlongher characterised the right-wing neglect, or celebration, of the crisis — in Argentina and Brazil as in the UK and US – as a tactic to suppress the erotic energy unleashed by the 1970s liberation movements. In response, he demanded that we view sexual identities not as static 'types' but as historically contingent, and adaptable to changing political circumstances, such as the fall of the Argentine and Brazilian military dictatorships – advice that is relevant now, in a time of far-right pushback against (even heavily commodified) LGBT+ identities.

Perlongher's prose spits off the page, especially when discussing the people he most cares for, in passages such as: 'the darling transvestite is not alone: she glides, on the prowl, among a multitude of comrades, each more extravagant than the next.' His politics were always poetic – because, as the introduction puts it, politics without poetics is merely bureaucracy. Besides the polemics and poems featured here, there are plenty of articles in which he creates a canon of Latin American authors whose fiction combined modern and postmodern literary techniques with a radically queer social critique, in a style he labelled as neo-baroque. The writers he mentions, such as Argentine playwright Copi, who (like Perlongher) wrote an inflammatory work about Eva Perón, and Cuban exile Severo Sarduy (who, Perlongher notes, was far more revolutionary than many authors based in Cuba after 1959) deserve, like Perlongher himself, to be more widely read outside Latin America. This anthology offers a valuable introduction to all of them.

Tribune Issue 5, Autumn 2019

TRYING TO SURVIVE 'ON VENUS': P. STAFF AT THE SERPENTINE

P. Staff's site-specific exhibition at the Serpentine Sackler Gallery, 'On Venus', deals with biopolitics, looking at the ways in which exchanges between bodies, ecosystems and institutions affect human consciousness and behaviours – especially for queer, trans and non-binary people. A new video work, also entitled *On Venus*, features two sections: the first presents warped archival footage of industrial farming for the production of meat, fur and hormones; the second features a poem about life on the uninhabitable planet Venus, conjuring a state of near-death that has parallels with trying to survive as a queer person in a heteronormative world. The surrounding installation impinges on the gallery itself, confronting entrants with a gargoyle weathered by acidic rain, a symbol of the worsening climate crisis, harshly lit against a reflective floor. The defamiliarising effect of Staff's intervention rubs up against the history of the building, which was originally used as a gunpowder store. Pipes suspended from the ceiling leak acid into steel barrels, at once evoking chemical corrosion, the sharing of bodily fluids, and the uncontrollable, networked spread of viruses and data.

Staff also uses acid for a less abstract part of the show – in a series of intaglio etchings documenting British tabloid articles from 2017, which wrongly claimed that Ian Huntley, notoriously convicted for the murder of two 10-year-old girls in Soham, Cambridgeshire, in 2002, planned to undergo gender reassignment in order to be moved to a women's prison. Pushed as part of a vicious, media-generated backlash against trans and non-binary rights and recognition, the mendacious story was eventually retracted, or deleted from newspaper websites, which of course garnered far less attention than the original headlines.

'I'm very selective about what I'll engage with, even within the trans community, let alone the British media's coverage of trans lives,' says Staff, in response to my question about how to cope with immersing oneself in transphobic discourses. (I'd ignored these headlines at the time, despite my long-standing interest in how the UK media frames trans issues, because I simply couldn't handle it.) 'To others, conversations about our lives are an intellectual game that bears no relation to anyone's lived reality but, even then, the Huntley story felt so cynical from the start. It was so obvious why the papers chose him, and that allowed me to disconnect a little and look at it analytically. I would have ignored it if I hadn't noticed all the clarifications and retractions.'

Trans and non-binary issues are most explicitly referred to in the etchings, but they also run throughout the exhibition, feeding into wider themes. In the video work, I noticed the extraction of urine from pregnant mares. This gets turned into Premarin – a key ingredient in oestrogen pills, on which I and many other trans women depend for our existence. 'In the film, I deliberately showed a range of animal commodification,' Staff tells me. 'I made a conscious decision to build in hormonal regimes as well as meat, leather, etc. For you and me, this has a meaning that it doesn't for others.' Until recently, many trans people – including myself – have felt excluded from, and unrepresented within mainstream cultural discourse. As such, it interested me that Staff's exhibition worked on two levels, with trans and non-binary people more likely to spot certain signifiers. 'In a way, that's a condition of our existence,' confides Staff. 'There is always a certain double-speak happening – questions of 'Do you read me? Do I read you?' I don't feel conflicted about that being part of the work.'

The depictions of slaughter in *On Venus* reminded me of a scene in Rainer Werner Fassbinder's *In a Year of 13 Moons* (1978), in which a transsexual woman who formerly worked as a butcher walks a friend through an abattoir, making a sledgehammer-subtle connection between the animals' bodies and her own. Staff hadn't seen the film, saying that, 'Often I'm trying to talk about biography and narrative when discussing transness; maybe a pharmaceutical regime rather than a surgical one.' They refer instead to theorists such as Donna Haraway or Paul B. Preciado, the latter of whose *Testo Junkie* (2008) combined personal reflections on using testosterone with a historical analysis of the pharmaceutical industry. These ideas, and the discomfiting tone of Preciado's text, inform Staff's work. Their previous video, *Weed Killer* (2017), 'put a narrative around chemotherapy into dialogue with a conversation about pharmaceutical regimes, knowing it felt uncomfortable,' as Staff explains. More present in this exhibition – and the catalogue – is Eva Hayward, whose work on architecture, sensation and transition has influenced Staff's efforts to 'trace a line between these newspaper stories and the erosion of a building, and the industrial farming methods seen in the video'.

Working with the Serpentine presented ethical challenges as well as philosophical ones. Last June, its CEO

Yana Peel resigned after media reports uncovered her financial links to the Israeli cyber-tech firm, NSO Group Technologies while, in April, the Sackler family suspended their donations to the gallery following a flurry of artist-led demonstrations over their company's highly addictive OxyContin painkiller, which is feeding into the US opioid addiction crisis. 'This is very present in the work,' says Staff, adding that the curator, Claude Adjil, who Staff first met in 2013, 'invited me to do the show knowing that my work often deals with pharmaceutical regimes.' 'We're in a moment of massive, and completely necessary restructuring in the art world, and it presents difficult choices for artists,' Staff continues. 'This is good. I want us to be faced with difficult decisions because everyone has been sailing through these issues as if they were meaningless for decades, letting money and influence ease them into comfort with things we shouldn't be comfortable with.'

Regarding their decision to go ahead with the show, Staff says that 'I made a conscious choice to talk about it sideways. If you're aware of the Sackler issues, there is a reading of the work that can emerge through that. I started working on the exhibition before we learned about Yana: what made me want to keep working here was having conversations with the curatorial team, admin staff and others about their thoughts on it. I was glad to have relationships with friends who asked me if I wanted to persist, but I think the most important thing is solidarity between artists and art workers, and I felt supported by the Serpentine staff throughout.'

Frieze, 20 November 2019

WRITE ALL THE OTHERS: MCKENZIE WARK ON THE FUTURE OF TRANS LITERATURE

Trans and non-binary people have long struggled to find effective language and useful forms to express themselves in the face of widespread transphobia in the media, politics and society. Throughout the 20th century, academics, activists and writers gradually shifted their focus from memoirs that would explain transsexual living towards more theoretical texts that incorporated personal material but eschewed the autobiographical form. Following Sandy Stone's imperative, in her influential '*The "Empire" Strikes Back: A Post-Transsexual Manifesto*' (1987), for such writers to create new genres in order to explore new genders, over the last 20 years this literary subculture has blossomed into a vibrant world of novels, short stories, poetry, plays, essays and journalism. *Reverse Cowgirl* (2020), the latest book by writer and scholar McKenzie Wark, follows in this tradition, while also subverting the linear form of transition memoirs, interweaving fragments of biography and auto-fiction with emails and Facebook posts. Wark began her literary and academic career in Australia during the 1980s, and is the author of numerous books, including *Hacker Manifesto* (2004), *Gamer Theory* (2007) and last year's *Capital Is Dead: Is This Something Worse?* Wark and I became friends in 2013, after I interviewed her about her work on the post-war *avant-garde* movement Situationist International.

Juliet Jacques: I'd like to ask you about the line on the back cover of *Reverse Cowgirl*, which says that 'the established narratives of being transgender don't seem to apply' to you. I think every trans person has felt like that – certainly any trans person who has ever picked up a pen and paper.

McKenzie Wark: I was interested in what could happen if traditional versions of the trans narrative got to play with other kinds of formally inventive queer and gender non-conforming nonfiction. I didn't see myself in most of the trans narratives to which I had access. Although, when I read your book *Trans: A Memoir* (2015), I thought: 'That's not my story but, because it exists, I, too, can exist.' Now, different ways of writing about being trans are adding new wrinkles to the narrative, rather than repeating the same stories that medical providers require of us.

JJ: You're 20 years older than me, yet there's a generational handover from me to you because of the weird things that transition does to your sense of lived time. And the fact that I transitioned earlier in my life than you did, partly because I had access to trans writers at a younger age. You situate *Reverse Cowgirl* within a certain line of trans writing by referencing contemporary authors who are not necessarily canonical. Leslie Feinberg is referenced, but not Kate Bornstein, Sandy Stone or other figures from the

1990s. Instead, you bring up Torrey Peters, Paul B. Preciado, Juliana Huxtable – people at the forefront of a new type of trans writing that doesn't use directly autobiographical forms.

MW: The text is meant to read a little bit like the Twitter feed of someone who's fairly literate. If I felt that a quote from another writer related to what I was doing, I included it, but I didn't feel like I had to mention everybody. Stone and Bornstein were very important to me, but didn't make it into the book. I was more drawn to what has happened with new North American trans writing. Imogen Binnie's novel *Nevada* (2013) was a turning point, at least in the world of trans writing that I ended up inhabiting. It's a story about someone several years after they've transitioned, who is not the ideal trans subject and is making mistakes in her life. It wasn't even marketed as a trans book: the cover has this really cool drawing, but doesn't say 'trans' on it in big letters, so you can read the book discreetly on the subway. But its circulation was somewhat limited to Brooklyn-based, white trans women and I wanted to counteract that a bit, so I've included references to Huxtable, a terrific black trans writer, in my book. I was interested in people writing now, some of whom I've met, giving an impression of a collective literary space.

JJ: A lot of older trans memoirs and texts have downplayed or avoided sex altogether, although Bornstein is a notable exception. In my memoir, I didn't talk about sex as much as maybe I'd have liked to. *Reverse Cowgirl*, however, is a book about sex as much as it is about gender, and how they intersect. How did sex open up new ways for you to think about gender and your own gender identity?

MW: I remember reading J. Michael Bailey's book about autogynephilia, *The Man Who Would Be Queen* (2003), which argues that there are 'bad' transsexual women who transition in order to become their own object of desire. I read it secretly in a Barnes & Noble bookstore. For years, that set me back, because I thought: 'Oh, I'm one of these autogynephiliac freaks and not a "real" trans woman.' I wanted to write about the possibility of figuring out that you're trans through gender euphoria experienced sexually. I tried to be a gay man but it never quite worked, and I think there's comedy in writing about that failure, and in writing about heterosexuality when you're trying to be the person that you want to have sex with.

There is a sense in the LGBTQ+ community that we have to move away from narratives of 'inversion' or the early-20th-century idea that gender variance and sexual diversity are always linked, and that's good. But it's constraining to conclude that being trans never has anything to do with sex. Here, I've mapped out a small corner of trans experience so that, hopefully, other people can think through their own gender and sexuality in relation to it. And go on to write about them.

JJ: One of the quotes I picked from your book is by Chris Kraus, who writes in *I Love Dick* (1997): 'My entire state of being has changed because I've become my sexuality: female, straight, wanting to love men, be fucked. Is there a way of living with this life like a gay person, proudly?' Kraus brings up the complications of gendered bodies, how they're received and how they interact with other people sexually, but also deploys an internalised stereotype of gay men. In your text, you start off by thinking of yourself as a queer man and moving within gay male circles in Sydney during the AIDS crisis.

MW: Kraus refers to 'a' rather than 'the' gay person, so readers can 'include themselves out' of that phrase. I think it's always more interesting to differ from, rather than identify with, the text, which is exactly what Kraus enables. She can conceptualise the specific thing she feels in relation to what it's not: the generic idea of gay pride. And she can then long for something like that but different from it, just as, if one were a gay man, one might differ from that received image. I tried to be gay. Being loved and lusted after by gay men made me feel like a woman – an emotional and sexual relation that's comically doomed. The pathos being that I attempted this just before the AIDS pandemic.

JJ: In a chapter titled 'Straight Life', you write about moving from primarily having sex with men to having sex mostly with women, although it's not a linear narrative. I particularly like this passage: 'Nobody needs to read another story by a man about, well, anything really, certainly not another story where the man fucks the woman. So let's just keep to this not novel but less storied dilemma: how does a man whose peak sexual experiences all involve being fucked in the ass go about having sex with a woman? Depends on the woman, of course. Also, here's another wrinkle that makes this maybe a less common story: what if the man in this story who fucks the woman is maybe not a man at all, and what if this man … sorry, this not-man, doesn't know it yet? At least, what if this human, let's say this egg, that wants not to hatch, this thing that wants not to be there, to not exist, is driven by a desire opaque to this human and to most of those around it?'

MW: I probably could've just written about my experience without that preamble, but I felt like there would be comedy in acknowledging what I'm sure is a pretty common experience in certain kinds of trans lives. The opacity struck me as useful: memoirs are so often about figuring oneself out. I wanted to write instead about how we never have any idea who we are. We just move through less or more useful patterns of misunderstanding.

JJ: There's a striking page titled 'You Are Your Attention: A Portrait of McKenzie Wark by the Facebook Algorithm.' It lists things that you've mentioned frequently on Facebook, ranging from left-wing politics, global warming, livestock and freight transport to Walter Benjamin, Lana Turner, hegemony, instant messaging, family, dresses, cashmere, psychoanalysis, gender and social class. Is there a sense that other people, and ultimately other technologies, know us better than we know ourselves?

MW: Facebook lets you see how it categorises you for marketing purposes. Those are some of the things that Facebook thinks of as being 'me', so it can sell me various products. I'm wearing a skirt right now that I bought through a Facebook ad from a brand called Current Mood. Trying to form an identity on social media when all it's trying to do is sell you stuff and monetise your attention can drive anyone – cis or trans – bonkers.

JJ: What has changed about the way that we now constitute our own identities on social media? What do you think about the possibilities of it, as well as the constraints, and the terrifying surveillance implications?

MW: I'm interested in the practice of constructing a subject in the post-broadcast era and the extent to which it's unlike the one we inherited from the golden age of mass popular consumption addressed by scholars at Birmingham's Centre of Contemporary Cultural Studies in the 1970s. When there were only five radio stations, all of them played the same Top 40 tracks; if you got lucky, you might hear a David Bowie song. Some of us figured out, by listening to his music, that we're at least not like straight people: 'Not sure if you're a boy or a girl.' Precisely, thank you.

Whereas now you can find any subculture or subjectivity online and create your own queer or trans sensibility out of them. But you can also make yourself into a neo-Nazi because that's easy to find, too. So, this new model of constructing bodies and subjectivities is definitely not an unmediated good.

JJ: My identity is not just determined by my queerness and transness. I'm really interested in the way *Reverse Cowgirl* also talks about Marxism and communism, and the affect of your politics – the feeling of constant defeat they bring.

MW: Having been schooled in an old-fashioned version of Marxism, one that was aware that its history was one of defeat, I always sensed who my real comrades were, because all the opportunists and optimists had already abandoned the project. It was important to be around people who lived through 1956 and 1968 – disaster years for international communism – yet who felt, as Samuel Beckett put it in *The Unnamable* (1953): 'I can't go on; I'll go on.'

I find myself a little out of tune with the current Marxist revivalism – people with hammers and sickles in their Twitter bios. How do you restart something you know has already been lost? You can't do it through cosplay; Marx talks directly about the problem of restaging the revolution in the garb of the previous one. But how, then, do you carve out a sense of the possibility of another life in a culture that you know you don't control, where you know your agency is limited?

JJ: There's a passage in the book where you start seeing a man called John, and you describe yourself as his plus-one, the 'handbag': 'I was the girl. This was quite educational. I was not expected to talk except for the purpose of social graces. I was not supposed to have opinions about things. It was permitted for me to agree with John's opinions or shades thereof. I was expected to smooth out disagreements between John and the others. Mostly, I just tried to blend in and observe, a closet communist. At some point, the men would just dismiss themselves to talk business or politics. I would be left with the wives.' Then you talk about how the wives' idea of women's liberation in this context was restricted to their own entry into the upper class.

MW: It's the most heavily fictional part of the book because of Australia's vicious libel laws. It's a composite portrait of some men I dated who have the means to sue me. It was interesting to see ruling-class gay culture; if you were doing the right thing as a property owner, then your sexuality could be overlooked. It was a little like Anaïs Nin's *A Spy in the House of Love* (1954) – I felt like a spy in the house of bourgeois sexuality.

JJ: I've been thinking a lot lately about *Females: A Concern* (2019) by Andrea Long Chu. The book's premise is that everyone is female because everyone is constituted by some sort of lack, which they fill with other people's desires that they then try to fulfil. We've already talked about the way in which your book addresses sexuality and desire. How do you feel about Chu's text and its relation to your own writing?

MW: I really enjoyed *Females* because it does what we did in 1980s theory: take an incredibly counterintuitive and ridiculous premise and build a conceptual language out of it that then collapses. It's theory as play. It's a rarefied taste to engage in theory that way, as if it's a branch of literature. People expect more rectitude or political guidance from theory than Chu is willing to offer. But I loved it because theory is literature. It's just another way of writing and has certain constraints.

JJ: In your recent interview for *Ssense* with Sanja Grozdani⊠, you talk about how scapegoating trans women has become a whole media industry. What do you think trans people, and trans women in particular, can do to combat this, both in our creative work and in the places where we publish?

MW: It's a double bind. There's this desire to engage with transphobia before it spreads further, but then you end up in a positive feedback loop by amplifying it. Yet, you can't ignore the hate, because it propagates. I really appreciate the way you've pushed back in a very public way, while remaining aware of, and navigating, the pitfalls.

You cannot engage with people who don't recognise your humanity, but you can address the people they're trying to persuade to see the way they do. I don't think we achieve that by seeking always to be exemplary subjects. I think we can write about ourselves as fully human, which also means fully flawed. We're more credible as humans if we're not attempting to be perfect and not claiming that, for example, sexuality isn't part of our experience. Yes, our sexualities may be weird, but so are everyone else's! Take autogynephilia, for instance – the moments when you're into yourself sexually. I hope everybody gets to experience that at least once, to look in the mirror and go: 'I'm hot in this gender!'

JJ: Instead, it's pathologised. Do you think that, through writing, it's possible to move the conversation beyond cisgender expectations of us and our need to challenge them? Are there any writers who you believe have managed to do that?

MW: It's important to be part of a larger literary conversation, but also that we have writing for each other. I'm looking forward to Peters' *Detransition, Baby*, which is due to be published in early 2021. It asks questions about what trans life is like ten years after transition, when you might just want to have a family and a stable life. Why should we be denied that?

JJ: As trans and non-binary literature develops over the next ten or 20 years, I hope you and I will continue to be part of it. It will be exciting to see what happens. I think new possibilities will open up.

Frieze Issue 210, April 2020

ON *FEMALES*
BY ANDREA LONG CHU

Andrea Long Chu's first book opens with a provocation: 'Everyone is female.' Soon after, she asserts that this '*everyone hates*' being female, but there are plenty more incitements before she begins to outline what she means by this, including the declaration that 'There are no good female poets, simply because there are no good poets'. To emphasise her point, there follows a 'list of things invented by females', of which (inevitably) some are good and some are bad, including 'the worst books' and 'great art heists', because if everyone is female then everything has been invented by someone female. Chu's list may seem random or even ridiculous, with items seemingly chosen for comic effect. It includes the H-bomb, Spain, telephones, feminism, the patriarchy, and – tellingly – stand-up comedy, before a conclusion calculated to wind up passionate Democrats and Republicans alike, states that 'The entire Supreme Court is female. The entire United States Senate is female. The president is, obviously, a female.'

Chu's short text argues that femaleness is an 'existential condition' in which all human beings are defined by other people's desires, hollowing out their own senses of self in order to make room for, and try to satisfy those desires: 'To be female', she writes, 'is to let someone else do your desiring for you, at your own expense'. Her fundamental provocation lies in her sidestepping of long-standing debates about the locus of desire by removing agency from the equation entirely, arguing that the social construction theory of gender is 'wildly incomplete' rather than untrue. This is because it has focused on how individuals construct their own genders, rather than how that construction is shaped entirely by our psychological need to react to other people's non-consensual social expectations and, especially, their sexual drives towards us. Here, everyone is the Other and everyone is othered; the origins of the desires that everyone projects towards each other can never be known, and nor can the forces that shaped them. This abjection does not apply exclusively to people who identify as women: again aware of the widespread irritation she will cause, Chu concludes her opening broadside by saying: 'I am female. And you, dear reader, you are female, even – especially – if you are not a woman.'

Given that Chu ascribes this abjection universally, *Females* is not and cannot be a call to arms, but it is inspired by Valerie Solanas' incendiary *SCUM Manifesto* (1967), which urged 'civic-minded, responsible, thrill-seeking females to overthrow the government, eliminate the money system, institute complete automation' and, most infamously, 'to destroy the male sex'. Chu argues that Solanas' manifesto 'effectively proposes *misogyny against men*', loathing men for qualities that had traditionally been ascribed to, and demanded from women – 'vanity, submission, narcissistic anxiety, and most of all sexual passivity'. Reminding us that Solanas also hated most women for displaying these characteristics, Chu separates femaleness from womanhood, defining femaleness as 'any psychic operation in which the self is sacrificed to make room for the desires of another'. This means sex is ontological rather than biological – 'to be is to be female', and everyone hates it because it means universal self-negation. It also means that what constitutes *gender* is the defence mechanisms that people adopt in response to this, whether they fight it – which, according to Chu, forms the basis of all politics, not just feminism – embrace it, or fight it at some points and embrace it at others. In this, Chu draws on Judith Butler's theories about gender as a public, performative act, but discards with Butler's ambivalence about its animus: whereas Butler is uncertain about whether gender identities are radical, personal choices or imposed by society, Chu sides unequivocally with the latter.

Written in a form that privileges irony over earnestness, Chu maintains plausible deniability over her words, and excuses herself from any obligation to provide any basis for a political programme. *Females* offers nothing but an ideological quicksand from which no-one can escape, a truth that can only be palatable when it is presented in jest: I picked 'stand-up comedy' from her list for a reason. Writing at Public Seminar, McKenzie Wark (who, like Chu and me, is a trans woman, a point to which I shall return) picks out Chu's discussion of 'commitment to a bit' – that is, setting up a central premise and following it to its logical conclusion, or an absurd conclusion that nonetheless follows discernible internal logic. This concept is drawn from comedians such as Bill Hicks who, if he felt his audience getting complacent, would 'walk the room' with interminable routines that were at best boring and at worst wildly misogynistic (especially his notorious 'Goat Boy' schtick), but in which the humour derived from its being delivered with the utmost intensity. Because it's so sharply funny, the issue of whether Solanas meant for the men-killing part of her *SCUM Manifesto* to be taken seriously has been a fifty-year debate – one that was not applied to the parts of her mission statement that anticipate the concept of fully automated luxury communism (which were largely ignored), let alone works that advocated such violence in the other direction, such as German Expressionist artist/writer Oskar Kokoschka's 1909 play *Murderer, Hope of Woman*, to name just one. My feeling is that it doesn't really matter, but she almost certainly did; Chu casts Solanas as a serious satirist, noting that 'commitment to a bit' means taking Solanas at her word, which is far more interesting than assuming she was joking and then dismissing her text. For her readers, 'Commitment to a bit' means not using Chu's sharp sense of irony as a reason not to carefully consider her argument; for Chu herself, it means stretching her 'everyone is female' premise as far as she possibly can.

It makes sense, then, that Chu decided against writing a manifesto, quoting more from Solanas' 1965 play *Up Your Ass,* about a lesbian sex worker who kills someone (the manuscript of which Warhol lost after Solanas gave it to him in person, which contributed to her decision to shoot him in 1968) than *SCUM*. Under Chu's schema, identity-based politics become impossible, not just because it means no-one can ever feel in control of their own identities, which essentially depend on the goodwill of others, but also because it removes the possibility of singling out any malefactors, or at least anyone who is more responsible for oppression than anyone else – although some people may still be responsible for *more* oppression than others, such as a cisgender man who refuses to acknowledge a trans woman's gender identity. Chu doesn't say it, but by her logic, materialist politics become more relevant as class differences and inequality clearly persist: the idea that everyone is female should not, in itself, prevent humanity from overthrowing the government, eliminating the money system and instituting complete automation. Chu argues that trans people are especially reliant on this goodwill, developing a point made in Julia Serano's *Whipping Girl: A Transsexual Woman on Sexism and the Scapegoating of Femininity* (2007) to say that we rely upon others not just to recognise but also to respect our gender identities in order for those identities to be validated – a kindness that can be, and often is, easily withheld or withdrawn.

In contemporary discourse around trans issues, the people most assertively withholding such kindness, for instance by ostentatiously refusing to use trans and non-binary people's preferred pronouns, are often called TERFs – Trans-Exclusionary Radical Feminists. (They are mostly, but not always, women; they are all female, obviously.) Believing that male and female were chromosomal and unchangeable, Solanas was not positive about trans women, despite being friends with Candy Darling – one of three trans 'superstars' who, like Solanas, appeared in Warhol's films – and suggesting in her manifesto that while such heightened femininity would be a bad model for women, men could 'fulfil' themselves as 'drag queens', even though this was a 'man-made stereotype'. As Michelle Tea points out in a sensitive essay on Solanas in her recent collection *Against Memoir,* which addresses the bad feelings evinced by Solanas' annihilationism and her proximity to anti-trans thought (although not the second wave feminist movement), 'faggot' in the US in the Sixties 'existed as a catch-all slur for anyone presenting as queer or genderqueer'. This means Solanas' grudging allowance for 'faggots who, by their shimmering, flaming example, encourage other men to de-man themselves and thereby make themselves relatively inoffensive' leaves a little room for trans women like Chu (and myself) to engage with Solanas, who was far more nuanced and less intolerant than Janice

Raymond, author of the notorious transphobic feminist text, *The Transsexual Empire: The Making of the Modern She-Male* (1979).

Chu doesn't spend much time on Raymond, who has been extensively discussed by other trans theorists, boiling Raymond's thesis down to the infamous assertion that 'all transsexuals rape women's bodies by reducing the real female form to an artefact, appropriating this body for themselves', which makes transsexuality 'the ultimate . . . conclusion of male possession of women in a patriarchal society'. Although he never expressed familiarity with this line of thought, Bill Hicks said that fundamentalism breeds a lack of irony, but Chu pulls out the core, and obviously unintentional and unspoken, contradiction in Raymond and her like with brutal ease: 'it is an eternal irony of the trans-exclusionary feminist that she regards nothing with greater horror than the prospect of someone's penis getting chopped off'. Having already said of Freud's famous complex that the anxiety is not so much the fear of being castrated as 'the fear that one, having been castrated, *will like it*', Chu both provokes the TERFs and challenges trans/non-binary people who have argued that we don't simply reiterate misogynist stereotypes of femininity by offering a spirited defence of transsexual YouTube star Gigi Gorgeous, whose make-up tutorials shifted into confessional videos and behind-the-scenes looks at gender surgeries without changing tone or intention. Gorgeous commits to her femaleness so much as to become 'a walking, talking advertisement' and Chu admits: 'I love this about her.'

That Chu can speak so intimately, honestly and controversially speaks to a growing confidence in transgender theory, as the growing number of voices finding an outlet means the burden of representation is not shouldered by a handful of people who feel compelled not to misrepresent the 'community'. This confidence is fragile, though, and a book such as this, aimed at a more knowing audience, may be a better forum to challenge its orthodoxies than in high-profile broadsheet op-eds, where Chu (and I, and many other trans/non-binary writers over the last decade) have attempted to convey our experiences, and which have often been the subject of heated debate about how they will lead outsiders to see trans and non-binary people – notably in a *New York Times* piece, entitled 'My New Vagina Won't Make Me Happy', published in November 2018, which was commendable for its raw honesty but caused anxieties about giving ammunition to conservatives who wanted to de-fund such surgeries and transphobes who wanted to outlaw them entirely.

In her 'Post-Transsexual' manifesto, 'The "Empire" Strikes Back' (1987), written in response to Raymond and various transsexual memoirists (but not Solanas), US artist/author Sandy Stone encouraged gender-variant people to use life writing as a basis for social change, constituting themselves as 'a set of embodies texts whose potential for *productive* disruption of structured sexualities and spectra of desire has yet to be explored'. Chu was not yet born when Stone's foundational essay was first published, but shares Stone's willingness to use Raymond as a launchpad for a counterpoint to existing trans writing, and to draw on her own life to disrupt preconceptions about sexuality and desire. What Chu shares with earlier trans authors such as Kate Bornstein or Leslie Feinberg is an understanding that the lines between memoir, political manifesto and cultural criticism are always blurred, and that finding spaces between genres can be just as productive for us as exploring spaces between genders.

Stone praised Chu's wide-ranging and widely-shared *n+1* essay 'On Liking Women' (2018) – which also responded to Solanas' work, suggesting that rather than thinking all trans women were men, Solanas thought 'all men were closeted trans women' – for 'launching the 'second wave' of trans studies'. Whilst *Females* contains some fascinating insights into the influence of *The Matrix* (1999) on misogynistic alt-right culture, written after both of its directors came out as trans women, I don't feel that it continues such a project, in part because Chu's theory doesn't account well enough for discrimination. Whilst family and friends soon granted me the goodwill of recognising my chosen gender after I came out, I resisted transition for years because nobody was actively encouraging me before then, and some people close to me questioned my decision when I did. My story is not unique, so while Chu talks about her need to transition being an external force in itself – a description that chimed with my experience – how to account for this drive persisting in the face of social and institutional resistance, and especially the idea, which I kept encountering, that transsexual women who didn't 'pass' as well as (say) Gigi Gorgeous were deeply undesirable? Essentially, this comes back to the age-old nature vs. nurture question which, as I said in my memoir about gender reassignment, is of far more concern to people like Raymond who wanted to 'mandate transsexuality out of existence' than to me, trying to navigate a transphobic society, but I could not answer this question even if I wanted to, and nor, I suspect, could Chu.

There are men, known in the community as 'chasers', who consider themselves heterosexual and who are drawn specifically to trans women, a drive that many of whom I've encountered want to conceal. Chu's theory may have been productively expanded with some thoughts on how *their* desires are constructed, given how interestingly and ironically she positions 'sissy porn' – a type of 'meta-pornography' in which women forcibly feminise men and humiliate and abuse them – as a parodic inversion of the alt-right's fantasies of dominating women, and something which misogynists, deep down, want done to them. This underlying proposition – that nobody actually *wants* power, no matter how much they say they do – makes it impossible to build much of a school of thought out of *Females,* and will doubtless infuriate as many people, of all political persuasions, as it intrigues, given its objective not to prove that gender is a social construct, but to expose its redundancy as a category of differentiated identity. And any objection, let alone resistance, proves her point – if we accept the 'bit' to which Chu has committed, then the only way to deal with femaleness is to accept it, however grudgingly, and move on – to the institution of full automation, elimination of the money system or anything else that may concern us.

Unpublished, written November 2019

INVENTING THE FUTURE

Issued as part of Jacaranda Books' #Twentyin2020 list, in which they are publishing twenty Black British writers in a year, Shola von Reinhold's debut novel, *LOTE*, is about exclusion, and how the rediscovery of art and artist marginalised in the past can provide an impetus for new creative cultures. Its queer, Black, working-class protagonist, Mathilda Adamarola, helps at an archive, where she explores her fascination with the 'Bright Young Things' – the bohemian aristocrats, socialites and writers of inter-war London – building a personal canon of lesser-known figures who she calls her 'Transfixions'. Some of these, by her own admission, are 'recherché white queers' such as author/aesthete Stephen Tennant, and the shipping heiress and *Negro* anthology editor Nancy Cunard. But Mathilda is already tiring of histories that don't include people like her when she finds a photograph of the long-forgotten Black poet Hermia Druitt, who lived on the edges of the Bloomsbury Group, Mathilda goes to a residency in a secluded Scottish town called Dun, where she devotes herself to learning all she can about Druitt, using a book entitled *Black Modernisms* as her guide to Druitt's work and its context.

This book within a book is quoted extensively, providing the basis for von Reinhold to examine processes of marginalisation through its detailed study of someone who (sadly) did not exist. Who was allowed to exist, in which circles, on which terms, and how did they affect who has been allowed to write themselves into history? These questions have always been pertinent for artists of colour, queer people and women, and von Reinhold engages with them on the level of form as well as content. Stylistically ornate if occasionally overlong, *LOTE*'s sentences are clearly influenced by the decadent writers of the *fin-de-siècle* and their 20th century inheritors, reflecting the way Mathilda values ornament at a residency founded in the 1970s, and heavily influenced by the 'Thought Art' principles of a minimalist theorist named John Garreaux.

Although her name is excluded from its official list, Druitt was involved with the short-lived, semi-secret Enochian Order of the Luxuries (or LOTE for short), based in Dun. Their presence infuriated Garreaux, who decried their proximity to capitalism, refusing to talk about them due to their 'entirely reprehensible' engagement with 'the aesthetic'. Consequently, evidence of her existence is so hard to find that Mathilda worries that Druitt, 'passionate about Sappho' (to use the inter-war euphemism), was a hoax. Mathilda eventually concludes that she was not – the descriptions of her clothing, and determination to match her contemporaries for extravagant style despite differences of race, class and wealth are too vivid for that. They are also among the funniest moments in a novel that is often hilarious, drawing on Wilde's dandyish humour but trans-posing it to the age of 'privilege discourse', which – as the narrator notes – annoy the many people she meets who live in the recent past, just before the 2008 financial crash.

Mathilda concludes that 'real, considerable efforts had been made at blanching [Druitt] from history'. *LOTE* is most intriguing when it blends its narrative with politicised cultural criticism: the conversation about how this absence is mostly the result not of organised conspiracies but of unconscious and often unchallenged bias is sharp and subtle; the explorations of Virginia Woolf's attitudes towards race in *Black Modernisms* are complex and impressively compact.

LOTE doesn't just explore processes of erasure, though: it asks how biases implicit in questions about art might be overturned, by considering who poses those questions, and why. Modernist art and literature, it reminds us, was largely European or North American, white and middle class, as are most of those interested in its legacies – the few people of colour in these circles were involved on other people's terms. Another of *LOTE*'s invented texts, 'White People Shouldn't Paint (or Write Novels, or Study Ancient Greek') proposes that the idea that painting is 'dead' ignores the fact that marginalised communities simply have not had access to the medium, which should not be declared over until they have had ample time to explore it.

All this may make *LOTE* sound studious and serious, but its strength lies in the lightness with which it wears its themes. Shola von Reinhold's next work could just as easily be shorter and tighter or a sprawling epic, but this is a first novel of considerable promise, and hopefully the arrival of a distinctive voice in British fiction.

Tribune Issue 8, Summer 2020

DISCLOSURE REVIEW: THE PROGRESS AND MISSTEPS OF TRANS REPRESENTATION ON SCREEN

Disclosure is a documentary about storytelling: who gets to tell stories about trans people, who gets to write and play the characters in those stories, how these decisions affect those stories, and how those stories affect trans people. It's a history of trans representation in film and TV, and the social uses and political limits of visibility.

Above all, despite its director Sam Feder having structured it as a straightforward combination of talking heads and archive footage, it's about complexity, calling for nuanced understandings of problematic aspects of pioneering works, the positive effects of negative portrayals, and the relationship between transphobia and racism.

Nobody is better placed to explore all this than Laverne Cox, who shot to fame for her role in the women's prison drama *Orange Is the New Black* (2013-19) and appeared on the cover of *Time* in 2014 when they declared the 'Transgender Tipping Point', the moment at which the trans rights movement had apparently become unstoppable.

Drawing links between screen portrayals (seldom written with trans viewers in mind), school bullying, street harassment and hate crime, Cox presents a comprehensive history of Hollywood tropes, from the trans woman as serial killer in films such as *Psycho* (1960), *Dressed to Kill* (1980) and *The Silence of the Lambs* (1991) to television programmes that repeatedly cast trans women as sex workers – without any explanation of the socio-economic reasons behind their doing sex work.

Cox and her many trans guests, including historian and filmmaker Susan Stryker, directors Yance Ford and Lilly Wachowski, artist/TV producer Zackary Drucker and actors Candis Cayne and Elliot Fletcher, talk persuasively about how important this representation is for trans people, who grow up, like most other Americans, not knowing any trans people, and so have their sense of self profoundly shaped by such material.

Disclosure goes as far back as D.W. Griffith's *Judith of Bethulia* (1914), in which the 'chief eunuch' leads Judith to behead Holofernes, thus connecting her act to castration and male femininity – a demonstration of how transphobic narratives were embedded in mainstream US film from its inception.

Transphobic representations, and their underlying assumptions, are not a thing of the distant past: many of the film's examples date from the last two decades, with TV hospital dramas still obsessing over the lurid details of 'sex change' surgery, or having trans characters get gendered cancers that don't match their identities or are caused by their hormone treatments.

The treatment in *The L Word* (2004-09) of Max, who transitions from female to male and becomes a "raging ape", comes in for heavy scrutiny, given the historic lack of representations of trans men – the show gave priority to the emotions of the women who felt betrayed by Max's transition. Similarly, the 'disclosure' trope, which casts trans people as shifty and secretive, rarely takes account of the consequences of being completely open about their identities in a transphobic society.

The exploration of the 'vomiting' trope – men's revulsion on learning they've kissed a trans woman, which moved from *The Crying Game* (1992) into 'gross-out' comedies from *Ace Ventura: Pet Detective* (1994) to *The Hangover Part II* (2011) – is especially powerful: outsiders, unaware how strongly such scenes affect trans people, making them feel unattractive or unworthy of love, may have their perceptions completely changed by the testimony offered here.

Questions about visibility underpin all these concerns, as well as the detailed conversation about who plays trans characters in films. From Chris Sarandon's Oscar for playing Leon Shermer in *Dog Day Afternoon* (1975), after trans actress Elizabeth Coffey Williams was turned down for looking too much like a woman, to the plaudits for Jared Leto and Eddie Redmayne for their performances of femininity in *Dallas Buyers' Club* (2013) and *The Danish Girl* (2015), the casting of cisgender men heightens preconceptions about the inauthenticity of trans women – a problem only now being circumvented by having trans actors, as well as writers and directors, for series such as Netflix's *Pose* (2018-).

Partly a response to Black trans people's complicated feelings about Jennie Livingston's documentary *Paris Is Burning* (1990), which provided access to drag ball culture even as it appropriated that culture, Pose is a welcome step beyond the chat shows that once offered the only chance to see trans people – even legends such as actor/model Caroline Cossey or writer/activist Leslie Feinberg – on screen.

As several interviewees note, increased visibility can mean increased danger: as transphobes learn more about our communities, they also learn more about how to oppress us. Cox is self-aware enough to ask what it means "when a few people are elevated while the majority are still struggling", while Stryker concludes visibility serves best in building support for policies that will improve material conditions for trans people.

The most fascinating question asked here, though, is: what if we never saw ourselves on screen at all? *Disclosure* suggests that, for all its pitfalls, trans representation does more good than bad, and the struggle to improve it has been, and will continue to be, worthwhile.

Sight & Sound, 28 September 2020

TORREY PETERS AND CONTEMPORARY TRANS LITERATURE

With her first novel, *Detransition, Baby*, recently published by Penguin Random House, Torrey Peters has established herself as an important voice in the burgeoning field of transgender literature. Over the last decade, trans and non-binary writers have turned their attention away from memoir and theory and towards fiction, and *Detransition, Baby* – about a love triangle between two trans women, one of whom has detransitioned, and a divorced cisgender woman, has become one of the first novels by a trans woman to appear on one of the "big five" US publishing houses.

Peters' success raises interesting questions about who these novels are for, the uses of writing for a minority community, and of aiming for a wider audience. In the preface to her first work – a self-published novella called *The Masker* (2016) – Peters expressed her excitement to see her work "as part of a conversation with … people like me".

The Masker was illustrated by artist Sybil Lamb because, wrote Peters, Lamb's novels and zines helped her to see what becomes possible 'when trans women write for trans women, rather than a larger commercial market'. *Detransition, Baby*, however, is dedicated to divorced cisgender women, who, said Peters, "must start over at a point in adulthood when they're supposed to be established," much like trans women.

An intelligent, funny and highly relatable work, *Detransition, Baby* has become a crossover hit, being optioned for a TV series and longlisted for the Women's Prize for Fiction in the UK. Peters' success, coming soon after Andrea Lawlor's *Paul Takes the Form of a Mortal Girl* was picked up by Vintage from small LGBT+ publisher Rescue Press in 2019, tells us plenty about the current place of trans and non-binary literature. It confirms North America, and especially the US, as its creative hub, as it has been since the 1990s. There, trans novelists and poets benefit from a well-developed infrastructure of small presses that allows them to flesh out their ideas within a community of trans readers, providing a platform to take their work to mainstream publishers if they wish.

Whether they do this depends more on their chosen genre and prose style than their choice of characters or themes: the skill of fiction and poetry has always laid in its authors' ability to convey highly particular experiences to a readership that has not known them, as well as in making them resonate with those who have. In *Detransition, Baby*, Peters expertly bridges the gender gap by combining experiences unique to trans women with insights into how being trans complicates more universal ones, around employment, family and relationships, making brilliant use of self-deprecating humour to disarm potentially hostile audiences, be they cis or trans.

Peters has always been vocal in acknowledging writers who paved the way for her, recognising that while we don't need specifically trans influences to create believable characters, construct compelling storylines or innovate with form, our predecessors have opened up possibilities. The earliest trans authors published memoirs, aiming to provide a more sympathetic account of their experiences than those in sensationalist news stories.

In the 1990s, trans theory grew out of critiques of those memoirs, which, the theorists argued, had not been truthful about what cross-gender living actually entailed for fear of enflaming anti-trans prejudices. As well as striving towards a political definition of 'trans' that could include as many people as possible, and publishing histories of this community, they tried to create 'a transgendered writing style', as *Gender Outlaw* author Kate Bornstein put it, often merging autobiography, cultural criticism and fiction in texts aimed primarily at trans readers and published by underground presses.

Throughout the 2010s, the novel has emerged as the form that can transcend this divide, from Imogen Binnie's acclaimed road-trip narrative *Nevada* (Topside, 2013) to Jordy Rosenberg's speculative history of an 18th century proto-trans man, *Confessions of the Fox* (Penguin Random House, 2018). Making this jump has brought new challenges: the demand for honesty made by the theorists, and the public, has led trans critics to worry about the political efficacy of writing, as Peters described her novellas, about "the ways in which trans women are fucked up and flawed" amidst a global effort to decrease trans visibility that has stretched from Putin's Russia to Trump's USA via Bolsonaro's Brazil and Boris Johnson's Britain, which has a small but vocal, well-connected cult of transphobic feminism.

There, in response to *Detransition, Baby* being longlisted for the Women's Prize, the 'Wild Women Swimming Club' published a letter condemning Peters' nomination, which they said 'communicates powerfully that women authors are unworthy of our own prize, and that it is fine to allow male people to appropriate our honours'. The Prize responded by recognising Peters' gender and disavowing the letter, which was signed pseudonymously by various dead female writers – an absurdity that points back to the tactic of writing honestly about our lives in the face of such hostility.

As Peters puts it in *The Masker*, a story of what happens when a cross-dresser tries to live out pornographic fantasies of forced feminisation, dedicated to 'my former self at my most afraid', there's 'a kind of safety' in being open about our deepest desires and secrets: protagonist Krys asserts that calling her "a faggot or perv" when she wears a sissy maid outfit is 'just redundant'. By now, it's clear that trying to placate transphobes is pointless: honesty like Peters' will give more confidence to younger trans writers – as well as artists, filmmakers, musicians and other creative people – and sooner or later, we'll reach the point where they can't shout us all down or shut us all out.

Schirn, 17 June 2021

BIBLIOGRAPHY

Not all of my writing about trans/non-binary issues and related subjects could be included in this anthology, for reasons explained in the introduction. This bibliography, then, only covers such work that has not been published here.

BOOKS

Jacques, J. (2015) *Trans: A Memoir*. London: Verso Books.

Jacques, J. (2021) *Variations*. London: Influx Press.

CONTRIBUTIONS TO EDITED COLLECTIONS

'Conundrum: The Dilemmas in Transsexual Narratives' in: Adusei-Poke, N. (ed.) (2012) *Das flexible Geschlecht: Gender, Glück und Krisenzeiten in der globalen Ökonomie*. Berlin: Bundeszentrale für politische Bildung, pp36-53.

'Foreword' in: Carroll, S. & Devine, M. (eds.) (2014) *Brighton Trans*formed*. Brighton: QueenSpark Books.

'The Holiday Camp' in: Waidner, I. (ed.) (2018) *Liberating the Canon: An Anthology of Innovative Literature*. Manchester: Dostoyevsky Wannabe, pp21–32.

'In Search of Gender Troublemakers' in: Eric-Udorie, J. (ed.) (2018) *Can We All Be Feminists?* London: Penguin Random House, pp149–160.

'Juliet Jacques' in: Sampath, S. (ed.) (2012) *Letters Lived: Radical reflections, revolutionary paths.* Toronto: Three O'Clock Press, pp66–75.

'Juliet Jacques' in: Craggs, C. (ed.) (2018) *To My Trans Sisters*. London/Philadelphia: Jessica Kingsley, pp120–122.

'On the Malleability of the Body' in: Jolly, M. & Russell, P. (eds.) (2020) *Unfinished Business: The Fight for Women's Rights*. London: British Library, pp54–61.

'Transphobia and the UK Media' in: Abraham, A. (ed.) (2021) *We Can Do Better Than This*. London: Vintage Books, pp92–108.

'The Woman in the Portrait' in: Horbury, E. & Yao, C. (eds.) (2020) *Transcribed: An Anthology of Trans Writing*. London: Polari Print, pp14–22.

ACADEMIC PUBLICATIONS

'Forms of Resistance: Uses of Memoir, Theory and Fiction in Trans Life Writing' in: McCooey, D. (ed.) (2017) *Life Writing,* vol. 14, pp357–370.

ARTICLES

'Working with Transsexual Patients'. *Student British Medical Journal*, 21 December 2010.

'The Uses of Role Models'. *New Statesman*, 12 November 2011.

'*My Transsexual Summer* appraised'. *Time Out*, 8 December 2011.

'Should trans screen roles by played by trans actors?' *The Guardian*, 14 January 2012.

'Trans Films at the LGFF'. *Time Out*, 8 March 2012.

'Five trans role models you should know about'. *The Guardian*, 8 June 2012.

'Xxxora's Newer Gender'. *Guernica*, 12 June 2012.

'Trans People, Pronouns and Language'. *New Statesman*, 16 January 2013.

'Reviewed: *Fanny & Stella: The Young Men in Women's Clothes*'. *New Statesman*, 18 March 2013.

'Sport is slowly catching up with transgender realities'. *The Guardian*, 16 April 2013.

'Chelsea Manning, pronouns and the press'. *New Statesman*, 5 September 2013.

'Is enough being done to remove unfair obstacles to trans people playing football?' *New Statesman*, 13 December 2013.

'He to She'. *Aeon*, 12 January 2014.

'Ten Great Transgender Films'. BFI, 13 March 2014.

'Trans People and Sport: The Stockholm consensus, ten years ago'. LEAP Sports blog, 30 May 2014.

'On the 'dispute' between trans people and radical feminists'. *New Statesman,* 6 August 2014.

'Top ten transgender books'. *The Guardian,* 21 October 2015.

'Under Cover: A Secret History of Cross-Dressers'. *Loose Associations* vol. 4:1, 2018.

'*The House of Impossible Beauties* by Joseph Cassara review – disco, drag and tragedy'. *The Guardian,* 24 May 2018.

'*Kiss My Genders* review'. *Frieze,* 14 June 2019.

'*Little Girl* review: a cinematic act of kindness to trans children'. *Sight & Sound,* 24 September 2020.

NOTE

'All pieces previously published in Frieze can be found at https://www.frieze.com/tags/juliet-jacques

ACKNOWLEDGEMENTS

This is an anthology, so as well as thanking Jenn and Ellis at Cipher Press for publishing the book and helping with the compilation, I should acknowledge those who commissioned and/or published the pieces in their original form. So, with apologies for anyone whom I've forgotten, gratitude is due to: Andrew Stevens (*3:AM*); Tom Chivers (*Daily Telegraph*); Sean Burns, Paul Clinton, Jennifer Higgie and Evan Moffitt (*Frieze*); Becky Gardiner, Gwilym Mumford and Jonathan Shainin (*Guardian*); Lina Romanukha (Izolyatsia Platform for Cultural Initiatives); Joanna Biggs, Thomas Jones and Alice Spawls (*London Review of Books*); Maria Dimitrova (*Mal*); Caroline Crampton and Helen Lewis (*New Statesman*); Tom Schneider (*New York Times*); Dimi Reader (*Newsweek*); Jane Gabriel (*Open Democracy*); Sahar Halaimzai (*PEN International*); Rebekah Weikel (Penny-Ante Editions); Katerina Gregos and Ioli Tzatenaki (Riga Biennial); Anuschka Berthelius (*SCHIRN*); Kieron Corless (*Sight & Sound*); Elnaz Baghlanian (*Swedish PEN*); Paul Burston (*TimeOut*); Sara-Mae Tuson (*Trespass*); Owen Hatherley (*Tribune*); Gareth Evans (*Vertigo*); Steve Levingston (*Washington Post*); and Željka Marosevic and Cecilia Tricker (*The White Review*).

Although I didn't include any of the pieces they commissioned in this anthology, I should also thank a few people who helped along the way: Torsten Hojer and Cliff James at Brighton-based LGBT publications *3Sixty* and *one80news*, who first asked me to write columns on trans people and politics; Kate Carter and Rachel Dixon at the *Guardian*'s Life & Style section, who took a chance on my *Transgender Journey* series and then let it run for more than two years; and Marco Zigiotti at *Filmwaves*, who let me write about anything to do with artists' film and video, no matter how obscure, and really helped me to find my way in journalism. So many people provided helpful feedback and conversations about these pieces, my work as a whole, and the nature of the industry, including the sadly departed Mark Fisher, Dawn Foster and Nila Gupta, as well as friends and comrades Fatema Ahmed, Chloe Aridjis, Manca Bajec, K. Biswas, Chris Borg, James Butler, Jasmina Cibic, Valeria Costa-Kostritsky, Jo Dawson, Yishay Garbasz, Laura Grace Ford, Fisun Güner, Emma Hannon, Roz Kaveney, Helen King, Alina Kolar, Pil & Galia Kollectiv, Ed Luker, Marie McPartlin, Douglas Murphy, Agata Pyzik, Ilona Sagar, Erica Scourti, Rachel Shabi, Tai Shani, Andi Thomas, Daniel Trilling, Zakia Uddin and Thomas Watson. Finally, thanks to my parents, for their support along several paths that were hard to navigate.